widescreen

Mark Cousins

widescreen
WATCHING. REAL. PEOPLE. ELSEWHERE

WALLFLOWER PRESS LONDON & NEW YORK

To be sung to Mogwai's music for *Zidane: A 21st Century Portrait,*
or Tanya's pianola…

Lyrics by Mark Cousins
Edited by Guy Bingley

First published in Great Britain in 2008 by
Wallflower Press
6 Market Place, London W1W 8AF
www.wallflowerpress.co.uk

A catalogue record for this book is available from the British Library.

ISBN 978-1-905674-62-6 (pbk)
ISBN 978-1-905674-79-4 (hbk)

Book design by Elsa Mathern

Printed in the UK by Cromwell Press, Trowbridge, Wiltshire

contents

REAL

PEOPLE

ELSEWHERE

CONCLUSIONS

acknowledgements

Not since school have I done chin-ups, and never in my life have I darkened the door of a fitness gym, but I've seen them in movies so I know that there's usually a trainer at the shoulder of the exerciser, entreating them to do just five more. You can do it, says the trainer (I'm thinking Ernest Borgnine or someone like that), you've got it in you. *Prospect's* former Deputy Editor Alexander Linklater toiled at my shoulder these last six years as my veins bulged with the effort of writing, telling me that I could do it, that I had it in me. He not only brought it out, but would see things in the film biz that I hadn't spotted, and suggest I write on them. I usually did. He rejected perhaps one sixth of my columns because they weren't good enough, and asked for improvements in another sixth or so, never failing to notice a limp thought or solecism. This was the best thing he could have done and I came to think of him as a dad (he's younger than me) whom I wanted to impress. I hated when he left the magazine, mainly because I missed him.

Behind him was superdad, *Prospect's* founder and editor David Goodhart, who's too much fun for someone you'd expect to be a brain in a jar. I'm sure I owe my longevity at *Prospect* to him, but he's always made me feel that they needed me, when in fact the reverse is the case. I'm surprised to this day when my copy of the magazine comes through the letterbox with a handwritten note, often from David, saying what he thought of my piece. I've written for loads of publications, and not once has this happened before.

Alexander Linklater's successor in the Deputy chair was William Skidelsky, who's as exacting as Alex – so I can't shirk. I recently wrote a piece on Danny Boyle; he told me exactly what was wrong with it, and he was exactly right. He was my new Ernie Borgnine. My thanks too to Senior Editors Ayanna Prevatt-Goldstein, Susha Lee-Shothaman and Tom Nuttall who have corrected my facts and grammar and been a pleasure to work with.

Guy Bingley agreed to copy-edit what follows and, within a few weeks, a padded envelope came through my door. It contained the texts, annotated in great detail, in neat red writing, revealing insights and an editorial eye of sophistication. I am very indebted to him and I look forward to reading his books, which will surely come.

More generally, my Deleuzean hermeneuticist of a film critic friend, Tony McKibbin, has improved my thoughts on movies and philosophy just by talking to me. He's influenced some of the ideas in this volume. Yoram Allon, Editorial Director at Wallflower Press, is now a near legendary figure in film publishing. Having worked with him on this book, I can see why. He made quick, supportive, cultured and insightful decisions from the start and this book would not exist without him. Jacqueline Downs at Wallflower Press was last but far from least to get her hands on the manuscript, and she improved it considerably.

Finally, thanks to GLM who kept me sane and made me happy throughout all this, and often read my raw texts and said when they were gash.

Mark Cousins
Edinburgh
September 2008

introductions

THE POINT OF CRITICISM

The sheer magnitude of social experience and organizational energy generated in the wake of a single painting by Velasquez so far outweighs and overrides the effort and intention that went into its creation as to make nature pale and angels weep. As a critic, I generate tiny bursts of this new organizational energy in hopes of generating more. 'Tis a small thing, but mine alone.

— DAVE HICKEY, *AIR GUITAR*

This book is a collection of short critical essays about cinema. I started writing them in May 2001 and in the intervening years, at regular intervals, I have been asked, usually politely, why I have never tried to make my own films. The point, a fair one, has been levelled at literary critics from, at least, the mid-nineteenth century. Isn't there something secondary about what they do? Aren't they coat-tailers?

Each time I have been asked variations on this question, my answer has been two-fold. Firstly, I do make films, documentary films. Secondly, I don't direct fiction films because, judging from what I've seen on the set, or from what I know from fiction director friends, you need to have the determination to insist on a retake when everyone is tired, cold and hungry, the actress's feet are killing her in her high heels and the crew is about to go into triple time. I don't have this determination. At moments like these I know I wouldn't care enough about the perfection of the scene as caught on that one last take. The agonies of the present moment would outweigh it, so I would simply call it a wrap.

Now, as I write this review of my own book on a misty day on the train from London to Edinburgh, having just re-read *The Function of Criticism* by Terry Eagleton, I want to justify being a critic by throwing the question back at the questioner. Why be a filmmaker rather than a critic? When most films are subject to market forces – extremely so, since they are expensive to make – why would someone want to make them rather than have the relative liberty of writing about them? Why do such a compromised thing – direct movies – when you could do a much purer job, which is just as close to the contours of cinema (and involves seeing many more films, which has to be a bonus)?

Filmmakers will respond that the creative buzz is worth the heartache, but few of the ones that I know are genuinely happy or creatively satisfied. They get to express themselves once every couple of years, when their new film comes out – if they are lucky – whereas I get to express myself – I get that lovely feeling of having made something, having given form to an idea – at least once a week.

Though my point sounds like one about personal fulfillment, it is more than this. Part of the reason why I have loved writing these small essays is because I believe, unfashionably, as Eagleton does, that criticism can have a social function. It did so when it began, in the eighteenth century in Britain, in that it opposed the authoritarian state. Critics then were people who used argument and reason to challenge the decisions of that state, the monarch and the church. From when I first started writing for *Prospect*, I felt that I was writing something oppositional. The title we chose for my column, 'Widescreen', tried to imply that I wouldn't stick to mainstream cinema or consensuses about it, but my editors and I never explicitly acknowledged at the time what became clear as my subjects mounted up – that my writing wouldn't so much be *centred on but broader than* mainstream, capitalist, entertainment cinema so much as *against* it. It soon became clear that I was writing from positions outside it, writing either about what I found 'out' there or about what the aforementioned mainstream looks like from there, looking in, or 'back'.

This oppositionalism represented a new stage in my career. I was 36 when I started with *Prospect*, had made documentaries on subjects such as neo-Nazism and the first Gulf War, had been director of the self-styled maverick Edinburgh International Film Festival, and had co-edited a book on documentary cinema with Kevin Macdonald, but I was best known as a presenter of serious film programmes on the BBC – the high end of the mainstream – a job I had done for five years. Like some of my filmmaker friends in their jobs, I felt a bit compromised by my TV presenting career; I was confined to interviewing English-language filmmakers and was under increasing pressure to engage with – or become part of the marketing department of, as I saw it – mainstream Hollywood. When my bosses forced me to do a long interview with Tom Hanks who had, in my opinion, still to prove his worth as an actor and who seemed to be making noticeably timid creative choices, I found myself on terrain that I didn't much like. Though I gave Hanks what I think was a good grilling, I retreated from this experience feeling grubby. I knew and loved many of the great films from Africa, from Iran, from Taiwan, China, Brazil, Mexico, Japan and Russia and yet I had just made an hour of television – which took three months of my life – which assumed, despite my questioning of Hanks himself, that he is a significant figure in the creative history of cinema. Which he isn't.

So by the time I started writing for *Prospect*, I had taken a vow not to add my voice to those around the world who clamour to talk about Western cinema, Hollywood and mainstream aesthetics as if they are all the movies entailed. I decided that, to use John Stuart Mill's phrase in *On Liberty*, there were 'sinister interests' in the world of film, and I wanted nothing to do with them. I was, to be honest, angry at how narrow was the talk about and awareness of movies – this was at a time when TV in the UK and elsewhere had pretty much stopped showing foreign-language films, before DVD had significantly broadened what we could see, and before the profusion of film criticism websites. I had come to the decision that Western cinema going on about itself – when its efforts were mediocre or cookie-cutting – was narcissistic self-regard and, worse, racism by omission.

Talk of racism and 'sinister interests' sounds melodramatic, I know, and I suspect 'sinister' had no gothic whiff in Mill's day, but I like the seriousness of these terms because they see mainstream cinema's problem as more than mere irritating shallowness. I follow in J. K. Galbraith's footsteps in believing that in capitalist societies, products have a built-in obsolescence. I want a new phone or new trainers not because my previous ones are done, but because their latest versions are slightly more up to date, more *me*. Writer Benjamin Barber thinks of this as infantilising taste. I wouldn't go that far, because there are too many exceptions (I know my PowerBook does a better job as a computer then its predecessors), but in general I would argue that permissive capitalism (the most recent model that will sell you child porn if you want it) inflames desires for trivia. It does so through aesthetic innovation. Just when you've bought your pair of low-rise, skinny jeans, Kate Moss turns up at some club in high-waisters, and you're needily out of the charmed circle again. Yet where fashion at least keeps moving, where it has kinesis and vectors, mainstream cinema is the opposite. It inflames desire by repetition – of genre, star image, sequels, remakes, formulaic storytelling, marketing techniques, poster design, CD tie-ins, and so forth. Its perfect consumer is the child in the 'Teletubbies' who, once they have seen the video insert, shouts '*again!*' And so we get *The Matrix 2* and *3*, remakes of whole genres (like 1970s and 1980s horror) and prequels, what you could call *Star Wars* minus 1, 2 and 3 (or minus 3, 2 and 1.)

Where high-waister jeans are, as I write, being sold on the precise idea that 'low-rise are passé, get with the new thing', when did a mainstream movie last sell itself on the same idea of aesthetic innovation? When did a poster for a mainstream film shout '*romcoms are so passé, get with this new style of cinema*'? Almost never. This bothers me a lot. It has turned me into a dissident from the movie world, the sort of dissident who borrows from John Stuart Mill again: I believe that liberty isn't only a matter of people being free from state oppression or interference; their creative impulses should also be free from what Mill called the 'despotism of custom'. I am also, therefore, against the odious unfairness of the movie playing field. In Edinburgh, where I live, the sides of buses, bill boards around town, bus shelters, burger bars, the advertising and editorial pages of newspapers, the banners of local websites and the façades and lobbies of the multiplexes are at the moment plastered with advertising for *Pirates of the Caribbean: At World's End*. At my local Cineworld multiplex it is playing on three screens today, at 11.00, 11.40, 12.20, 13.00, 14.20, 15.00, 15.40, 16.20, 17.00, 18.20, 19.00, 19.40, 20.20 and 21.00hrs. At the Odeons in town it is playing a further 15 times today. At the Vue cinemas in the city, it is showing 23 times today. At the independent Dominion cinema it is showing twice more. A fair proportion of the advertising space in this city at the moment is exhorting me to see a film that is showing 54 times *today*. And the film has already been showing for two weeks. And Edinburgh is a small place. This push to maximise awareness and minimise choice smells like bullying and an unfair playing field to me. It would be less so if the film merited its blanket availability, if it was an efficient piece of popular entertainment. Is it? Let's look not at what the critics thought of it (they detested it), but ordinary movie goers – that seems fair since it is they who are being bombarded by its marketing campaign and it is they who are paying £6 a ticket. An audience pole on the first website I look at averages 5.2/10. You'd expect a genuinely popular film to score at least 7/10. They, the movie-goers, describe it as follows: 'Trash', 'wooden script', 'mind numbing', 'crap', 'separates us, the suckers, from our hard earned money', 'an ungodly directionless murk', 'abysmal', 'an utter waste of time', 'totally lame', 'non-sensical', 'a waste of money', 'pitiful', 'stupid', 'it left me angry', 'a three hour bore', 'senseless drivel', 'lousy', 'I want three hours of my life back', 'a horrible mess', 'a true piece of crap', 'the worst film I've seen in years', 'truly awful', 'avoid at all costs', 'an insult to film-making and filmgoers', 'I was cringing and squirming in my seat', 'I wouldn't recommend it to my worst enemy', 'moronic', 'terrible is an understatement'.

Terrible is indeed an understatement. I would defend this film's failure to engage its audience if it was born out of a sincere attempt to be fun and exciting but, without a shadow of a doubt, it was made to hoover up the hard-earned cash of those around the world who liked the first film in the trilogy and thought the second was OK. In this it has been successful. The third film cost about $260m to make, about $300m will have been spent on marketing worldwide, and has taken $624m at the time of writing. This means for all the coaxing and cajoling, the blanket booking and audience bombardment, it is just $64m in the black so far (ha ha) but, of course, will mint it on DVD because supermarket chains will put it at kids' eye-level and millions of hard-pressed parents will buy it to get some peace. *Pirates of the Caribbean: At World's End* is bad because its story was at world's end. It had run out of creative juice. It cynically, avariciously repeated an aesthetic formula. How could someone who cares about cinema not be angry about this? How could such a person not pack their bags from the mainstream, move out of town and become a dissident, hollering treasonable ideas about innovation, meritocracy, variety, inspiration, imagination, honesty, relevance and curiosity from outside?

So, seven years ago, *Prospect* gave me the chance to do something like that, to write about innovation in any area of cinema (not only production), that I could find; documentary, the ne'er do well genre which had, at the end of the 1990s, started to do well; the compelling aesthetic properties of film; cinema from Iran, China, Japan, Senegal, Mexico and anywhere 'unexpected'; movies in relation to the real and the social; and some of the philosophical implications of the medium. These would be the positions I mentioned earlier. It would be from these that I would launch my attacks.

The seventy or so pieces – many expanded from the originals – fall into four broad categories. The first is about the process of cinema watching and how movies affect our feelings and thoughts; I have called this section 'Watching', and the films referred to in it are more mainstream than in the rest of the book. A second is about documentary and how film is tethered to the real world; this section is called 'Real'. The third is a series of portraits of filmmakers and actors, and is called 'People'. The last is about places where films are made; as I live in Scotland and as few of these pieces are about here, and as I think of neither Hollywood nor European film as *cinema nostrum*, our cinema, and as much of the writing in this section is about Asian, African or Middle Eastern film – though Britain features substantially – it is called 'Elsewhere'. *Watching Real People Elsewhere*: what cinema affords.

Whilst the point of view and perspective of these articles were there from the start, the style of the pieces took a while to snap into focus. I stumbled around for a while, writing lists of important points that weren't linked by strong enough arguments. My writing lacked drive. Then I realised that a thousand words are about enough to do a thought experiment. I'd start with an uncontentious observation about cinema – say that Billy Wilder is a master director – then try to marshal the case against, because I thought there was a case against. I'd been a reader of *Prospect* from the start, so was perhaps tipsy from its heady tilt against received opinion, but it was the *form* of this tilt that I so enjoyed. 'On the surface of things, the following seems to be so but, when you think about it, the opposite is more likely to be the case, and the implications of this for the movie world are quite profound' was a shape, an engine to drive my writing. Each month, as I sat down to write my column, whether I was in Iran, India, America, Cannes, wherever, I could hear its argument and my purpose was to articulate it in an interesting manner, then type it up. I'd click into *Prospect* mode – condensed, accessible, discrepant – and, mainly to please my formidably brainy and exacting editors, did some of what I think is my best work. My writing wasn't beautiful, but it was hard. Though my theme was often aesthetic, my style was masculine.

What have I achieved? Little, I think. I was selling thoughts about cinema to busy people who knew they should mistrust what the cinematic mainstream offered them but hadn't time to wade through film culture to find what and where was good, thoughtful or maverick. This sounds good, I know. And from the start, I was aware that *Prospect*, its scepticism and the readership it created and fed themselves constituted a marketplace, a smallish but very influential one. I go to parties often and, very regularly, someone comes up and talks to me about these essays. I love this, and it speaks well of *Prospect*'s reach, but does not mean that I am having any effect. For a number of reasons, my dissent will have had little of the impact Terry Eagleton envisaged when he wrote about oppositional criticism. First-ly, because much of what I am writing about is not easily seen. To see it you'd need to go on-line and buy DVDs of films by Ritwik Ghatak, Djibril Diop Mambéty, Youssef Chahine and the like, and I suspect few have ever done so. We considered including a DVD of film extracts with this book, but clearing the rights would be a pain, and expensive. Secondly, I write too fast and can't stand re-writing, so there is a feeling of dash about what follows, which might have some virtue in it I suppose. Thirdly, I have a tendency to empty proph-ecy and *ex-cathedra* pronouncement, especially in my last paragraph, which is usually too grand. Fourthly, and this will sound paradoxical, I suspect I have travelled too much to write brilliantly about world cinema. What I mean is that, for me, writing is like travel-ling – pacy, impressionistic, exciting, sexy even – and these pull in the opposite direction to the deepest consideration. I think I care about world cinema and the diversity of movie dialectics as much as anyone writing in the English language, and have chased that passion (or it has chased me) to India, to Tehran, Egypt, Cannes, La Ciotat, Sarajevo, Mexico, Ber-lin, London, Copenhagen, Paris, New York, Los Angeles, Beijing, Shanghai and anywhere where movie people are, or were. But someone needs to lock me in a room a bit more. I am always packing a bag, always walking away from the page, from writing, to cinema. Walter Benjamin said that a critic must be 'a strategist in the literary battle'. I think I have failed to be a strategist in the cinematic battle. I am romantic, not strategic. I praise or excoriate. Though I would like to create greater awareness about forgotten cinema, to challenge the canon, to broaden what is known and shown, I do not work out what I should do, how I should write, where I should speak, in order to have these effects.

Maybe I am being too downbeat. I do get people saying 'I saw such and such a film because of your recommendation.' Regularly when I teach, students come up to me (of-ten trembling or blushing – TV can make anyone a micro-celebrity) to tell me that they watched *Moviedrome* or *Scene by Scene* (both of which I presented on BBC2) as a kid (which makes me feel ancient), and that it got them into movies. The editor of this volume, Guy Bingley, says that there are repeated themes in what follows: what he calls 'the stylistic extremes of recent cinema' and the impact of Computer-Generated Imagery (CGI); the aesthetics of Asian cinema; violence, war and the humanism of movies; adaptability and experimentation; cognition and what we take from films after they have finished; the im-pact of DVD; real versus forms of fakeness; and the mechanics of film industries. If so, I am well pleased. What I do immodestly believe is that these writings buzz and shadow cinema from just before 9/11 to the present day. In doing so they notice a shift in the direction of the real over those years, but chart the wobble in the other direction caused by CGI. They are by someone who was watching as wide a range of movies as anyone in the last decade, who was snobby about nothing, who was massively curious about the form and content of cinema (and the relationship between the two) in the new millennium, and slotted that curiosity into one of the most readable magazines in the English language. Perhaps they 'generate tiny bursts of new organizational energy', to use Dave Hickey's phrase from the quotation at the beginning of this chapter. And note the word tiny. What follows are snippets, glimpses and glances.

Still immodestly, I'd add that there's insight into world cinema today here and for that reason (as well as the fact that I use the word 'stooshie' a bit), I hope you read on.

THE LAST THIRTEEN YEARS

What has happened in the movie world in the last thirteen years? In 1995, *Heat*, *Seven* and *The Usual Suspects* were all riding high at the box office. America had rediscovered the intelligent thriller, it seemed, and *Braveheart* quickened the pulse. Mainstream cinema wasn't in bad shape, but movie-land hardly noticed because it had bigger concerns. The sand was shifting under its feet. Film was changing, but few would guess how momentous those changes would be.

Consider, for a start, the landmarks in film history of the last thirteen years. A new film studio – DreamWorks SKG – emerged. The first fully computer-generated film, *Toy Story*, was released in 1995. Not only did it show us what films would look like for a generation to come, it revived the animated movie genre which had been in the doldrums for decades. As a result, a new Academy Award category – Best Animated Feature – was created. At the very same time, a group of Danish directors launched Dogme, a back-to- basics manifesto that seemed to revile *Toy Story* and evangelically set cinema on a march towards reality.

And that was only 1995. In 1996, the first DVDs were sold; 400 million of us have since bought machines to play them, and they have become the fastest growing entertainment technology of all time. In the same year, *Titanic* became the most expensive film in movie history, and the one to take the most at the box office.

Two years later, the Dogme-influenced *The Blair Witch Project* showed that from then on the internet would be crucial to the reception of cinema. In 2000, Clint Eastwood's *Space Cowboys* became the first Hollywood feature to be shot on High Definition Television (HDTV). In another world from Hollywood, Iran in these years was the most innovative filmmaking nation, *Wo hu cang long/Crouching Tiger, Hidden Dragon* brought Chinese aesthetics to the attention of international filmgoers, and Mexican and Taiwanese cinema became centres of innovation. Since then, documentary, which has almost never been commercially viable in theatres, became so. The success of films like *Être et avoir/ To Be and To Have* (2002), *Spellbound* (2002), *Touching the Void* (2003), *Fahrenheit 9/11* (2004) and *La Marche de l'empereur/March of the Penguins* (2005) (cost €8 million, took $55 million in the US) revived the genre as *Toy Story* did for animation.

Not since the 1950s and 1960s had a movie generation been so intriguing. Some of the significance of the story of film since 1995 is easy to see. The digitisation of the film process was certain to shift the shape of cinema, and it is doing so. Eventually, it is to be hoped, digitising films will future proof them against decay. Eventually, it is to be hoped, Hollywood will stop treating CGI as a new toy and use it intelligently and subtly. DVDs continue to confuse cinephiles: we love the magical way they store good sound and picture but hate the thought that home-cinema might kill cinema-cinema.

Less obviously, there are two aesthetic facts that in the DVD age we must face: the first is that the canvas of cinema – its screen size – is getting smaller. In the past we saw films on a white rectangle ten metres wide, now we are more likely to see them on a black rectangle less than one metre wide. This has profound implications for background composition, the scale of events within the frame, and so forth. The second is that a movie is no longer a one-off, linear experience. We watch it, then listen to the director's commentary, or watch excised scenes or a 'making of'. As such, filmmakers will be braver in the use of story and character points that are too hidden or complex to see on a first pass.

Even these subtle shifts in the art of cinema over the last generation were partially predictable. No-one, however, could quite foresee the dynamism of the global film world. Amongst the most exciting directors working today are Michael Haneke, Tsai Ming-liang, Abbas Kiarostami, Aleksandr Sokurov, Samira Makhmalbaf, the Dardenne brothers, Fatih Akin, Pedro Almodóvar, Gus Van Sant, Lars von Trier, Hou Hsiao-hsien, Cristi Puiu, Claire Denis, Florian Henckel von Donnersmarck, and Carlos Reygadas. An Austrian, two Taiwanese, two Iranians, a Russian, two Belgians, a Spaniard, an American funded by HBO, a Dane, a German, a German Turk, a Romanian, a French woman and a Mexican. Not since the 1920s has innovation in cinema been so globally dispersed. Some of this can be explained in money terms – Taiwan's top-gear economy, the Mexican and Iranian governments' decisions to invest in film, and so forth.

Least predictable of all has been the mainstreaming of documentary. The first films were documentaries, as are some of the best. They have been made, regularly, since the 1930s yet only in 2002 did they build a critical mass. The fact that history got bigger since the millennium, that 9/11 out Hollywooded Hollywood, image-wise, and made the real world feel suspenseful and unfolding like a narrative, made fiction cinema look ersatz.

Only in tying these three things together – digitisation, the re-emergence of non-Western aesthetics and the return of the real – do we get the full, complex picture of cinema since 1995. That the central tool of the filmmaker is no longer a camera but a computer means that much more than that which is merely filmable is showable. Anything goes. Yet, wading through that anything, what we find valuable in movies these days is the filmic voice of a young female Tehrani director, or an Austrian's austere essays on the nature of violence or a French documentarist's portrait of a rural infant school. Film, in the last, ontological, decade, has been more diverse, in almost every sense, than it's ever been.

watching

eighteen glances at the medium of film, in the era of CGI

8½

This piece was not written for *Prospect*. It is a response to a letter actor and film activist Tilda Swinton wrote to her eight-and-a-half-year-old son, in answer to him asking his mum what people dreamt before cinema was invented. As I don't have a son, I wrote to my eight-and-a-half-year-old self. I hope it tells you something about the writer of this book.

Dear Eight-and-a-half-year-old Mark,

You are in Belfast. It is 1974. The city is a war zone, dead and locked up at night. You are living in that house on the Crumlin Road. You do not know it yet but in two years time, a bomb will damage it. Don't worry, you will all be evacuated and, as a result, you will start a new life on a housing estate in a town called Antrim.

There will be lots of Belfast people there – thousands, in fact, but Antrim will have no cinema. You will see movies on TV – BBC2. You are about to fall in love with two directors – Alfred Hitchcock and Orson Welles. In Belfast in three years time you will see a film called *Jaws* (1975), but it is one by Welles – *Touch of Evil* (1958) – that will change your life. It will make you fall in love with the drug of cinema, the feeling it gives you.

How will cinema change your life? It will stop the world feeling scary. You will discover a quietude in cinemas, in the dark, before the lights go down. In a letter to her son, who is the same age as you are, a friend of mine called Tilda Swinton called this feeling 'ecstatic removal'. My friend Tony McKibbin says that in life people should protect their nervous systems. Looking back, I can see that you were a nervy wee boy in the 1970s so maybe you went into the Odeon on Great Victoria Street in Belfast to protect yourself in the way Tony describes. But protect isn't quite the right word. You will find, as you grow up and become a man, that *release* is what you will feel in cinemas, the sense that your nervous system, which is usually defended, in the ready position, stops shrinking and opens out like a flower.

To what will it open out in the coming years of your life? Tilda tells her son that he will discover 'the promised land of freedom', and that's what you will find too. So unfettered is cinema that you will feel imaginative fireworks explode in your head. You will feel the rush to tears at the beauty of Claudia Cardinale in *C'era una volta il West/Once Upon a Time in the West* (1968) but then, later, you will realise, with life-changing consequences, that it was only partially her that brought those tears. It was also, impossibly, ridiculously, the exalted sweep of the film's image up into the air, over the railway station and further still to reveal a frontier town being born.

You will run like a sprinter with this realisation that form, camera moves, what Daniel Frampton romantically calls the *thinking* of the film, moves you and sustains you. You will come to find, as a teenager and in your early twenties, that you need cinema, the way you need to dance, to remind you of the bodily and mental liberties that existence affords you.

This sprint, this dance, this love will become your life. And here's something you could never guess, living where you are, in working-class Belfast, a planet away from Hollywood: you will earn your living in cinema, close to its contours. Are you shocked? I'd expect so. You'll discover that documentary films – in which the director is really co-director, with life itself – suit your sense of not wanting to be in full control, and you'll make some daring ones. You'll write and talk about films in newspapers and on TV but, soon, you'll find that you have made a vow to yourself not to be part of the marketing of mainstream cinema, so you will sprint some more and find that suddenly you are amongst the films of people with names like Weerasethakul, Tsuchimoto, Kiarostami, Sokurov, Dumont, Almodóvar, Chahine, Farrokhzad, Mambéty, Imamura, Kötting, Douglas, Jarman and Malick. By the time you realise this, you will be miles from anywhere. You will feel lonely there – so letters like Tilda's will mean a lot – but dead happy too, alert, paying attention, as John Sayles would say, astonished, as Jean Cocteau exhorted.

You will start to write about the fact that invigorating movies get squashed, or outrun, by steroid-boosted cookie-cutter ones. Tilda talked about her work as being an act of resistance. Your work will feel like that. As a passionate, decentred, curious critic, you will try to articulate an opposition to the dead contrivance of dominant cinema.

So movies will do something to you and, eventually, you will begin to do something back to them. But what, for now, at the age you are now, do I wish for you? I wish you had more film books at hand than *Halliwell's*. I wish the world of cinema would open up faster for you. You found your way to Iran and its cinema, the work of Ghatak and Dutt, Gerima and Muratova, all on your own. But, tying Tilda's thoughts and mine together, I wish for this: something called the 8½ Foundation. A trust, based in Scotland perhaps, where Tilda and I live, which would make twenty films available for free on DVD to children around the world, on their 8½th birthday, their movie day. These films would be the best, most imaginative, movies of all time – directed by Miyazaki, Norman McLaren, Buster Keaton and Michael Powell – films with titles like *Palle alene i verden/Palle Alone in the World* (1949), *Le Ballon rouge/The Red Balloon* (1956) and *Das Singende, klingende Baumchen/*

The Singing Ringing Tree (1957). They would be available subtitled in fifty languages. The Foundation would be funded by film studios around the world, to enrich the culture in which they operate, a gesture of optimism about their medium.

8½ is the perfect age to fall in love with cinema. It was the name of a great film. I found out only last year, in the dark, when someone recognised my voice at a firework display, that the Indian family who ran the Curzon cinema in Belfast in 1974 – which is now, for you – ran spectacular Indian movies in the morning back then, before the doors opened. They are running them now, as I write. Isn't that remarkable? The 8½ Foundation could be remarkable.

You lucky thing. You are about to discover your passion.

Mark

THOUGHT

Most of us have at some point used cinema to alter our mood. Despite my belief that film's value lies in its connections with reality and ideas as much as escape, I, too, often use it as a quick fix. If I'm sad but want to be happy, *Singin' in the Rain*'s enthusiasm will transform my thoughts. If I'm sad and want to indulge that sadness, a Bette Davis melodrama scored by Max Steiner will deliver the desired release. Bracing films like *Force of Evil* (1948) or *Y tu mamá también/And Your Mother Too* (2001) will give me an expresso hit. *Vertigo* (1958) or *Blue Velvet* (1986) will quickly defocus life around me and wrap me in a dream blanket.

Even the very first filmmakers noticed that the illusionistic and present-tense qualities of cinema gave it a very direct vitality. By the 1920s, experimental French directors like the underrated Germaine Dulac, were trying to tailor their movies to mental processes. In her Madame Bovary-like *La Souriante Madame Beudet/The Smiling Madame Beudet* of 1921, when the eponymous Beudet sees a handsome man, Dulac slows her imagery to capture the reverie of Beudet's erotic gaze. A term from painting – impressionism – was borrowed to describe the result. Cinema had taken an important step in approximating consciousness.

But Dulac was attempting to capture a purely present-tense mental event. Just two years later, Abel Gance went further. In his *La Roue* from 1923, when a character is dangling over a cliff, Gance edits images from previous events in the movie at the impossibly fast rate of 1/24th of a second to create the effect of life passing before him. His character's inner-eye was overwhelmed. Gance had hit upon the idea of a flashback not as a narrative sequence belatedly revealed, but as an undigested memory that intrudes on the present; 42 years later (see 'Trauma', below), Sidney Lumet closed the gap further. Where Gance's character saw flashes from his own, *un*traumatic past because he thought he was going to die, in *The Pawnbroker*, Lumet edited silent half-second intrusions from Rod Steiger's character's time in concentration camps into the flow of his somnambulant life in present-day New York.

Films like *The Pawnbroker* showed cinema's natural affinity with the involuntary aspects of mental activity. The ease with which it jumped about in time and space mirrored the tardis-like quality of consciousness. But cinephiles have to face up to a converse quality in the medium. Hand in hand with its brilliant affinity for the gurglings and zappings of mental activity is a weakness at what you could call the voluntary aspects of consciousness, in other words cognition. We know what the images are in Steiger's head but what if he decides to try to think himself out of his trauma, how does a filmmaker show that? Obviously they could film him discussing his problems with a councellor or friend, or writing a diary that records his struggles to understand and surmount their problems. But in each case he would, of course, be using words. A novel could do this just as well, if not better, as could a play on stage or radio. What does the pure medium of film bring to the depiction? Compared with speech-based art forms, when it comes to rationality, shots and cuts seem *maladroit*.

Many film experts would dispute this. The whole point about the *nouvelles vagues* that swept through the world of cinema in the 1960s and 1970s was that they tried to make shots more like sentences. Filmmakers as varied as Jean-Luc Godard in France and Djibril Diop Mambéty in Senegal wanted to think with the medium of film, and I doubt that there'd be serious film writing if they hadn't been rather successful in that regard. But here's the rub: yes, you need to keep your brain switched on to understand a Mambéty film, or an Ingmar Bergman one or Alain Resnais' *L'Année dernière à Marienbad/Last Year in Marienbad* (1961), but there's a difference, surely, between saying that a film can inspire thought and that it itself behaves *according* to reason. I can make a logical argument using mathematical symbols or words but not with strips of film, exactly. Don't get me wrong. I believe passionately that cinema is fantastic at making us think, at presenting elements of story or space or time to us in such a way that we have to use our brain to make sense of them. Moreso, I'd say, than theatre, for example. And I also know that some of the best filmmakers are great thinkers and use the full power of their brains to come to an artistic decision. But that's not the same as saying that if you inspect the shots and cuts in their film, you find thought there. Instead, I believe, you find *evidence* of thought, just as when we look at an Egyptian pyramid we conclude that a great ramp must once have existed to enable it to be made.

The films of master directors like Carl Theodor Dreyer, Orson Welles, Elem Klimov, Abbas Kiarostami, Yasujiro Ozu, etc., are like pyramids whose thought-ramps have disappeared. I love them for this, the nostalgia for cognition that they evince. They are memorials to thought, but not thought themselves.

Cinema is better than any other art form at the repressed, sexual, damaged, dreamy, Freudian aspects of the human mind but it doesn't look or feel rational because it isn't. This is why it's undervalued. This is why it doesn't have the prestige it deserves.

SPEECHLESS

No one seems to have commented on this, but there have been too many of them not to notice: the great films of late summer and early autumn this year have been almost speechless. Literally. They have little or no dialogue.

We have had *Vendredi soir/Friday Night* from Claire Denis, the French director renowned for her sensual wordless scenes. It is about a woman daydreaming in a Paris traffic jam, picking up a man and having sex with him. It has the odd sentence, but nothing of consequence. The animated feature *Belleville Rendez-Vous*, an instant classic, has a few mumbles and some radio commentary, but the characters say not a word to each other. Matthew Barney's majestic three-hour centrepiece to his *Cremaster* cycle – involving the building and destruction of the Chrysler building, scenes of Masonic ritual, the legless Aimee Mullins, bagpipes symbolising the creative cycle and the transformation of the Guggenheim in New York – features about three lines of dialogue. And Jean-Pierre Melville's reissued 1970 heist film *Le Cercle rouge/The Red Circle* has perhaps ten pages of dialogue. Most films of its length would run to 150 pages.

These films are too diverse to suggest a change in the zeitgeist, or a meaningful trend in the way cinema is being conceived by filmmakers. But four of them in a row, each deriving its power from the fact that its characters are almost mute, is a coincidence worth noting.

As the great Danish director Carl Theodor Dreyer observed, 'the picture, far, far more than the spoken word, penetrates deeply into the spectator's consciousness.' Within minutes of looking at the face of Valerie Lemercier in Denis' film, we are in that daydream with her. If she had spoken, we would have become snagged on elements of her consciousness; but her aphonia allows us to drift deeper. A technique used by some film editors helps explain this. Before David Lean became a director, he was a celebrated cutter of films such as *Pygmalion* (1938) and work by Powell and Pressburger. His approach was to learn the dialogue of a scene by heart so that he could then switch the sound off and cut purely visually, hearing the words in his head but attending primarily to the rhythm of gestures and camera. In this way he was able to discover a deeper sense of movement in a scene than the surface talk suggested.

And in the films Lean was dealing with, the dialogue was rather good. This has not usually been the case. As Dreyer again put it, 'words gushed forth from the empty faces' of actors in Western sound cinema, and we were left with no underscore whatsoever. Like *Vendredi soir*, Matthew Barney's *Cremaster 3* is pure underscore. It plays as if its conscious surface has been stripped off, exposing a vivid work of unconscious forces composed of base notes. Though Barney is a visual artist who has strayed into the movies, his film is sufficiently powerful for its lack of dialogue to act like a manifesto for mute cinema.

Not that there haven't been such rallying cries before. The German director Wim Wenders insisted that the screenplay is the vampire which sucks life from the film. His own commentary-heavy documentaries of the 1990s splendidly demonstrated his point. Bernardo Bertolucci's undervalued *The Sheltering Sky* (1990) achieves greatness in an extended mute sequence where Debra Winger's character loses herself – a kind of daydream, again – after her husband, played by John Malkovich, dies. Bertolucci here demonstrated with bravura the connection between silence and high cinema. The reissued *Le Cercle rouge* is itself a homage to a famous case of extended cinematic muteness. One of the most talked-about sequences in French film is a 25-minute silent robbery of a jewellery store in Jules Dassin's 1955 film *Rififi*. Watching this today is still a gripping experience. You can hear your own heartbeat. *Le Cercle rouge* is the best of its many imitators. It too features a hit on a jewellery store. The sequence is again silent, except for two words. And it is more than a coincidence that the procedure also takes 25 minutes.

Such lessons about the psychological and narrative power of visual cinema are scattered throughout film history, yet one national film culture has been noticeably reluctant to learn them. Two of these great speechless works which are playing at the moment are French, one is Franco-Canadian and the fourth is American. By contrast, British cinema has in general skated on the surface of the well-made screenplay rather than dug into film's deeper terrains. There have been exceptions, of course. English director Nic Roeg's Australia-set *Walkabout* (1971) had a 15-page screenplay, and features long wordless sequences in the outback. Alan Clarke's Northern Ireland-set *Elephant* (1989) made a point of having almost no dialogue whatsoever. And *The Sheltering Sky* was produced by Britain's Recorded Picture Company.

But more films made on these islands should learn the lesson of Dassin, Melville, Roeg, Clarke, Denis, Bertolucci and Barney. Isn't it time for producers to stop flying off to Euro-funded courses on screenplay analysis and the three-act structure and concentrate instead on more filmic approaches?

The film industry's public sector body, the UK Film Council, should announce a scheme to fund films without words.

EMPATHY

The award-winning new British film *My Summer of Love* starts with a young red-headed girl lying in a field. We see a huge upside-down close-up of her eye, then, again upside-down, what she is looking at. A posh girl on a horse. Immediately this visual couplet – an example of field/reverse-field shooting, in film parlance – positions us as the looker.

Perhaps more than any other art form, cinema trades on empathy. People pay a fiver to be Luke Skywalker or Scarlett O'Hara. Certain directors, like Ken Loach in his latest film, *Ae Fond Kiss*, use minimal lights, camera moves, music and acting rhetoric to reduce the aesthetic hurdles between audience and screen and further facilitate identification. The Japanese former documentarist Hirokazu Kore-eda employs similar techniques to almost pointillist degree in his forthcoming masterpiece, *Dare mo shiranai/Nobody Knows*.

Moralists have rightly been concerned about cinema's magnetic appeal, particularly in the area of politics. Leni Riefenstahl's *Triumph des Willens/Triumph of the Will* (1935), in which we empathise with the crowd, usually carries a warning before screenings. *Braveheart* (1995) tipped the needle in favour of the Scottish National Party for a bit. The first of these examples makes the obvious point that in unscrupulous hands movies can spread lies or half-truths about the real world. More subtly contentious, however, have been those films in which empathy is used to make a well intended point. Think of the cycle of 1980s anti-apartheid movies whose general form was that of a white person in the foreground of the story entering the world of black South Africa and discovering its injustices. We coat-tailed them and were expected to have our eyes opened.

Two recent movies represent interesting twists to this formula. The first, *Diarios de motocicleta/The Motorcycle Diaries*, could unkindly be summarised as a rich guy, Che Guevara, learning that there are poor people in the world. As such, it is only a journey of discovery for those who, like Che, do not know this in the first place. Walter Salles is too talented a director to rely solely on such a template, so he uses the changing light and landscapes of South America in his film to vary the tone of Che's journey. Still, the strategy of empathy in the end fails him, I believe, because we already know what his main character doesn't. Only when Che realises that he wants to do something for the poor – as the film is finishing – do his thoughts and feelings become compelling.

If *The Motorcycle Diaries* was a kind of *Bildungsroman* in reverse – rather than learning the values of society, its main character unlearns those values – director Antonia Bird and writer Ronan Bennett's *The Hamburg Cell*, which was shown on Channel 4 recently, was even more so. An account of one of the 9/11 suicide bomber's induction into terrorism, its main character, Salim, was a gnomic, middle-class, Catholic-educated Lebanese man who is taught by radicals to believe in jihad, the evil of America and the paradise which awaits those who sacrifice their lives for Islam. Bird usually hurls us into the lives of her central characters, but this time she and Bennett stood back somewhat. In terms of filmic empathy, this was interesting. Salim was one of the few characters in recent cinema whose journey was virtually unfollowable. Raised in the ambivalent political climate of Lebanon, he was something of a void at the start, but the mental steps he took were not ones we could completely understand. Speaking as an atheist, I find few films about religious conversions intelligible. (The exceptions are von Trier's *Breaking the Waves* (1996), Dreyer's *Ordet/The Word* (1955) and Bresson's *Pickpocket* (1959)). Their characters' gradual abandonment of logic makes me gradually abandon interest. What made *The Hamburg Cell* unusual was that Salim's religious conversion was coupled to an increasing disregard for life, a double barrier. Bird and Bennett's film became a sober essay, then, in the limits of filmic empathy.

Cinema has occasionally gone against the grain of its impulse to identify. *Citizen Kane* (1941) was about an essentially enigmatic and unknowable man. John Ford's equally famous *The Searchers* (1956) centred around a racist outsider – Ethan Edwards – whose journey we watched but did not quite follow. Most intriguing of all was Luchino Visconti's vast film of the life of the nineteenth-century Bavarian king, *Ludwig* (1972). For the first hour or so we are invited to share the aspirations and opulent lifestyle of the monarch. As Ludwig begins to go mad and build his fantasy castles, Visconti seems to accept that no member of the audience will see things as his character does. So, remarkably, he uses him less and less. The king gradually disappears from the film – an anti-climactic dead end, if Visconti had not had a brilliant ace up his sleeve. As the king goes, the castles become characters. Ludwig is dispersed into architecture.

David Lynch did a similar thing in *Lost Highway* (1997), where one character morphed into another. Both movies were rejections of cinema's bent towards identification. They flaunted the norms of filmmaking – particularly political filmmaking – and were the better for it. That may be the danger of filmic empathy. It can take you almost anywhere, even places where you shouldn't go. The small group of good films which refuse to do so more than merit their reputation.

TOM CRUISE'S FACE March 2002

Susan Sontag once wrote an article about the death of cinephilia. But what if everyone stopped going to the cinema altogether, if even the Boulevard St Michel cinémathèques with their Preston Sturges retrospectives sold (as they say in Scotland) hee-haw tickets? What might make people re-enter movies as if for the first time? This occurred to me last night as I contemplated my own re-entry into cinema. After six months of not seeing movies, I wondered if I had forgotten how to understand their language. Would I re-member the difference between a good cut and a bad one, how to see the formal system of a film?

My friends might at least have warned me that *Vanilla Sky* (2001) was not perhaps an easy choice. I figured that since I'd been in Iran and India, a plunge into mainstream Americana might be more bracing than a paddle in something British, so I bought a ticket for the top grosser of the day. Almost uniquely for me, I knew neither who the director was or what it was about, only that *Vanilla Sky* is the event movie on which Tom Cruise and Penélope Cruz became a couple (you hear this stuff even in Rajasthan) and that the critics slated it.

Here's what I saw: a mental collage of *Time* magazine, Mount Rushmore and Sigmund Freud. This astonishingly ambitious and humiliating film takes a face –Tom Cruise's – and writes the secrets of the American heart over it. It is as zeitgeisty as *Time* tries to be and as consciously symbolic as the Presidents' heads on the cliff.

As *Vanilla Sky* is not the sort of movie that you might have flocked to, here's the pitch: Tom Cruise is a publishing mogul whose jealous ex-girlfriend drives both of them into a brick wall. She dies, his face is ruined, he toys with plastic surgery; but when this doesn't work he has his body frozen and enters a world of dreams and nightmares.

What makes this failure of a film compulsive is the anxiety it expresses about Tom Cruise's face. That face has been with us for two decades, since *Risky Business* (1983). Even then, the blank beauty of Cruise's features contained the idea that they must not re-main so. The risky business was sex and capitalism, and there was the hint that America, while it loved this fresh face, would eventually punish its owner for cornering the genetic market. Twenty years later, that hint has culminated in this film about the desire to see Cruise's face ruined. It's another example of cinematic 'want see'.

I once made the simple point that America in its movies likes to see the things it has built up ruined. The destruction of the Twin Towers had been pre-imagined by Hollywood because they were, in some Freudian way, death-defying. Now the cathedral of Cruise's face

Take a human face, film it in close-up, project it on the big screen, and you have cinema, of a sort: Tom Cruise in *Vanilla Sky*

has hit the imaginary mangler. In hindsight it's obvious that this would happen. In films like *Born on the Fourth of July* (1989), the actor began the process of despoiling his looks on camera but, like the taste of a forbidden drug, that only led audiences to want to see more, to go further.

In 1956, this game was played out for real. Montgomery Clift, the beauteous star of *Red River* (1948), *A Place in the Sun* (1951) and *From Here to Eternity* (1953) blacked out at the wheel of his car whilst driving down to Sunset Boulevard and smashed up half his face. The film *Raintree County* was only a month into filming. When the production recommenced, Clift the left side of whose face had been paralysed tried to disguise the damage. The same thing happens in *Vanilla Sky*, but, of course, fictionally. The film's director is cinephile Cameron Crowe, who peppers his films with movie and rock music references – this one quotes *Sabrina* (1954), *Jules et Jim* (1962) (which is very much about Jeanne Moreau's face) and *À bout de souffle/Breathless* (1960) – and who did a book on Billy Wilder. It's impossible to imagine that Crowe didn't think of Clift when writing this film for Cruise, who, incidentally, used to be called a kind of anti-Clift, but whose career is now incorporating more and more of the earlier actor's anguish.

The face of Tom Cruise floats in a different place to that of Russell Crowe. The latter's success has re-masculinised Hollywood, reintroducing a McQueen-like force and realism. As Stanley Kubrick's *Eyes Wide Shut* (1999) showed, Cruise is best at being pre-sexual. In that film he was always about to have encounters, but didn't. His then-wife Nicole Kidman stripped off with real erotic charge, but he was more symbolic. The best scenes were at the orgy, where he wore a literal mask. Cruise wears a mask for perhaps a fifth of *Vanilla Sky*.

In censored cinema, an actor's face is forced to become a symbol of the sexual business that's supposed to be taking place. This was as true of Garbo in silent American cinema as it is of Hindi actresses in mainstream Indian movies today. Perhaps more surprising, the French New Wave, which many misremember as sexually explicit, actually used the faces of Jeanne Moreau and Anne Wiazemsky to express their new, free, intellectualised sexuality.

One of the biggest box-office names in American cinema is locked into a similar 'over-determination' of his face. In films like *Vanilla Sky* it is called upon to express so much, yet because the actor himself has such a charmingly limited range, at least two directors – Kubrick and Crowe – have put a mask on it.

BISEXUALITY

When Bertolt Brecht said that art is not a mirror to reflect reality but a hammer with which to shape it, he clearly hadn't seen *Top Gun*. The whole point about Hollywood blockbusters is that the audience – primarily the people of non-coastal America, but nowadays everyone from Johannesburg to Moscow to Taipei – has its hopes and fears reflected back at it.

Tinseltown's latest blockbuster, Oliver Stone's *Alexander* (2004), is already the subject of much mirror/hammer debate. Its depiction of an epic defeat of the Persians is being seen as a reflection of our Rumsfeldian times. From Tehran and the Middle East, such scenes will look ominous indeed. There was, of course, barbarity in Alexander's campaigns – as the remains of Persepolis in central Iran continue to show – as well as tactical brilliance. The balance Stone strikes between heroic and sadistic Alexander will reveal whether he is playing to coastal America or the middle states. Reports that Ptolemy (played by Anthony Hopkins) dismisses in a single sentence the charge that Alexander was a tyrant suggest the latter.

But it is not only the idea of conquering Iran that gives the film a dark injection of the zeitgeist. Alexander's bisexuality also feels of the moment, perhaps in a more complex way. Despite an apparent shift away from gay rights in many US states, and the hilarious writ issued by a group of Greek lawyers against Warner Bros. for portraying Alexander as gay, the film gives homoeroticism considerable airtime – more than any previous Hollywood epic.

This is not surprising. Popular culture in recent years has been unexpectedly progressive about sexual minorities. Television programmes like *Will and Grace* in the US and Britain's *Big Brother* made gay and transgender themes mainstream, and we didn't even hear the hammer clang. Hollywood has been more cautious, but *The Birdcage* (1996) and *In and Out* (1997) broke new ground by having a laugh with gay characters, none of whom were victims. By the end of the 1990s, many female film characters had a gay best friend.

Nevertheless, the case of *Alexander* reveals the liberal/conservative gridlock that still underlies the issue of homosexuality on film, and that makes it a key mirror/hammer theme for Hollywood. Home to bisexual stars like Marlene Dietrich, Greta Garbo, Rudolph Valentino, Danny Kaye, James Dean, Anthony Perkins, Laurence Olivier and many others, it could hardly ignore the subject. For many years it was borderline taboo, but nowadays bad-boy stars like Colin Farrell, who plays Alexander, see no shame in doing the odd gay film. As if to prove the point, Farrell has just done a sort of gay turn in *A Home at the End of the World* (2004). Doing so showed his range and, oddly, his balls; and to Farrell's nonchalance you can add the bullish liberalism of Oliver Stone. Never afraid of the hammer approach to art, as his hagiographic *JFK* (1991) showed, you'd expect Stone to show some boy-on-boy action, especially if he had final approval over the film, as the New York Times recently reported. This is where the gridlock comes in. Stone has, apparently, voluntarily trimmed the homoeroticism. *Rolling Stone* says that Alexander and his lover Hephaestion 'exchange hot looks, but Stone – perhaps unwilling to kill the film's box-office chances among homophobes – stops there'. Yet the screenplay, which Stone co-wrote, has Aristotle (Christopher Plummer) aver that sexual relationships between men will 'build a city-state and lift us from our frog pond'. They certainly did Hollywood no harm.

Behind star and director, of course, there are the less measurable forces of studio and moneymen. Since the time of Bogart and Cagney, Warner Bros. has been associated with gritty stories torn from the headlines, and so if depicting sexual minorities is becoming less taboo, it might be expected to be the first to hold a mirror up to these changes. Yet its owners have, by association, the most to lose by alienating conservative customers. Warner Bros. is embedded in one of the entertainment world's biggest conglomerates, Time Warner. You might expect Murdoch-owned Fox to be more cautious still, but its specialist division Fox Searchlight has just produced *Kinsey* (2004), in which the main character's bisexuality is dealt with more frankly even than Alexander's.

For Hollywood-watchers, this question of whether films reflect or initiate social change is intriguing. Take the world of crime precognition in Steven Spielberg's *Minority Report*, which was seen as being eerily connected to the principle of military pre-emption when the movie came out in 2002. It is on this level that *Alexander*'s connection to Iran and to bisexuality may be understood.

Then again, the whole point about movie stars is that we want to be them and be with them. Isn't there something essentially 'bi' about that? We are attracted to beautiful people in cinema but we also, if we identify with them, look at the world through their eyes. If Oliver Stone has made an effective film, we will not only experience the thrill of being Alexander, we will feel his sexual longing for his boyhood friend. I hope this is the case, but judging by the American reviews (the *Village Voice* called it 'a festival of risible wiggery'), perhaps it won't be.

TRAUMA

Steven Spielberg's *War of the Worlds* is Hollywood's big, veiled portrait of 9/11. It is surprising, in a way, that it has taken this long. Traumatic experience has been Hollywood's bread and butter since the same Spielberg had his main character face death in the form of a great white shark in *Jaws* (1975). Only a matter of weeks ago the number one film at British and US box offices was *Batman Begins*, whose wellsprings are two distressing experiences of a young boy – the murder of his parents and his falling into a nest of bats. Nearly ten million people around the world have seen this film so far. Another forty million are likely to in the next few years.

Such examples are not unusual. The intensity of mainstream cinema, its adrenaline-charged quality, has explained its licence to print money for decades. Hollywood is, let's face it, a kind of traumaland, a Disneyworld of distressing events. Sometimes it's even serious about such events. The climax of Alfred Hitchcock's *Marnie* (1964), for example, depicted what psychologists call *in vivo* exposure: to find out what is causing his wife's sexually unresponsive, kleptomaniac behaviour, Sean Connery's character takes her back to her mother's house where, he believes, she witnessed something mentally disruptive.

Marnie at least had a crack at depicting the cause and effect of mental life in a grown-up way, but it was still unconvincing. Mature filmic treatments of traumatic events are to be found elsewhere. In the world of documentary, John Huston's *Let There be Light* (1946) and Kim Longinotto's *The Day I Will Never Forget* (2002) – to name just two – brilliantly conveyed, respectively, the treatment of traumatised Second World War GIs and the agonies of female genital circumcision. Forget the rollercoaster ride of sensation that is mainstream cinema. These and many other documentaries showed that filmed imagery could render painful human experience credibly and precisely.

The best example I know in fiction cinema is Elem Klimov's *Idi i smotri/Come and See*. Filmed in the Soviet Union in 1985, it is set in Byelorussia in 1943, as the Nazis sweep eastwards, sacking villages as they go. One 15-year-old boy's whole family has been murdered. The film shows his flight through bogs, his disorientation and tinnitus – the way his head seems to flood with panic and mental noise. There is something fundamental in this. In fact, I believe that cinema is itself structured like traumatic experience.

Sidney Lumet's *The Pawnbroker* helps explain what I mean. Made in 1964, it depicts the dull, repetitive life of New York City pawnbroker Sol Nazerman, played by Rod Steiger. We see him at his store everyday, talking to his customers in a monotone. Then mental images of Nazerman's days in Auschwitz-Birkenau intrude silently, with increasing persistence, into his numb daily life. Psychologists call these intrusions 'flashbacks', of course. So do filmmakers. This is no accident of terminology. Just as traumatic memory is discrepant and nonlinear, so is film editing. No other art form can jump about in time and space as film can. As if to prove the point, there are no records of traumatised patients reporting flashbacks that pre-date cinema. There are no flashbacks in Shakespeare.

But there's more. Film is naturally capable of depicting the more permanently altered states in which traumatised people sometimes feel that they live. Krzysztof Kieslowski's *Trois couleurs: Bleu/Three Colours: Blue* (1993) portrayed Juliette Binoche's grief at her husband and daughter's death as a somnambulation interrupted by a series of blackouts, signified by fades to black and musical intrusions. Most of these involved close-ups of Binoche. Right from the earliest movies, especially at the time of silent cinema with its huge close-ups of Greta Garbo, it became clear that the magnified human face was distinctly new in human culture. Never before had human beings been offered the chance to inspect faces like their own in lit, flickering, available close-up.

Cinema can do two things at once. It can represent experience in a way that feels direct, but has no real consequences. It feels like living while not actually being like living, because in life you have to deal with the consequences of a terrible event, whereas in a movie you watch its repercussions – and then the credits roll and you're out the door. Movies allow us to enter disturbing experiences in a uniquely vivid way without breaking down, or hyperventilating, or having feelings of being unable to cope. Indeed, at their best, they are like the moment at which a traumatised person feels that they are beginning to recover.

If this is so, then the closeness of cinema and trauma should be explored. Might movies even help with treatment? No clinical studies have asked this question; perhaps it is time to do so. Movies take us on the trauma ride and let us see where that ride goes, without being hurt. If any art can help, movies can. They, as much as any, plot the path to recovery, show that it is possible, that people have traversed it, that it is safe, even when it is frightening.

CINEMASCOPE September 2003

CinemaScope is fifty years old this year. In 1953, 20th Century Fox trumpeted *The Robe*, the first film in the new format, as 'the modern miracle you see without glasses'. The film premiered on 16th September of the same year in New York's Roxy cinema, on a screen measuring 65 x 25 feet. Cinemas around the world quickly refitted, widening their screens and curving them in concave imitation of CinemaScope's famous perspectival logo. So encompassing was the new heightened experience of going to the cinema that it led to a shift towards epic settings and spectacular shooting styles and briefly halted the decline in cinema going.

But CinemaScope and its variations represent an ambiguous revolution in style, because they exposed a repressed anxiety of cinema: 'What is it we can do that television can't?' The answer both purified and vulgarised the medium.

The vulgarisation is well known. *The Robe* itself and films like *How to Marry a Millionaire*, released in the same year, look today like stage plays photographed by a camera plonked in the front row of the stalls. Film historians refer to the frieze-like way that actors were strung along the width of the screen as 'washing line' compositions. Focus was very shallow, forcing everyone to act in a flat plane. Directors thought that cutting between shots on such a huge screen would jar audiences, so they kept editing to a minimum.

Luckily, however, widescreen cinema aesthetics predated CinemaScope, and there was an older tradition of directors engaging with the wide rectangle rather than the near square. As early as 1897, a now long-forgotten filmmaker called Enoch Rector photographed a Nevada boxing match in a widescreen process (which he called Veriscope) on a 63mm negative rather than the 35mm that would become industry standard. This is perhaps the first example of a filmmaker changing the shape of their canvas in order to find a better fit between it and the event he was trying to capture.

Three decades later, one of France's most innovative directors applied the aesthetics of the extended horizontal to epic subject matter with such flamboyant success that the widescreen image became associated with spectacle thereafter. The film was *Napoléon*. The director, Abel Gance, used three adjacent cameras for scenes such as Napoleon's departure for Italy. He then projected the footage from each of the cameras onto a single very wide screen. In the same year, the Parisian inventor Henri Chrétien found a way of doing something similar but with one camera rather than three. He devised an 'anamorphic' lens, used both in the camera and the projector, which squashed a wide vertical image on to a standard 35mm negative, then reversed the process, 'desquashing' it onto a wide screen. Chrétien's innovation made Gance's avant-garde technique commercially viable. It would be 26 years before another country – America – realised its potential. Among the few who did so creatively was director Nicholas Ray in films like *Rebel Without a Cause* (1955). Ray had studied with one of the twentieth century's greatest horizontalists, the architect Frank Lloyd Wright, and he applied the aesthetics of Lloyd Wright's buildings to the new compositional world of widescreen. The year after *The Robe*, director Stanley Donen made *Seven Brides for Seven Brothers*, the first good widescreen musical. The fact that there were 14 characters in this film made it a horizontal shoo-in. Years later, when shown on television, its edges were cut off. The result might be accurately renamed 'Four Brides for Four Brothers'.

This misfit between cinema and television, their failure to talk the same compositional language, was the very point of the commercialisation of CinemaScope and its variants (though some canny mainstream directors in the US started keeping the essential story information in the centre of the frame). In Japan, meanwhile, the bravura of master wide-screen directors like Kon Ichikawa and Shohei Imamura was derived in part from other art forms. The tradition of horizontal scroll illustration was a clear precedent and the Zen idea of *mu*, which argues that empty space is a positive compositional element, provided such filmmakers with a rich conceptual palette. In one astonishing shot in Ichikawa's *Yukinojo henge/An Actor's Revenge* (1963), the screen is empty except for a figure so tiny in the up-per left corner that the effect would be similar if the double page before you was blank except for a single letter, top left.

By the 1970s, widescreen had become the norm and filmmakers were experimenting with other tools such as telephoto lenses and louma cranes. By the mid-1990s, cinematic horizontality had become so much part of the lazy rhetoric of conventional cinema that that group of innovative Danish pranksters, headed by Lars von Trier, banned its use in what they called their vow of chastity. They saw the near-square screen ratio as purer and more fundamentally cinematic than widescreen which, they argued, was a decadent per-version of the medium.

The fact that variations in the ratio of width to height in film can raise such fundamen-tal questions about the nature of cinema is one of the reasons I like it so. Might we not also mention the matter of the squareness of the edges of the movie screen? The peripheries of human sight are soft and rounded. Shouldn't filmmakers take this into account, and con-sider replacing the rectangle with the oval and ellipse? To do so would restart the question of centre and edge in film, and another compositional rethink.

MOVIE HOUSES

Exactly a century ago, the first of a new type of building that would transform our cultural lives was constructed. At 8am on Monday 19 June 1905, on Smithfield Street in Pittsburgh, the first purpose-built movie theatre, a 96-seater, was opened by local entrepreneurs Harry Davis and John Harris. They called it a 'nickelodeon', combining the cost of admission with the Greek word for theatre. On the first day, 450 people queued, in 32-degree heat, to see the 15-minute programmes of shorts and 'funnies', repeated over 16 hours. On day two the numbers grew to 1,500. Such was the cinema's success that by 1907, 2,500 of these buildings had appeared in the US. The new downmarket, democratic medium of film had found an architectural-psychological home.

The nickelodeon was particularly popular with immigrants (the films were silent), kids and the working classes. Almost at once, social activists were concerned that such people – and single women too! – were gathering together in the dark. Surely the effects on society would be detrimental? But in the century that followed, once movies shook off their initial social stigma, the buildings in which they were projected began to be seen not as a threat to community, but a constituent of it. Many examples of this remain today. In Darwin, Australia, a major attraction is the Deckchair cinema; during the siege of Sarajevo, an underground cinema kept going, projecting movies on video; in 1996, when the owners announced the sale of the Plaza cinema in Liverpool, local volunteers set up the Crosby community cinema trust and ran the place themselves; in many towns, the façades of long-abandoned cinemas are listed buildings.

Three architectural trends emerged: the gothic-baroque movie palaces of the late 1910s and 1920s, such as Grauman's Million Dollar Theater in Los Angeles; the modernist art deco theatres of the 1930s and 1940s, with their soaring fin towers and Frank Lloyd Wright horizontals; and the suburban multiplex barns of the 1980s. Each reflected the intentions of the movie world of its time. Grauman's resembled the central portal of Notre Dame in Paris. Cinemas were cathedrals; people went there to worship. But in towns of the 1930s that needed cinemas only half that size, the solution was the geometrics of art deco, exuding Europeanness and luxury. The opening of New York's Radio City Music Hall in 1932 captured something of the speed, vitality and optimism of cinema in the sound era. Film revenues were still in ascendance, and as deco came to influence the production design of movies themselves, the fit between medium and architecture seemed complete.

Then came the slow decline in filmgoing. In 1949, as a result of antitrust legislation, the main Hollywood studios were ordered to divest themselves of their movie theatres, so third-party developers bought and ran them. From the 1950s to the late 1970s, the movie cathedrals were bulldozed or converted – Grauman's ironically became a church – and deco cinemas around the world were closed or became bingo halls. The revival of moviegoing in the late 1970s – inspired by *The Exorcist* (1973), *Jaws* (1975) and *Star Wars* (1977) – caused a rethink. When the devastated and desperate Hollywood studios discovered to their relief that they had an audience again, they looked at that audience and discovered that it was male, teenage and suburban. Middle-aged people, who liked a bit of comfort, were nowhere to be seen. Then Reagan's 1986 antitrust reforms allowed studios to reacquire cinemas, and a massive building programme took place. This time cinemas were small and unadorned. Six or more would be housed in a single space with a central or electronic projection box, massively reducing projectionists' salaries. The foyers of these places looked as if they were designed by Willy Wonka: all neon, spun sugar and fizzy drinks. This was cinema architecture in its third manifestation: industrial and infantile. It is easy to see the pattern: a return to cinema's profane and ignoble origins. The prestige-less architecture of the multiplex reflected the opprobrium the film world had incurred.

In the 1990s, the pattern of the 1910s and 1920s continued to repeat itself. The prestige of the movies began to return. The Odeon chain rebranded itself 'Fanatical About Films'. The second-generation multiplexes made a bit more effort with seating and lighting. Older moviegoers returned and added to the fragmentation of audience demographics. So where does that leave cinema design? If history is anything to go by, if the industry is to capitalise on the revival of its prestige, a new idiom is needed. Something that leapfrogs the baroque uncertainties of the movie cathedrals and finds a twenty-first-century equivalent of the deco cinemas.

There are many possibilities. Edinburgh's art cinema, Filmhouse, and the Edinburgh International Film Festival have combined forces to look at new types of movie buildings which rethink exhibition and combine it with a festival centre, production companies, rooftop bars and restaurants. The architect Richard Murphy has proposed a series of au-ditoria with open outlooks to Edinburgh Castle that close as the movie is about to begin, thus reversing the idea of the womb-like black cinema box. Such rethinks are desirable if we are to attract people back to cinemas and remind them why DVD is only second best.

LOCATION

Think of *Taxi Driver* (1976) and its unforgettable depiction of the teeming nightlife in Manhattan's Hell's Kitchen district. Or the Rome of *Ladri di biciclette/Bicycle Thieves* (1948). Or Los Angeles in Michael Mann's *Heat* (1995). Or the Iranian villages in the films of the Makhmalbafs. In each case the setting is not just the world out of which the characters grow, but also, somehow, the reason why the film exists.

This is not always the case with great movies. The oft-quoted example is *Casablanca* (1942), not a foot of which was shot on location. Studio filming lent it a seductive veneer. The flaws and accidents of real life were nowhere to be seen.

Conversely, real locations can generate vitality. Our eyes dart around the screen, fixing on the details of street life and real faces. Roland Barthes used the word 'punctum' to describe the piercing effect that such unplanned photographic detail can have.

All this is relevant again because of two new trends in mainstream cinema. The first is 'runaway' production, where cities like Toronto are used to stand in for Manhattan to save money. In 1990, no Hollywood movies with budgets over $25m were filmed abroad.

In 1998, 24 were, and the figure is rising (the number of smaller-budgeted runaway films nearly doubled in the same period). The state of California reckons that nearly $10bn of its $34bn film and television industry is being lost as producers go elsewhere. Anthony Minghella's *Cold Mountain* was a particular bone of contention last year when it used Romania to stand in for North Carolina, thus slashing its $150m budget to around $80m.

The second trend is just as significant. The newest instalment in George Lucas's *Star Wars* saga was shot almost entirely against green screens, with computer-generated locations 'added in post', as was the recent Jude Law vehicle *Sky Captain and the World of Tomorrow*. Neither of these films have radically new content – they derive from serials like *Buck Rogers* and city movies such as *Metropolis* (1927)– but when you add together the influence of CGI backgrounding and runaway production, you begin to reduce the role that real locations play in the cinema.

The obvious response to this is concern that films are getting less authentic. But it is hard to get worked up about such authenticity in cinema. The opening twenty minutes of one of Roman Polanski's best films illustrates a more interesting issue. In *The Tenant* (1976), the main character Trelkovsky, played by Polanski himself, is looking for an apartment to rent. He arrives at a run-down nineteenth-century courtyard tenement in Paris. The landlady closes a window to get rid of him, but he opens it again and persists. So she brings him upstairs, fiddles with the lock, enters the gloomy flat and lets him in. She opens French windows to show him where a previous occupant fell. He moves in and explores the place, opening a wardrobe where he finds a dress, looking out into the courtyard to see who is using the toilet on the landing opposite.

The apartment in *The Tenant* fascinates us because the actors interact with it. All that opening and closing of windows and wardrobes make it a real place, full of noises and mysteries. And looking out across the courtyard or up the stairwell establishes the sightlines of the building, who can see whom. The theme of the film is how a place can drain the life out of a person. It becomes vivid as Trelkovsky becomes absorbed into its secrets. In the era of the green screen, with its post-hoc backdrops, actors can't interact with the scenery as they do, brilliantly, in *The Tenant*.

But Trelkovsky's apartment in the film was only a very carefully designed and dressed set: the location does not need to be real to be alive. Sets and locations can be alive in different ways, and it is the interactions which count. In Bernardo Bertolucci's *Strategia del ragno/The Spider's Stratagem* of 1970, a son returns to the town of Tara where his father, Athos Magnani, is worshipped as an anti-Mussolini hero. Magnani was nothing of the sort and the town has been in a state of somnambulant denial since his death. To depict this dream-like state, Bertolucci filmed the whole movie in Sabbionetta in Emilia-Romagna, an extraordinary colonnaded town. Bertolucci has real villagers stand statically as Magnani *fils* runs past them through motionless piazzas. The first time we meet the main female character, who was in love with the father and will soon fall for the son, she is standing still in the distance in a garden. The camera sweeps right to find her and, as if brought to life by its motion, she suddenly walks forward at its pace.

If the Polanski example shows that actor interactivity and sightlines are key elements in rendering a space alive in a film, the Bertolucci movie reminds us that sets and locations can be alive in different ways. In the end, the creative question for filmmakers is not whether Toronto looks like Manhattan or whether Jude Law can make us believe in the CGI world behind him. Rather it is how to make sure that the settings for their films are not passive. The set sucks the life out of Trelkovsky. The son of Athos Magnani wakes up the town which he visits. The locations in the best films do something to their characters or, even more interestingly, the characters do something to their locations. The relationship between the two is what fascinates us.

RAIN

Name a great painting about rain. Scan the history of classical, renaissance, or modern art and you'll find very few important examples. Wind, yes. Sunshine, of course. And fog (Oscar Wilde's quip: London was not foggy until Whistler), but not rain. We get its aftermath, wet streets and biblical floods, but seldom have painters looked at rain in the present tense, as a visual moment.

In painting, rain is very hard to do. In cinema, rain is another matter. The title scene of the MGM musical *Singin' in the Rain* (1952), where Gene Kelly dances in a downpour shot on a studio set, is one of the most kinetic in movie history. The camera swoops, the dancer runs, jumps and spins, and the image itself gleams with the reflections of the studio lights in the pools of dappled water. It's absurd in a Hollywood way because getting drenched is seldom much fun, but 'golden age' cinema has always structured its feelings in a utopian way, stripping out the unpleasant parts of real life and building in safety and forgetfulness.

This applies even more to mainstream Hindi cinema. Seldom in Bollywood is a good soaking anything other than exhilarating or symbolically erotic. Mira Nair's *Monsoon Wedding* (2001) climaxed with a cathartic cloudburst in New Delhi. *Dil*, the biggest Hindi film of 1990, a kind of *Grease* remake, had a splendid one too, as did 1983's *Betaab*, where the lovers duet in a glass cabin during a shower. The rain song, as it came to be known in the biggest film industry in the world, has become a narrative structural device, like the action sequence in Hollywood.

The optimism and manageability of mainstream movie rain is thanks in part to the cinematographer's best friend, the rain machine. For years in American musicals, a shower would be turned on like a tap and would soak the stars fetchingly, while the rest of the street stayed dry. The shower that soaks John Wayne and Maureen O'Hara in John Ford's *The Quiet Man* (1952) was a rugged spin on this; it made her hair straggly and sexy and showed his physique beneath his shirt. But rain-machine rain started to look very false by the late 1950s, when more films were shot on location. It took the British director Terence Davies to turn things exquisitely full circle in his *Distant Voices, Still Lives* (1988), where, as the doors of a cinema opened and the audience flooded out, an instantaneous downpour started with the perfect timing and effect of the movie those who were entering it had just watched. We were to notice it and regret how realism had swept away the phoney rain.

In American film noirs of the late 1940s, night-time city streets were the sleek visual analogue of their detectives and femme fatales. As Brylcreem was to John Garfield's hair and satin to Gene Tierney's costumes, so rain was to the studio sets of Chicago and New York. The reflections on the road always glowed as if it had just finished pouring.

Shichinin no samurai/The Seven Samurai (1954) tells the legend of the end of the samurai era of the sword. Director Akira Kurosawa wanted the climactic scene where the samurai is shot by a bandit, and the musket triumphs over the sword, to be both pathetic and heroic. He drenched the action in rain. Everything was tonally mid-grey, the opposite to the colour enhancement of rain in Hollywood or Bollywood. The samurai is shot, he curses through sludge, and he falls as the incessant rain turns everything into monotone.

In Alfred Hitchcock's *Psycho* (1960), as Janet Leigh drives, she thinks about the money she has just stolen. As she becomes more worried about the consequences, it gets dark and starts to rain. The camera looks through the wet windscreen at her as her eyes widen with fear. As the wipers swish we see her clearly, then not, clearly, then not. The rain is like a judgement. Famously, the next downpour of water, in the pristine white bathroom, comes after she has decided to return the money. She is happy and begins to cleanse herself – until she is interrupted. The rain and the shower bookend her moral choice.

In Andrei Tarkovsky's Russian films, it sometimes rains inside rooms. In Powell and Pressburger's *Black Narcissus* (1947), rain clears the air. In Nic Roeg's *Don't Look Now* (1973), rain on a puddle in England is used as texture throughout. In *The African Queen* (1951), it raises the level of the water so that Humphrey Bogart can get his boat out of the reeds. Rain moves, and cinema is drawn to anything that moves. By rolling over and around things, it describes the shape of objects and people. It renders clothing translucent. It throws melodramatic shadows into an unlit room, heightens colour and reflection. There is something rainy, flickering and silvery in the medium itself.

Still, whereas the rain in Indian and British films is understandable because both those countries have so much of it, the preponderance of rain in Hollywood films is more surprising. The very reason for making films there was its lack of rain. The earliest directors used only natural light; the early moguls set up shop where light was everywhere. Nevertheless, rain machines became one of a filmmaker's favourite toys. While rain in India and Britain is just a fact – as this summer has made clear – in California, it is a longing.

VIOLENCE

December 2003

With Clint Eastwood's *Mystic River* and Quentin Tarantino's *Kill Bill: Vol. 1* near the top of box-office charts around the world, the nature of screen violence is once again the central social question in Western cinema.

In Eastwood's early spaghetti westerns and mid-period 'Dirty Harry' films, we saw brutal killings but neither their psychological causes nor social effects. By the early 1990s, with *Unforgiven* (1992), the actor-director had undergone a change of heart. In a key scene, a gunman is shown to be worried about having killed an innocent man. Eastwood's recent *Mystic River* continues this recantation, the slowest apology in modern American cinema. In it, the sexual abuse of a child leads inexorably to other crimes in later generations. It flows through America like the river in the title.

The problem with the film, one of Eastwood's best, is that out here in the real world we already know that violence has consequences. He is among the few still discovering this. If he is to advance at all as a filmmaker in the final phase of his career, he must address the question of how the apparent inexorability of violence can be stopped.

Kill Bill, Tarantino's latest film, one of the most violent ever released in Britain, is *Mystic River*'s intellectual correlative. Where Eastwood has progressed to the point where he understands that violence matters, Tarantino presents it abstractly, like music. In several interviews, he has said that he films his sword fighting scenes of decapitation and multiple amputations as if they are musical numbers. It has always been aesthetically interesting to borrow form and apply it to unfamiliar content in this way, but his doing so ignores the obvious fact that in musical numbers people dance, where in fight scenes they die. The consequence of the former is tiredness; of the latter bereavement and trauma. Tarantino's scenes are structured like those of Gene Kelly, as a crescendo. They finish without repercussions.

This sounds like I'm taking *Kill Bill* too seriously. It is, after all, offered up as comic book neo-violence, its purpose being to exhilarate. An artist has a right to choose whether or not his or her work is social and psychological. But *Kill Bill* is plainly not a comic book. It is photographed, not drawn. It is far more representational than cartoon violence. Unlike the visuals of Tom and Jerry, its images capture the texture of Uma Thurman and Lucy Liu's skin, and present these on a massive screen. That is the magic of film. It is tied to the real world in a way that drawings only partially are and music is not at all.

This is not to say that film must be serious or literal in its depiction of human suffering. *Scary Movie 3*, which has just broken box-office records in the US, features the slaughter of gormless teenagers, but is plainly a comedy. The films of Sam Peckinpah were among the first to find balletic beauty in violent death, but the agonies of those deaths were clearly apparent. Brian De Palma's *Dressed to Kill* (1980) and Alfred Hitchcock's *Psycho* (1960) both found something thrilling about the slaughter of a vulnerable woman, but that thrill, it is revealed, expressed the impulses of a voyeur. *Kill Bill* is neither ironic, savage nor voyeuristic. It has no point of view whatsoever. Some have argued that as its action hero is a woman, it is a work of revenge feminism, but to be feminist you need first to be human. Despite its photographic representationalism, it never manages to be so.

Film theorists have long debated this relationship between the representational and abstract elements in cinema. The most distinguished contribution came from André Bazin, whose starting point was that 'photography affects like a phenomenon in nature, like a flower or snowflake'. His central claim, elaborated in more than 2,000 ontological articles, was that this meant that cinema has an innate, inescapable duty towards the real. With this in mind he saw Orson Welles, Roberto Rossellini and Jean Renoir as central to the canon, but his argument applies to all but the most purely experimental abstract cinema. So influential was this ethical position that, as Colin McCabe's book on Jean-Luc Godard shows, it became the founding principle of Godard's work and the New Wave as a whole.

In one scene near the beginning of *Kill Bill*, Tarantino appears to be on the verge of acknowledging Bazin's insight. As Thurman brutally stabs and murders a young woman, he cuts to the victim's small daughter, who has been watching the mayhem. Even if the idea that photographed cinema can be a comic book was tenable – which it isn't – surely this hint at the consequence of witnessing a violent act undermines the argument. Rather, while acknowledging that damage will be done, Tarantino shows that he isn't interested in that damage. This callousness wounds us, because Bazin was right. Cinema affects us like nature.

Bazin would have approved of *Mystic River* on ethical if not artistic grounds, but it seems likely that he would have detested *Kill Bill*. The irony is that Tarantino named his production company A Band Apart after Godard's *Bande à part*. Godard would hate the dishonesty of Tarantino's vision and his absurd conflation of dance and death.

FEATURE LENGTH

Exactly a hundred years ago, an Australian director, Charles Tait, made the world's first feature-length film, *The Story of the Kelly Gang*. Before 1906 there had been short and medium-length films, but nothing approaching 100 minutes, the length we in the West now associate with cinema. Judging by the surviving reactions to it, Tait's 1906 film was no masterpiece, but it had 'found' the running time that is now the industry standard, the commercial norm and the duration for which most moviegoers seem willing to escape real life.

The more you think of Tait's feature ideal, however, the less clear it becomes why we have settled on 100 minutes. The first movies were just a few minutes long, shown in circuses or rooms behind shops and aimed at working-class audiences attracted by novelty and quick thrills. Soon canny producers realised that they had to broaden their audience, and so started turning plays and literary subjects into prestige productions with elaborate costumes and name actors. Films became longer to become more middle class.

Duration has long represented prestige. D. W. Griffith's 1916 film *Intolerance* ran for over 190 minutes. In 1927 Abel Gance's *Napoléon* topped it by clocking in at more than five hours. By comparison *Gone with the Wind*, made in 1939, was a breeze at under four hours. B-movies tended to come in at the seventy-minute mark while 'Best Picture' Oscar-winners are often a stately two hours-plus.

The 100-minute standard came about for commercial reasons. Exhibitors like to show a film twice in the evening: at 6pm and 8.30pm. Add time for adverts and a quick clean of the auditorium, and you are left with 100 minutes. There is also a vague stylistic reason: three thirty-minute acts plus ten minutes of scene setting 'feels right,' perhaps fitting Aristotle's unity of time.

But you can equally argue the opposite, that there's nothing natural about 100 minutes. At short length – say ten minutes – filmmakers need to be less concerned with sustaining audience interest. Single-act dramas are more about creating worlds than obviating boredom. The filmmaker or writer is freed to become the architect of a parallel universe, or find a better balance between story, mood and aesthetics.

We tend to meet at cafés for periods of around forty minutes, so why not have a film industry organised around thirty- to forty-minute blocks rather than 100–120 minute blocks? We could pop in for a twenty- to thirty-minute film costing a pound or two, then, refreshed, head out to do other things. The impact, aesthetically, would be enormous. Plot would cease to be the be-all and end-all of commercial cinema. The cinema of sensation – car chases, dinosaurs and the like – would no longer dominate.

If it could work for shorter-form filmmaking, what about the longer form? The assumption is that long movies are bad for box office. But even this unravels under scrutiny. In the West, the two most commercially successful movies of all time came in at 194 minutes (*Titanic*) and 222 minutes (*Gone with the Wind*). And how long is the average film in the biggest film industry in the world, India's? About three hours. People in India bring food to the cinema, they talk throughout the movie, and expect musical numbers to interrupt the story. Crucial to the business plan of Indian cinema is that people go in large groups. Western cinema's two screenings in one evening isn't the only way to structure a hard-nosed exhibition business.

Long films, paced unlike Hollywood, separate you from the outside world so completely that they slow your heartbeat and sharpen your ability to look at an image. The films of Michelangelo Antonioni in the 1960s and Theo Angelopoulos from the 1970s onwards each insisted that we look at his imagery as we might a Mark Rothko painting, sustainedly, alert to existential as well as narrative content.

But if you rethink 100-minute cinema, there are further possibilities to consider beyond just shorter or longer. Adam Curtis's *The Century of the Self* (4 x 60 mins) and Alan Bleasdale's *Boys From the Blackstuff* (5 x 55 mins) , showed how well four- and five-part mid-length work deals both with unfolding drama and ideas-driven documentary. That they were both made for television should not lead us to believe that cinema has nothing to learn from them. Why can't the movie world offer its work in mid-length triptychs? We have the *Lord of the Rings* trilogy (combined running times of the special editions, 682 minutes), Krzyzstof Kieslowski's *Three Colours* trilogy (each a Tait-like 100 minutes or so) and trilogies by the likes of Baz Luhrmann, Abbas Kiarostami and Lars von Trier. But each of these was designed to be seen as three one-off experiences, years apart. Why doesn't an innovative filmmaker like Mike Figgis make a five-part movie designed to be seen on five consecutive weeks, the story and ideas flowing between each part? Would this not bind audiences into moviegoing, just as the Saturday morning serials, with their inevitable cliff-hangers, did in the earlier decades of the movies?

NOVELS

Woody Allen once said that if he had his life to live over again, he'd want it exactly the same, but without seeing the 1968 film version of John Fowles' novel, *The Magus*. Michael Caine thinks it is the worst film he's been in, which is saying something. Fowles, who himself adapted it for the screen, called it 'a disaster all the way down the line'. *The Magus* stands out from cinema's long line of botched filming of books because of the particularly wrong-headed way in which Fowles tried to shoehorn all the layers of his complex 600-page novel into two hours of screen time.

The Magus comes to mind because another complexly layered, 'difficult' novel, Michael Cunningham's *The Hours*, is currently gracing our screens. Adapted by David Hare, it is directed by Stephen Daldry, who made *Billy Elliot* (2000), and stars Nicole Kidman, Julianne Moore and Meryl Streep, who also appears in the original novel as herself – in a way. In the film she doesn't play the part of herself. Rather, she is the character who, in the book, thinks she sees Meryl Streep on the street; except that this incident doesn't occur in Hare's adaptation. Following this so far?

The Magus isn't the only ominous sign that complex novels can make ropey films. The movies of Boris Pasternak's *Dr Zhivago* (1965), James Joyce's *Ulysses* (1967), Milan Kundera's *The Unbearable Lightness of Being* (1988), Marcel Proust's *Swann's Way* (1984) and Émile Zola's *Germinal* (1993) were all bad or worse, and they are just the tip of an iceberg. The film versions of these novels added nothing to the literature; even if they had been good, they would have been superfluous.

Those who disagree would argue that books like Cunningham's, Joyce's or Kundera's are so good that they overspill the minority literary world and enter the broader culture. If they become part of the landscape of our lives (as *Sophie's Choice* and *Catch-22* certainly did) then cinema, which prides itself on being contemporary, has every right to deal with them, just as it does with news events, scandals and changing trends. I would go further. Where a novelist has only one medium (words), a filmmaker has four: photographed images, dialogue, music and even written words (captions and titles); quadruple the expressive means of novelists. Words are intrinsic to thought, but they can only imply space, visual appearance, colour and light. Film can be precise about these things but can only imply thought. Cinema stands on the edge of a dark crater of thought, moved by its silence, brushed by its breezes. The problem comes when you take an object of thought – a literary novel – and treat it with something cinema – for which thought is only a yearning. Why yearn for it when you have it between the covers?

In Cunningham's book, Streep's character, Clarissa, a fiftysomething New York lesbian publisher, goes out to buy flowers. The novelist catches the rapture of her walk. As she is about to step out of her apartment, she 'delays for a moment the plunge, the quick membrane of chill, the plain shock of immersion. New York in its racket and stern brown decrepitude, its bottomless decline, always produces a few summer mornings like this.' Lovely thoughts. A film cannot generalise about the New Yorkiness of that morning, nor the contrast between decline and momentary transcendence. If Stephen Daldry had filmed Streep pausing for a moment, then cut to swirling camera moves, we would have scoffed. He does not, because he is a very good filmmaker. *The Hours* does not fall into the trap of trying to match the fleeting joy Cunningham describes in this scene, but at times we can feel paragraphs behind shots. *The Hours* is a moving film which reaches for complex ideas; in its pacing and pauses it sometimes feels like an elegy for the novel from which it was adapted.

Cinema's relationship to novels, literary and otherwise, has always been a series of ram-raids, head butts, genuflections and bear hugs. In the first type, producers smash and grab a book because it is a bestseller, or because it has a good title or characters, plot twist or scandalous theme. The famous example of this is Ernest Hemingway's *To Have and Have Not* – far from his best work – which Hemingway bet director Howard Hawks he could not translate to the screen. Hawks took up the challenge, turned it into a vehicle for Bogart and Bacall and won the bet. But he threw out most of the plot in the process.

The second method is radical inversion: reverse key elements of the novel to accommodate the fact that films start from the outside and work in, where books do the opposite. In Mary Shelley's *Frankenstein*, the monster is talkative and eloquent. In James Whale's film of the book, he is entirely mute, which works beautifully. Usually, characters who are quiet in books but think a lot, talk more in films. With *Frankenstein*, it is the other way around. In *The Hours*, David Hare makes the famous climax of Cunningham's story talkative rather than mute. Just to complicate matters, I would say that, while the *Frankenstein* inversion works very well, Hare's, in the opposite direction, does too. It is the biggest change between book and film and the moment where both work best.

Another, extremely rare kind of adaptation is the literal one. The Soviet film theorist Vsevolod Pudovkin dreamed of film versions of books where every sentence would have its equivalent shot. This is roughly what happened in *Greed* (1924), the silent masterpiece by Erich von Stroheim, a meticulous transcription of Frank Norris' great work of nineteenth-century naturalism, *McTeague*. Attempting to match the novel's detail, von

Stroheim nearly bankrupted his studio. The film originally ran for eight hours but, even in its massively truncated form, it is a marvel.

Then there is the most productive exchange between page and screen: the analogous adaptation, where the film replaces the literary structure of a book with a cinematic one which symbolises the original. *Apocalypse Now* (1979) did this, substituting Conrad's journey up the Congo in *Heart of Darkness* with Martin Sheen's journey into Vietnam. The most famous example of analogous adaptation is Harold Pinter's screenplay of *The French Lieutenant's Woman* by, of all people, John Fowles. Pinter has written 24 screenplays, every one of them being an adaptation of 'difficult' material, either other people's novels or his own plays. His *Go-Between*, from the L. P. Hartley book, is perhaps his best, but *The French Lieutenant's Woman* illustrates more clearly the principle of analogy in adaptation.

The problem facing Pinter and director Karel Reisz was this: Fowles' book told the story of a Victorian Englishwoman, ruined by an affair with the lieutenant of the title, who enters into another relationship. To contrast the mores of the past with his own time, Fowles filtered his nineteenth-century narrative through the prism of the 1960s. Plus, he intended a pastiche of Thackeray. Plus, he wrote alternative endings. Pinter's analogy? He invented a modern story in which Meryl Streep – who plays the Englishwoman and who is becoming the patron saint of literary cinema – is making a film with actor Jeremy Irons, about the characters in Fowles' book. In this new story they begin an affair. The film narrates the characters' story and the actors' story simultaneously. It worked not only because there were two interlocking plots, but because the second contained the first – a richer philosophical premise. Fowles called Pinter's screenplay 'a brilliant metaphor' for the book.

The Hours does not attempt such a rethink. In a way, it does not need to, because the novel's cutting between the lives of three woman in three different time periods seems custom-made for cinema. From D. W. Griffith's *Intolerance* of 1916, filmmakers have delighted in the almost magical way that film can act like a time machine, connecting temporally distant events. The book of *The Hours* does this, and so does the film, almost giddily. In the novel, a disturbed and unravelling Virginia Woolf lowers her head into a washbasin, then pauses, afraid to look up again to face herself in the mirror. In the film, when Nicole Kidman as Woolf does this, director Daldry cuts to Meryl Streep lifting her head. Such editing links between the women happen frequently at the beginning of the film.

The creative challenge in adapting *The Hours* was not to be faithful to a great book, but to work out why that book is great and, as Pinter, Coppola, von Stroheim and James Whale did, reinvent that greatness for the movies. Film history is full of very talented people like Daldry, Streep, Kidman and Julianne Moore facing that creative challenge. Many fail because they are respectful or tentative.

Amongst the very best films derived from literary novels are these: *Journal d'un curé de campagne* (novel by Georges Bernanos, director Robert Bresson, France, 1950); *Solaris* (novel by Stanislaw Lem, director Andrei Tarkovsky, USSR, 1972); *Le Mépris* (novel by Alberto Moravia, director Jean-Luc Godard, France, 1963); *Crash* (novel J. G. Ballard, director David Cronenberg, Canada, 1996). Notice one thing: none of them are Anglo-American commercial films. An astonishing three-quarters of Oscar-winning films have been adaptations of books; and, during the 1950s, the same proportion applied to all American films. Yet it is with the middlebrow novels of Graham Greene, Dashiell Hammett, Raymond Chandler, Patricia Highsmith, James M. Cain, John Steinbeck, Ernest Hemingway and Robert Louis Stevenson, rather than more highbrow fare, that Hollywood has distinguished itself. Mainstream cinema has almost completely failed to achieve anything creatively from more difficult literature. It is too afraid of ambiguity to do so.

So why try? I think the answer lies in a starchy 1908 film called *L'Assassinat du duc de Guise*. Before it, cinema was a medium of sensation, a fairground attraction. This film was a self-conscious adaptation of a semi-literary work and, when it was released, a new audience came to the cinema: the middle classes. There had been literary adaptations before the *Duc de Guise*, but it rang the box office bell and replaced sensation in cinema with a certain type of contemplation.

This has been very good for the art of cinema, except that since then too many people in the film world have felt that they must go eight rounds in the ring with big intellectual books. Cinema's inferiority complex has been plain to see since its earliest days. Few countries respect their films as much as their novels; when it comes to the crunch and national film industries have to prove their worth, many still point to their literary adaptations. When they do not feel threatened, when they are buoyant and on a winning streak – as France was in the 1920s and 1960s, Germany in the 1970s, Iran and Denmark in the 1990s and Latin America today – they seldom adapt literary books. Or, if they do, they tear into them with the hungry conviction that there's cinematic meat in them somewhere.

The adaptors of *The Hours* were mostly up to their material, but part of me is with Woody Allen's hero, Ingmar Bergman. 'Film has nothing to do with literature', Bergman said. 'We should avoid making films out of books.'

ENDINGS

Far be it for me to suggest that you don't have your fingers on the pulse of popular cinema, but in case you haven't seen all Hollywood's blockbusters this year, I have selflessly done so on your behalf. The summer is nearly over, so I've bagged all the biggies. What, then, is the state of American popular cinema in 2005?

At first sight, things seem like business as usual. The most successful cultural export industry in the world has churned out loads of rubbish. In the last year, the Hollywood sausage machine has given us *Robots*, *Mr and Mrs Smith*, *Star Wars Episode 3*, *Fantastic Four*, *Wedding Crashers* and *The Island*, all 'high concept', all low achievement. If the *Star Wars* film had been in French, it would have been accused of being ponderous and plotless. But instead it was ponderous and plotless and hugely successful, taking $810m in cinemas around the world, which makes its DVD rental and sales estimate an additional $1bn. Of the above six stinkers, the first four, it should objectively be noted, were made by 20th Century Fox. Good to see Rupert Murdoch's empire contributing as much to the art of cinema as it does to that of television and newspapers.

But mainstream cinema in 2005 was different from recent years in a number of ways. For a start there were fewer sequels, which is great, except that there was also a downturn in box office. If the industry concludes – as *Variety* did – that takings fell because there were fewer sequels, then we can expect more next year. More encouragingly, three of this year's big hits were actually quite good. *Batman Begins* (Warner Bros., £18m in Britain so far), *War of the Worlds* (UIP, £32m) and *Charlie and the Chocolate Factory* (Warner Bros., £19m) were each distinctively mounted and – in parts, at least – intelligently spectacular. Three good Hollywood blockbusters in one year is rare, but these films were intriguing in other ways. Each used production design to signify the dysfunction of its dark-haired, central character. Lighting and colour expressed his mental problems, so much so in the case of *War of the Worlds* that some multiplexes stuck notes on their doors telling audiences that the dark look of the film was 'as its director intended'. More significantly, as many commentators noted, two of the films were veiled commentaries on America today. Johnny Depp's infantile, squeaky-voiced man-child who has created a Neverland for himself and who can only engage with children, usually sadistically, could not fail to call Michael Jackson to mind. And the brilliant first hour of *War of the Worlds*, where America is invaded by beings from elsewhere, is a dead cert 9/11 allegory.

Even these good films were frustrating, however. Two of them in particular stumbled where mainstream American films really intend to succeed – in their third acts. Los Angeles is the Mecca of story structure in screenplays. It may not be the most creative place in the film world, but it prides itself on being the home of narrative cinema. Its screenwriting gurus preach a three-act creed, where the final act resolves the hero's journey satisfyingly, answering the psychological and thematic questions established in act one and explored in act two. Act three is – according to Robert McKee and Syd Field – not a place for subplots (they should be resolved at the climax of act two), but for the deep, meaty revelation of the solution to the problem which will restore order to our hero's life and world.

Neither *Batman Begins* nor *War of the Worlds* quite afforded these satisfactions. The former asked very engaging questions about its central character, Bruce Wayne. How should he grieve for his murdered parents? How can his father's philanthropy adapt to modern life? How can the son's rage be channelled into something good? But when the third act kicks in, *Batman Begins* becomes too manic in its determination to build to a big climax to complete what it had set out to do. And this was as nothing compared to *War of the Worlds*. Not since *Saving Private Ryan* (1998), also directed by Steven Spielberg, has a film started so well and ended so badly. The first hour was even better than *Batman Begins*. Spielberg's trademark broken family is once again the focus. Dad has the kids for the weekend, but he knows nothing about them and cares little. Spielberg is the master of such somnambulant Americana, terrifying his complacent world – ripping it up, hurling objects through it with Old Testament wrath. As with *Saving Private Ryan*, when a filmmaker does this to you in act one, he has you completely. So what does Spielberg do? He throws it all away. When the tripod extra-terrestrials invade, the psychological and social richness goes. Act one of *War of the Worlds* treats you as an adult, but half way in it assumes you are a child, trowelling on the absurdities in set-piece after set-piece. In fact, it's difficult not to conclude that failure to bring its planes in to land has been the central creative problem in Hollywood for a generation. Since the earliest days of CGI and before, mainstream American filmmakers have not so much resolved their dramas as abandoned them in favour of the new fifth gear that CGI affords – impossible, melodramatic otherworldliness.

So what can be done? Something radical perhaps? I'm all for the *droit d'auteur* not to have his or her film tampered with, but if the great mainstream American films are too over-the-top at the end, too well-endowed with action and multiple endings, why doesn't someone – for the sake of moviegoers and in the interests of the filmmakers themselves – quietly return these films to the cutting rooms and, er, improve them? There are copyright issues involved, and such action might well attract the attention of the odd Hollywood lawyer, but putting that aside, wouldn't cutting these movies make the world a better place? Maybe the BBFC, which has the right to ask porn directors to remove scenes before certification, could do the same on aesthetic grounds? It could email Spielberg saying that *War of the Worlds* will get a 12A certificate as long as he agrees to make act three a bit more believable. Then, in order not to incur the costs of reshoots, the offending directors could ask someone like Jean-Luc Godard to make the new endings. He could then simply excise the offending scenes, insert his signature black screen and a quotation from Howard Hawks or Louis Althusser (either would do) and we'd have a better result.

War of the Worlds and *Batman Begins* might be *films maudits* after Godard got his hands on them, but they are *films maudits* anyway, and my suggestion would make them *maudit* in more palatable ways. If summer movies were started by Spielberg and finished by Godard, they might turn out to be the best ever made.

EPICS

As I've said before, the whole point about cinema, surely, is the close-up of the human face. Huge images such as the Sphinx, Mount Rushmore and the colossal statues in Greece and Rome established the sense of wonder to be had in gazing at magnified physiognomy, but until the movies, such depictions were rare. Even in vast paintings – of battles, landscapes, coronations – the human beings tended to be no more than twice or thrice our size. But Greta Garbo's inscrutable face was hundreds of times bigger than that of those who read their own thoughts into it. Therein lies the wonder of the movies.

It is perhaps surprising, therefore, that cinema is currently undergoing a flight from close-ups. It does this every now and again, as if bored with the effortless way in which macro-imagery can enrapture. Instead of bringing the camera close, as Alfred Hitchcock did in *Vertigo* (1958), Sergei Eisenstein did in *Bronenosets Potyomkin/Battleship Potemkin* (1925), Ingmar Bergman did in *Persona* (1966) and Carl Theodor Dreyer did in *La Passion de Jeanne d'Arc/The Passion of Joan of Arc* (1928), movies today are retreating to the apparent splendours of the wide shot, the panorama, the spectacular vista intended to make us say 'wow'. This was the *Lord of the Rings* trilogy's technique, and is that of the Brad Pitt-starring *Troy*, and the eco-disaster picture *The Day After Tomorrow*. Even that barometer of US cinema's artistic ambitions, Martin Scorsese, has been framing more widely recently, as *Gangs of New York* (2002) showed.

This trend towards wide shots is in part explained by the landmark technological changes which cinema is undergoing. Those who doubt that the digital revolution is significant should consider the fact that the two previous occasions on which film 'went wide' and turned to stories set in classical times were the 1950s – after the switch to the various widescreen processes such as CinemaScope – and the very first decades of filmmaking, when audiences were still agog and directors such as Cecil B. DeMille presented frieze-like tableaux of classical excess. Both were formative moments, and so is the present one. In each of these three periods, producers and directors who were faced with a new technology fell back on primitive, likeable, pre-cinematic ideas of showmanship. At times of great change in cinema, it seems, the movie world abandons its unique selling point, the close-

A blank background and the contours of the human face: anti-tableau filmmaking in *Battleship Potemkin*

up, to impress audiences in more conventional ways. In retrospect, *Titanic* (1997) – still the most commercially successful film ever made – was e-cinema's declaration of intent.

What makes me approach multiplexes with a heavy heart these days is that every filmmaker wants a go at CGI. I like landscape and cityscape cinema, but the current tableau filmmaking is a digression. The moment when it dawned on big-budget directors that the computerisation of the movie process meant that they could show all those things they couldn't show before was probably an exciting one in Hollywood. Loads of dinosaur/cyborg/city-destruction movies were submitted and green-lit. But as is often the case with adrenaline rushes and creative stampedes, good old-fashioned inventiveness got lost in the process. For those of us on the receiving end of the movies which resulted, there was a limit to the number of times we could gasp at a flyover of the Colosseum, or at vast marauding armies or the (unconvincingly weightless) destruction of one of the world's famous buildings.

In the current rejection of the close-up in mainstream cinema, filmmakers seem to have learnt nothing from the past. The 1950s epics now seem stolid, and most of DeMille is unwatchable. In a few years' time, *The Phantom Menace* (1999), George Lucas's first *Star Wars* prequel – which was filmed almost entirely in medium and wide shot – will look like one of the most boring movies ever made. Entranced by his ability to show Hieronymus Bosch-like scenes of myriad complexity, why would Lucas do anything as boring as bring the camera close to the faces of his actors? Future audiences will be un-impressed by such CGI showreeling and will be perplexed by the film's lack of foreground. What made the *Matrix* films visually interesting, despite their sonorous verbal gobbledygook, is that the Wachowski brothers cast a wide range of facial types, lit them from above to emphasise the texture of each and then photographed them so that they filled the screen.

What, then, of the most talented directors at work today? How have they responded to the new possibilities of digital filming? One of the best, Iran's Abbas Kiarostami, made his first significant digital film, *Ten*, two years ago. His budget was far lower than Lucas's, of course, but his technique was nonetheless remarkable. He made a film in which every shot except one was a medium close-up. Just as Hitchcock, Dreyer and Eisenstein in their bravest, most driven projects reached for cinema's unique selling point so, in *Ten*, did Kiarostami.

When cinema next reinvents itself, that will be the lesson to remember.

CHILDREN

Children's films seem to be on a roll. Exactly a decade ago, *Toy Story* married kids' themes with adult jokes and CGI and created what has since become a dynamic, shiny, intelligent formula. It revived the animation genre, took $360m in cinemas around the world and made it fun again to take kids to the movies.

Then came *Toy Story 2* (1999), *Shrek* (2001), *Shrek 2* (2004), *A Shark's Tale* (2004) and *The Incredibles* (2004): high-quality American family fare for the computer age. Defiantly post-Disney (whose wholesomeness they lampooned), they were marketed aggressively and drove the DVD boom. At last American family cinema had ditched its Eisenhower-era cosiness.

Ten years later, the wonders of CGI no longer surprise us. We are used to seeing toys, cartoon characters, dinosaurs and spaceships in three dimensions and photorealistic detail. Does this render earlier kids' films so pictorially primitive that they will no longer speak to young people? Imagine the birth of a child – perhaps your own. Now put in a sealed shoebox a DVD of a film for them to watch on their seventeenth birthday and another, in another box, on their fourteenth. What would each film be? *A Shark's Tale*? *Toy Story 2*? Each of these would capture some of the cinematic dynamism of our age, our knowingness and sense of fun, but is that enough of a gift to seal in a shoebox and donate to the future?

I'm not sure. Here are a few films I'd donate to tomorrow's children.

Albert Lamorisse's *Le Ballon rouge/The Red Balloon* (France, 1956). Compare it to Chaplin's films about kids and you see how great it is. Seen entirely from the perspective of a six-year-old boy, it shows him finding the balloon of the title, befriending it and losing it. He isn't allowed to take it – his metaphorical pal – to school. Schools are no place for poetry. Like many great children's films, it has little dialogue and deals with feelings of loneliness. *The Red Balloon* was much copied, never bettered.

Dorota Kedzierzawska's film *Wrony/Crows* (Poland, 1994) is also about loneliness, and the most moving children's film I know. It tells the story of a neglected ten-year-old girl nicknamed Crow who kidnaps a toddler and tries to mother her. Its title sequence is copied in *Billy Elliot* (2000), and it would appeal most to girls of around twelve. Brilliant and devastating.

Das Singende, klingende Baumchen/The Singing Ringing Tree (East Germany, 1957) was based on stories by the Brothers Grimm, bought by the BBC in the 1960s, dubbed and chopped into a children's television series. It was, for many of us, our first sip of neat surrealism and caused many a nightmare. Yet looked at now, at full length, Francesco Stefani's original is a remarkable piece of communist-era European fantasy. Its low-tech aesthetic hardly detracts from the mysterious appeal of its story.

Hayao Miyazaki's *Tonari no Totoro/My Neighbour Totoro* (Japan, 1988). Unlike Miyazaki's recent *Hauru no ugoku shiro/Howl's Moving Castle* (2004), which was far too long, this mid-period masterpiece goes by in a breeze. It has hardly been marketed in the West, yet it sells like hot cakes because, quite simply, it is a wonder. Satsuki and Mei's mother has been taken to hospital, their father tells them not to go into the vast forest, but they do, where they discover *totoros*. Miyazaki's films are mostly about little girls and many feature ecological spirits, but this is his most uplifting.

Then, dare I say it, a Japanese silent movie. *Otona no miru ehon – Umarete wa mita keredo/I was Born But...* was made in 1932 in Japan by Yasujiro Ozu. Rarely seen, it's about two grumpy brothers who move to a new town and get into fights. Their father is a salaryman, but when they compare him to their friends' dads, they are ashamed of his lowly status. The film charts their slow realisation that social status isn't everything. If you think Henry Thomas is good as Elliot in *E. T. The Extra-Terrestrial* (1982) or Jean-Pierre Léaud is great as Antoine in Truffaut's *Les Quatres cents coups/The 400 Blows* (1959), look at Hideo Sugawara and Tomio Aoki as the brothers. Their performances are as fresh and convincing as it's possible to imagine, and the camera – always at their height – captures it all.

Is there more at stake here than a shoebox game? The government seems to think so. The UK Film Council, with the encouragement of the Department of Culture, Media and Sport (DCMS), is producing a new media literacy charter, drafted by a task force from Ofcom, Channel 4, BBC, the British Film Institute and Skillset, on the premise that teenagers should be able to read moving imagery as much as words. This used to be called cineliteracy, then media literacy and now – a catch-all – twenty-first-century literacy.

The assumption is familiar: that television and cinema are such a presence in young people's lives that we should teach them to be discerning about both. Left to the market alone, kids will see only the cinematic equivalent of a Big Mac. Which is not to say that CGI children's cinema is the movie equivalent of fast food. But if we believe that film is the language in which countries of the world increasingly speak to each other, then we need to retain scepticism of the kinetic sheen of CGI. *Toy Story* isn't bad for us. But other kids' films, such as the ones above, are more complex and make us feel more human.

Get the shoebox out.

FESTIVALS

The London Film Festival has just celebrated its 50th year. The Edinburgh International Film Festival was sixty this summer. Venice turned 63. Cannes is sixty in May. The film festival regulation body, FIAPF (Fédération Internationale des Associations de Producteurs de Film), reckons there are 700 of them in total; the *New York Times* claims over 1,000. The number of festivals has rocketed in the last decade.

Venice, Edinburgh, Cannes and London are right to celebrate their longevity. But as the elite of the festival circuit clink champagne glasses, it would be surprising if their smiles weren't a little strained. Despite their glamour and ubiquity, festivals are in crisis. There are just too many of them, and they are too political and colluding.

At least 3,000 films are made each year. Film festivals are the shop windows for such production – visible and glamorous, but also powerless in that they (mostly) only respond to it. Since only around 150 of the 3,000 films are of real artistic merit, the thousand shop windows have to fight tooth and claw to showcase the best. When I was director of Edinburgh, I frequently locked horns with the then director of London. Cannes tends its relationship with Pedro Almodóvar with great care, but if he doesn't win the Palme d'Or soon, might he switch allegiance to Venice? Venice has long been Woody Allen's festival of choice, but might Toronto be making approaches behind the scenes?

To make things worse, FIAPF operates a pointless A-list of the 12 festivals it thinks deserve top ranking: Berlin, Mar Del Plata (Argentina), Cannes, Shanghai, Moscow, Karlovy Vary, Locarno, Montreal, Venice, San Sebastian, Tokyo and Cairo. The omissions are glaring – no Sundance, London, Rotterdam or Toronto. To qualify, each of the 12 must have a competition section containing at least 14 world premieres. So the A-listers alone have at least 168 slots for new films to fill, which means that in theory all 150 of the good movies get swallowed up.

That the film festival circuit is political with a big 'P' isn't surprising. The Italian fascist government meddled with the programming at Venice way back in 1938; the interference led to the founding of Cannes the next year. In 1995 and 1996 a major start-up festival in Prague tried to replace Karlovy Vary (established in 1946 in the province of Bohemia) as the region's main film event, on the grounds that Karlovy Vary was tainted by its past as a showcase for Soviet cinema.

Such catfights are exacerbated by the amount of public money at stake. Few film festivals raise more than twenty per cent of their income from box office sales. Most of the funding comes from the public sector or sponsorship. Of the thousand or so festivals, a handful have budgets upwards of £10m, two of Britain's festivals cost over £1m, and the smallest are in the £10,000 bracket. If the average budget is, say, £400,000, then the total cost of the circuit is £400m. (This excludes the cost of trips by PRs, journalists and so on.) Perhaps forty per cent of this £400m comes from the private sector, which leaves £240m from the public purse.

How is this spend justified? The festivals argue that they are net contributors to their local economies, that they raise the profile of their cities and that they develop audiences' taste for non-mainstream films. All true, but in the last decade, the first two reasons – economic and PR – have taken precedence. Film festivals have proliferated because economic development departments and tourist boards understand them.

The implications are significant. Festivals grew out of the film society movement of the 1920s. Their original purpose was, in the words of Venice director Marco Müller, to 'reveal what the markets hide'. I have argued before that the international film industry is boosted, as if by steroids, by Hollywood's massive advertising spend on its own product. The film festival circuit is, then, a counter market, itself boosted by an annual steroid injection of £240m. Piers Handling of the Toronto Film Festival called this counter-market an 'alternative distribution network'.

But is this how festivals now operate? When the latest *Matrix* film premiered at Cannes, as did *The Da Vinci Code*, it was clear that the festival was spending some of its (public) money to subsidise Hollywood publicity budgets. If that is what is needed to draw the world's media, which will then cover the alternative films on offer, then fine. But festivals are becoming too collusive, and seem to have forgotten their original *raison d'être*. As well as showing new films, festivals have always had retrospectives, masterclasses, tributes and so on. But why are so many of these about first world directors who are already part of the canon? Another Cocteau season? Another Bergman or Kurosawa retrospective? This conservative programming is the heart of the problem. African filmmakers, or the great Indian directors – with the exception of Satyajit Ray – don't get a look in.

If festivals are to justify their existence, they need to engage with the history of film in the broadest sense, not simply enjoy the glitter of the mainstream. Only then will they reveal what the market hides.

real

glimpses of life beyond the movies

JAZZ

Ken Burns' massive documentary about the history of jazz, which ran on a BBC midnight slot till June, tripled sales of jazz CDs in the US. It is one of the longest single-subject documentaries ever shown on British television, and in scale and gravitas gives *The World at War* a run for its money. Whilst the jazzerati noted its various weaknesses and ellipses, television critics were largely exuberant. The consensus was that this is what quality television should aspire to. It has been seen as a brave, defining statement in Jane Root's new BBC2, aimed at baby boomers with attention spans longer than Channel 4's Generation Y-ers.

It had the same impact in the US. There, Ken Burns is the imprimatur of the Public Broadcasting Service: he is its licence to continue. I bet he's mentioned in the introduction to its annual report. His trademark marriage of the epic and the pedagogic has defined the high style on which much of PBS's often routine programming coat-tails.

Jazz was sponsored by General Motors, a fact that produces a wry smile among documentarists. GM once, indirectly and unwillingly, made a less public-spirited contribution to the documentary form in Michael Moore's 1989 film *Roger and Me*. In the 1980s GM's Chairman, Roger Smith, and his new regime axed 30,000 jobs in Flint, Michigan. The dogged Moore tried to confront him with the social damage done. The film was a hilarious, rage-fuelled letter bomb about how one town became a rat-infested crime capital.

Consideration of *Roger and Me* casts *Jazz* in a less flattering light. Moore's film was edgy, filmic and first-person, as its title suggests. In comparison, *Jazz* is aesthetically stolid. It chooses a very conventional explicatory mode and sticks to it. It is vanilla documentary, bloodlessly, grandiosely schoolmarmy. It misses by a mile most of the great things that documentary films can at their best do and falls into all the formula traps. As a vehicle for information, a conveyor belt, it is exceptional and I too will buy more music because of it. But it never becomes more complex than that. It has no shape, no driving energy, nothing pre-intellectual.

Jazz's recent overvaluation raises a perennial problem for documentary and, perhaps, criticism in general. Films which are even halfway good are feted because the great stuff, the electrifying films, are seldom-seen, decaying in bad prints, unyieldingly long, resistant to television slots and under-scheduled by art-house cinema programmers. It is not only in comparison with the wit and passion of *Roger and Me* that *Jazz* falls down. Consider Kazuo Hara's *Yuki Yukite shingun*/*The Emperor's Naked Army Marches On* (1987); Viktor Kossakovsky's *Sreda*/*Wednesday* (1997); Claude Lanzmann's *Shoah* from 1985 (and his new postscript to it, *Sobibór, 14 octobre 1943, 16 heures*/*Sobibor Oct. 14th 1943, 4pm* from 2001); Juris Podnieks's *Hello Do You Hear Us?* (1990); the Maysles' *Grey Gardens* (1975), Mikhail Kalatozov's *Soy Cuba*/*I am Cuba* (1964); Marcel Ophüls' *Le Chagrin et la pitié*/*The Sorrow and the Pity* (1969); Shohei Imamura's *Nippon Sengoshi – Madamu onboro no seikatsu*/*History of Post-war Japan as Told by a Bar Hostess* (1970); John Huston's *Let There be Light* (1946); Lindsay Anderson's *O Dreamland!* (1953); or Maximillian Schell's *Marlene* (1984). Compared to these dazzling documentaries (which, I repeat, are seldom shown), *Jazz* looks very ordinary indeed.

So what makes the others extraordinary? It's hard to generalise, but I'll take a deep breath and try.

(1) Their shapes are not discernible from the start. Their ends are unforeseeable. They change shape. (2) Unlike planned fiction films, which sometimes steal documentary's clothes for a bit of edge, they have uncertainty built into their structures. (Ken Burns' intellectual surety precludes this.) (3) They avoid 'slot aesthetics', the ways in which films are tailored to fit into a television schedule. These include 'grabbiness' at the beginning, stating your theme up front then simply repeating it in the body of the film, and resistance to ambiguity. (4) Less tangibly, the movements of these films are contained within them. *Jazz* moves to the beat of something external (history): it creates no inner pulse and, ironically, no syncopation. (5) These films are 'messy', not everything fits the structure (as in point 2). (6) None of them are pedagogic. This should be obvious. If a film sets out solely to impart information, it is no more important than a training video. (7) They are not reducible to what they are 'about'. This is the old 'subject shouldn't be contained within form' rule. (8) They all have action in the present, even when they are relating past events. We must see decisions being made on camera. (9) They all contain some kind of gap, something lost, unfilmable, inexpressible. (10) Their commentaries, if they have one (and most don't), couldn't be stripped off and used as a radio play in itself.

It's remarkable, in fact, how much can be generalised about this random selection of documentaries. What is more, these ten commandments can be boiled down to just two. Great documentaries must build on the uncertainty of the process, and they must not contain their subject matter as a jug contains water; they must be it.

Jazz fails on both counts, so it could be a book, or a radio series. Great films could not possibly, ever, be either.

FRIEDMANS

It has long been the immodest contention of this author that the changing relationship between escapism and realism is becoming the defining issue for modern cinema. Movies have always idealised their subjects, but the digitisation of the filmic process, the triumph of the Iranian para-realist directors, and the rhetorical challenge of Lars von Trier's Danish movement Dogme – all of which took place in the late 1980s to mid-1990s – as well as the more recent revival of pure documentary, constitute a cinematic reorientation towards the real which is rarely paralleled in film history. The naturalist directors of the 1920s didn't have anything like the same impact, nor even, arguably, did the Italian neo-realists or the *cinéma vérité* movement of the early 1960s. Peter Jackson's jokey campaigning for what he called the 'f-word' – fantasy – at the recent Oscars shows that even the director of the *Lord of the Rings* films knows how much realism is making the running in twenty-first-century filmmaking.

Cinephiles should be delighted. The technological, aesthetic and audience barriers which have for years dogged the movie world seem to be melting away. A new candid cinema of the unfeigned and the raw is the result.

Its trump card is its ability to astonish and its latest exemplar will do just that. Andrew Jarecki's documentary *Capturing the Friedmans* won the grand jury prize at Sundance 2003 and electrified the festival circuit thereafter. A detailed portrait of the breakdown of an apparently normal, if somewhat exhibitionist, Long Island Jewish family, it is certain to become a talking point when it is finally released in Britain in April. Its subject matter – the father Arnold's paedophilia, the possibility that he abused his son Jesse, the allegations that together they then sexually assaulted boys in Arnold's computer class – alone is the stuff of tabloid headlines. But when you throw in the fact that eldest son David is New York's most successful birthday party clown and, most remarkably, that the Friedmans filmed the twists and turns in their fortunes – particularly, with inexplicable good humour, the awful bits – the fascination becomes understandable.

Its relevance to the broader question about realism in modern cinema becomes clear when it is compared to another award-winning film about paedophilia, Clint Eastwood's

Mystic River (2003). Eastwood is old school and his movie is about the damage and violence that flows through subsequent generations when a child is abused. Its seriousness and grandeur impressed many in the film world, as its recent Oscars for Sean Penn and Tim Robbins show. Others were concerned not only by the fact that Penn's and particularly Robbins' performances were actually rather awkward, but also that Eastwood's interest in moral archetype, and entertainment cinema's tendency to classicise story norms, seriously reduced the film's ability to deal with the messy realities of abuse. It felt, rather, like one of those 1950s problem pictures – concerned but aloof.

What makes *Capturing the Friedmans*, by contrast, an outstanding work of (documentary) film is that it not only has room for the spiky, ambiguous bits of paedophile cases, but seems to find dignity in them. It does this in two ways. Firstly, flaunting the traditions of neatness in movie storytelling, it undergoes no fewer than seven consecutive narrative transformations: first it is a character study of an abuser, then a miscarriage of justice tale which segues into a surreal family portrait, then an account of an extraordinary psychohistory involving a 13-year-old having sex with his 8-year-old brother, then a campaigning piece about false memory syndrome, then an anti-oedipal narrative where Dad is beloved and Mom is the villain, then an essay on filial imperviousness to truth, then an account of the competence, or otherwise, of a sex crime unit. Each contains revelations, each is undercut with comedy.

Secondly, its characters are far more unusual than those in fictional cinema. Arnold plays 'Heaven, I'm in Heaven, and my heart beats so that I can hardly speak...' on the piano the night before he begins his sentence for ninety cases of sexual assault. Normal character expectations are thwarted. One of the few victims prepared to speak to director Jarecki gives perhaps the least believable interview in the film. And one of the sex crime professionals makes the alarming assertion that you have to interview a possibly abused child by telling them what happened. Jesse is videoed singing and dancing on the courtroom steps just hours after he has been sentenced, aged 19, to 6–18 years in prison. Many films have dealt with child abuse (the issue's arc of horrific revelation is almost generic) yet none until *Capturing the Friedmans* has captured it in the round. And none would dare take as its main character a clown-paedophile-videographer-escapist.

To contrast *Mystic River* and the Friedmans film reveals a vital point: since new candid cinema respects the surrealism of the truth and the messiness of real life, it could play a crucial role in the continuing maturation of film. If *Capturing the Friedmans* does well at the box office, its honesty may prove infectious and, as a result, well-meaning movies such as *Mystic River* will engage, in the future, more vitally with their subject.

FAHRENHEIT 9/11

November 2003

Eight months before the Weinsteins left Miramax
and the company was downsized…

For the first time in a decade or more, the frenzy caused when 5,000 film and showbiz journalists gathered in Cannes this May had some substance to it. Usually the big story is that Madonna wore a basque to a screening or that Lars von Trier fell out with Björk. But in 2004, unathletic critics were sprinting up the steps of the Palais du Festival to see a serious documentary with no stars in it.

Michael Moore's *Fahrenheit 9/11* has already stacked up the column inches. His apparent hubris has been dissected, but his new work's innovations as a film, and its potential effect on the film industry, have been overlooked.

Its first innovation is based on one of the oldest tricks in the journalistic book: the 'fine-toothed comb' rule. We have all seen the footage of George W. Bush in a classroom as he is told of the attacks on the World Trade Center. You would think that nothing more could be gleaned from these moments of video, but Moore's researchers discovered something in the material which produced an audible gasp at the Cannes screening.

Dazed, Bush scans around him and spies a children's book about a goat. He starts reading. Moore's commentary gives Bush the benefit of the doubt, at first: maybe he's just doing something with his hands as he processes the problem. But the President keeps reading, apparently engaged by the tribulations of the goat in question. Moore puts a clock on the screen to count the time. For seven full minutes, Bush reads this children's book.

For ironist or journalist alike, this is a real *coup de cinéma*. Moore's adroit use of such moments begs the question of why the US networks, who shot this footage and must have noticed Bush's prevarication, didn't use it.

And his eye catches other telling moments. The photographs from Abu Ghraib emerged as he was editing, but Moore had something more. With crews in the field, he sought out details such as a drunk Arab who falls asleep in the sun, under a blanket, and gets an erection. US soldiers see it and touch it, handling it like a joystick. A single incident in the flow of many, but cinema can capture such indicators of disrespect, and concretise them.

In an equally disturbing vein, Moore has his reporters quiz US troops on what it was like being in the tanks as they went into battle. Several describe how they were able to wire their CD players into the helmet talkback system inside the tanks. They describe excitedly how they played, at full blast, a heavy metal track by a group called the Bloodhound Gang containing the lyric, 'Burn motherfucker burn', as they raced towards Iraqi cities. The bleak poetic point is that armies have always used battle cries, and popular music has produced much that is suitably aggressive and reactionary.

Moore's longish pre-title sequence describes the relationship between the Bushes and the Saudis in the years and months before the attack. In his account, Moore brings us to the morning of 9/11, then runs the title sequence of his film and only after that does he present the most graceful sequence in the whole film. He plays the sound of the planes crashing into the twin towers and the screams of shock on Manhattan's streets, but over an entirely black screen. We don't need to see the images because, of course, they are burned into our minds. This is a simple but remarkably effective cinematic idea which should influence the portrayal of that day hereafter.

As cinema, *Fahrenheit 9/11* breaks some new ground. It also looks like it might bring about some changes in the film industry. The first is, with reservations, a good one. As I write, the trade press are announcing that Moore's film will be the first theatrical documentary feature to be released in the Middle East. There have been many great non-fiction films about this region – Borhane Alaouie's outstanding *Kafr Kassem* (Lebanon, 1974), which depicts an Israeli massacre of Arabs in 1956, is the first that comes to mind; but these are never shown in cinemas there. Since Moore is careful to show not only liberals who oppose the war in Iraq but also middle-American Republicans and families closely associated to the military, this might challenge the opinion of audiences in the United Arab Emirates, Syria, Jordan, Lebanon and Qatar that Amrika is monolithically supportive of Bush.

The second implication for the film world is that *Fahrenheit 9/11* could bring about the sale of its production company, Miramax. There has long been tension between Miramax and Disney, who acquired the distributor-producer in 1993, but the *New York Times* reported recently that Disney boss Michael Eisner has been talking of a sale because of the 'accumulated aggravation' he felt at Miramax co-chairmen Bob and Harvey Weinstein. *Fahrenheit 9/11* might just provide the final push.

Though Miramax has released many sentimental and po-faced literary films over the years, it helped to lift the studios out of their 1980s obsession with teenagers. It created a middlebrow in US cinema whose lasting value has been to pave the way for the country's more innovative, intelligent directors. Anything which shakes the foundation of the company could have a negative knock-on for mature American filmmaking, which would be just one of the ironies of Moore's film. It already looks like a landmark in documentary history.

LENI

For dynamism alone, no female film director has matched the shots and cuts of Third Reich propagandist Leni Riefenstahl, who died on 8 September this year, aged 101. But the obituaries have missed a further and more curious point – that no female artist of the twentieth century has taken so much pleasure in looking at men. Essentially, she was an erotic artist.

In a different age Riefenstahl might have made porn movies, although she would have considered herself too classy for that. *Triumph des Willens/Triumph of the Will* (1935) had the suspense and build-up of sophisticated pornography, and photographed men in partial erotic archetypes. Her two Olympic films (1938) stripped the athletes bare then exalted their bodies. Her still photographs of the Nuba tribespeople of Sudan, a project she began in the 1960s, again centred on active, naked males. Yet, as if to prove Roland Barthes' point that pornography has no subtext, this bravura gallery of diverse masculine display is, in the end, a narrow body of work. The artist's eye does not stray beyond the immediate erotic force field. There is no flicker, no insight captured by chance – Barthes' 'punctum' again, the unconscious detail in a photograph that 'pricks' or 'bruises' you.

This absence of uncertainty does not consign Riefenstahl to the dustbin of film history. Ingmar Bergman, Billy Wilder and Busby Berkeley were great filmmakers, yet their work contains nothing extraneous to the main story or idea. What is more distinctive about Riefenstahl's career – given the events of her life, it is astonishing – is that she had no aesthetic breakdown. Third-rate directors plough the same furrow all their lives, and some first-rate ones, such as John Ford, remain classicists to the end. But most great artists transform their work. In the world of film, directors as varied as Bergman, Hitchcock and Powell/Pressburger came to a stylistic crisis and changed direction. The themes which interested audiences shifted, technology changed, and they adjusted their aesthetic accordingly. Yet Riefenstahl, whose way of making movies was allied to a national regime which became an international byword for monstrosity, sallied forth, when she was allowed to, in an arrow-straight line and made imagery of the exact same kind as she had while under the spell of the Nazis. There was not a kink in her path. There is no conceptual or compositional difference between the early shots of *Olympiad*, for example, and her Nuba pictures. She believed in the sublime (in the Burkean sense) in the 1920s, 1930s, 1940s, 1960s, 1970s, 1980s, 1990s and, presumably, in the 1950s too, when we heard nothing of her. She did what the poet Rainer Maria Rilke wrote of: she praised human beings. She framed and lit them to express their grandeur. That there are no signs of rethink or despair in her work, when there clearly is in those less tested by the times in which they lived, is what is hardest to understand about Riefenstahl.

Her 1943 film *Tiefland*, in which (whether knowingly or not) she used concentration camp inmates as extras, is rightly cited as the most abhorrent of her mistakes. Yet her utter failure to demonstrate any interest in the flux of new visual ideas that flowed through the twentieth century suggests another species of error. Riefenstahl could not have been unaware of the Nazis' famous Entartete Kunst ('Degenerate Art') exhibition, held in 1937, which denounced modernism and abstraction. If she went with the Nazi flow then, scoffing at such work, might she not have looked again after the war and perceived an intellectual alternative? The themes of the divided self, and the despair which underscored modernism, went straight over her head. And even sticking closer to her beloved subject, the grandeur of the human body, might she not have shown more interest in Picasso's monumental nudes?

Riefenstahl, of course, was not a painter. But by the time she returned behind a camera, even cinema had become modernist. Antonioni, Godard and Fellini had all appeared. There were new ways of portraying human beings on film. Riefenstahl ignored them all. Perhaps it was too late in her career to change. Maybe, not being an intellectual, she did not follow or understand the latest trends in picture-making. But most likely, she did not realise that she was tainted by more than her personal association with an ideology; she had made an artistic form itself guilty by association. In her hands, classicism was corrupted.

To these possible explanations must be added a fourth; that – again at the level of form (not content, not politics) – she considered herself to be right. To the extent that she worked out a rationale for her eroticising, classicising sensibility, she convinced herself that it was somehow perfect.

Riefenstahl's refusal to take any responsibility for the culture of National Socialism remained the ugliest aspect of her persona. What made her interesting is that this ugliness was layered on to an extraordinary, once-in-a-generation talent. That has guaranteed her a position of ambivalence in the history books. But the bitter icing on the cake in the case of Leni Riefenstahl was a blinkered stylistic arrogance. Her inability to modify the form of her work is her concluding artistic indictment.

NO MORE SEX

What with Ang Lee's sexually explicit *Lust, Caution* winning this year's top prize at the Venice Film Festival, and *Atonement*'s cautionary sexual tale doing rather well in the cinema, questions of eros are in the air. Lee's previous film, *Brokeback Mountain* (2005), was praised for its discretion with cowboy-on-cowboy action (though rumours persisted that a more explicit version of the sex scene in the tent was shot), yet here he is, one of world cinema's masters of the image equivalent of the *mot juste*, deciding that uncoy sex scenes would not disrupt the aesthetic decorum of his period film. And Christopher Hampton and director Joe Wright insisted that novelist Ian McEwan's use of the word 'cunt' was exactly what was needed to disrupt the decorum of their film, which ended up with a Certificate 15.

Rather than rehash those lads' mags' and TV lists of best sex scenes in the movies (*Betty Blue* (1986), *Don't Look Now* (1973), *Body Heat* (1981), *Out of Sight* (1998) and *My Beautiful Laundrette* (1985) usually figure), or re-open the debate about censorship, let's imagine what cinema would be like without sex, if the erotic had not been central to its gaze and sales pitch.

From the earliest days, American epics directed by Cecil B. DeMille were strewn with babes lolling in the buff. Such scenes, and the early French porn films recently released as the compilation *The Good Old Naughty Days* (which featured equal opportunity combinations of nuns, priests and dogs) show that, right from the start, movie-makers had one foot in the sex business. If movie depictions of sexual activity or longing had not been allowed then Marilyn Monroe, Johnny Weismuller, Brigitte Bardot, Jane Russell, Kim Novak, Sharon Stone and Brad Pitt, for example, would not be household names. Hyphenates like Mae West, who wrote as well as performed, might well have made it, and Marlon Brando, who got his leg up because he looked great in a ripped T-shirt, is likely to have changed the acting world nonetheless. The real losses would have been people like Monroe, a brilliant, erratic comedienne.

On the directing side, would a de-sexualised cinema have Alfred Hitchcock, Bernardo Bertolucci, Nic Roeg, Nagisa Oshima, Rainer Werner Fassbinder, Luchino Visconti, Pier

Paolo Pasolini, David Lynch, Federico Fellini, Shohei Imamura, Paul Verhoeven, Lars von Trier or Derek Jarman in its pantheon? Hitchcock and Lynch are likely to have made it because they were driven by fear as well as sex. Pasolini and Imamura would have done so too, because their dualism was class and sex. But the will to form of Bertolucci, Fellini and Jarman seems so driven by eros – and the way the world composes beauty around eros – that their unforgettable talents might not have been recognised in our hypothetical regime.

More striking, perhaps, is the converse. Many would argue that the 1960s in Europe and the 1970s in America were amongst the greatest periods in movie history, but look at some of the headline talents from those eras: Martin Scorsese, François Truffaut, Ingmar Bergman, Francis Ford Coppola, Steven Spielberg, Wim Wenders. More than a hundred films between them, yet relatively few sex scenes. Scorsese in particular seems to avoid them. And if we open out further to those who many consider the greatest directors of all time – Orson Welles, Yasujiro Ozu, Carl Theodor Dreyer, Robert Bresson, F. W. Murnau, etc – there's relatively little sex in their hundred plus films either. Of course this last bunch mostly worked at a time when censorship forbade direct eroticism, but there's no doubt that Welles was more interested in power than sex, Ozu in family equilibrium, Dreyer and Bresson in spirituality, and so forth.

Eviscerate the movie world of its sexuality, then, and you get some surprising results. On the down side, the star system would lose key figures like Monroe, Novak and Bardot. And it would seem obvious that by ignoring the force field of eros, and its disruptive power, we'd be left with a bland, Eisenhowerian, worldview. But this is one bit of the hypothesis that we don't have to imagine because, since 1982, Iran has banned depictions of sexual activity or longing and the result has been a generation of films about learning, community, friendship, poetry, co-operation and spirituality which sounds deadly dull but, in fact, has produced some of the greatest glories of modern cinema. One of the most famous of film theory essays helps explain why. Laura Mulvey's 'Visual Pleasure and Narrative Cinema' argues that movies stop, as it were, to stare at women, that narrative and point of view in cinema is, therefore, gendered, and that such gendering and halting warps film form and film culture. If Mulvey was right, and many believe she was, then the richness of Iranian filmmaking seems to derive from the lack of a structuring, sexual gaze at its heart.

So are we on to something here? If many of the greatest filmmakers of all time disavowed sexual activity, and if one country's forced avoidance of it has resulted in great art, then here's a proposal: a voluntary vow of cinematic chastity. Perhaps, for two years, we could submit ourselves to a sexual detox? Doing so might rid Bollywood of its wet sari coyness and French and American cinema of its sexism. A temporary cinematic celibacy would surely mean that actresses of all ages would be cast more interestingly. It would force our writers and directors to explore more diverse aspects of human nature. It would take some of the heat out of cinema but, perhaps, replace it with light.

DISASTER

Television schedulers know more than any of us about cinematic tone. Imagine that you worked in programme acquisition at BBC2 and were planning to screen *The Towering Inferno* (1974) on a dull Wednesday night in September 2001. Then 9/11 happens. You cancel the screening in a heartbeat. Its Hollywood pathos, its movie-star versions of real lives, its artifice, are suddenly plain to see.

The same applies to the 1968 movie *Krakatoa, East of Java*, a juicy depiction of the 1883 volcanic eruption that caused a massive tsunami and killed thousands. I saw it as a boy and was thrilled by it, but remember little now except actor Sal Mineo's face. Doubtless some television station somewhere in the world scheduled it for the week after Boxing Day – and quickly pulled it. But why is *Krakatoa, East of Java* (it is actually west of Java) unshowable at the moment? And for how long?

The first question is easy to answer. *Krakatoa, East of Java*'s purpose was to deliver pleasure to people long after the grief caused by the real disaster had faded; 85 years on, aware that audiences like to experience horror vicariously (the poster's tag line was 'You are Engulfed by a Terrible Tidal Wave'), Hollywood could step in, dress history in production design, throw in movie stars and serve up the result. Our television scheduler knows that actual human pain abhors such dressing-up. Only when it subsides can the aesthetes tiptoe in with their costumes and squibs and rehash what happened as fantasy.

The second question, about the duration of a disaster movie's unshowability, takes us into more interesting territory. Can we reschedule *Krakatoa, East of Java* in a few months, at Easter perhaps, when the kids are on holiday? Or, when we look into Mineo's big eyes, will we just think of the recent news footage and feel the shock of kitsch? Maybe summer or autumn would be better. But certainly not next Christmas.

The more you follow this line of thought, the more the apparently harmless idea of the disaster movie unravels. If we are honest about the nature of human fantasy we must accept the principle that storytelling will always involve vicarious jeopardy. Yet the cycle of late 1960s and 1970s films like *The Towering Inferno* and *Krakatoa, East of Java* are different from modern disaster movies. They have none of the seriousness of *Titanic* (1997) or the ecological drive of *The Day After Tomorrow* (2004). Their movie stars – Paul Newman and Faye Dunaway in *The Towering Inferno*; Sal Mineo and Diane Baker in the Krakatoa film – are more clearly used like baubles on a Christmas tree, to glitter and catch our eye. Their lack of immersion in the world of the story gives these films a smooth surface, a Warholan blankness. But there is something else. They were made at a time before live, rolling television broadcasts from disaster sites. We hadn't seen 'rough' imagery of sky-scrapers falling or tsunamis hitting, as we have now; 9/11 television footage will be in our heads for the rest of our lives, and so will the Indian Ocean footage. Its ability to move us will wane, of course, but it is locked in. Contemporary Hollywood cinema acknowledges this inescapable visual recall. If our inner eye has been permanently changed by 9/11 and Aceh, aren't we close to concluding that *The Towering Inferno* and *Krakatoa, East of Java* are permanently unshowable?

So a world disaster renders some film aesthetics less valid – perhaps invalid. But it may also do the opposite. Take the films of Iranian director Abbas Kiarostami. In 1987, he made *Khane-ye doust kodjast/Where is the Friend's House?*, about a boy who mistakenly takes home his friend's school jotter and tries to return it to him. Soon afterwards, an earthquake hit the region in which the film was shot, ruining the boy's village. Kiarostami returned to the location to see if he could find the boy, and, in 1991, made a film about his return in which real villagers were asked about the real boy. *Zendegi va digar hich/And Life Goes On* is set mostly in the director's car as he (played by an actor) drives along damaged roads, asking for directions from displaced people, exploring temporary settlements, talk-ing to his own son about what they are seeing. I watched the film again last week, and, in the wake of the tsunami, its argument was electrifying. Human life flows unstoppably, it says – it is observable in tiny details. Though the earthquake killed thousands of people, the process of milking goats, of carrying food between villages, of noticing girls out of the corner of your eye, of seeing in nature the answers to human problems, continues. In *And Life Goes On*, a maze of journeys evokes the life of the village with unforgettable optimism.

Kiarostami went on to make a third film, *Zire darakhatan zeyton/Through the Olive Trees* (1994), about a director making a movie after an earthquake. One of the great trilo-gies of film history, it will be the centrepiece of the National Film Theatre's Kiarostami retrospective in the spring. How has an impoverished, censored national cinema such as Iran's made work so relevant to our times? By contrast, it seems that a Western inclination to wish-fulfilment has squandered cinema's power to depict life as it really is. If the evolu-tion of imagery has made *Krakatoa, East of Java* unwatchable, then maybe it is because American producers' ambitions have been too low. They don't know what magic they have in their hands.

DARKNESS

As your multiplex moocher, I would like to report a trend in mainstream cinema: it has darkened, both thematically and psychologically. The trailer for *Spider-Man 3* shows that in the next instalment, arachno-man merges with a black creature from another world. The film's tagline is 'The Battle Within'. In 2005, *Star Wars: Episode III* depicted Anakin Skywalker's own battle within. The same year, Bruce Wayne in *Batman Begins* saw his parents slain and had a traumatic experience in a dark cave, setting him on his, and the film's, tenebrous course. Also in 2005, as I've mentioned before, *War of the Worlds* was so visually dark that cinemas put up signs explaining that the projection wasn't at fault. *The Passion of the Christ* (2004) was one of the most downbeat mainstream films ever made. Currently showing in the multiplexes are *The Prestige*, which is stygian in the extreme, and *Casino Royale*, which treats us to 007's battle within.

It was a surprise to discover that the movie Bond even had a within, but there's no doubt that the tone of mainstream cinema has darkened: nearly all its franchise characters – those heroes who blow in the direction of cinematic and social prevailing winds – have undergone traumas of late. Sunny disposition is out. Black is the new lack. It has happened before. In the 1940s and 1950s, European *émigrés* and filmmakers who saw combat made more than 300 shadowy films about venality and lust that became known as the film noir cycle. In the 1970s, a more pessimistic view of human nature emerged blinking in the Californian sunshine, lasting for about a decade. And for thirty years now, tinseltown's legend-maker-in-chief, Steven Spielberg, has seemed profoundly undecided about trauma and darkness.

What is behind this new spate of mainstream movie noir? The obvious answer is 9/11, but other issues should be considered first – like demographics. Between 1990 and 2000, the percentage of US movie tickets sold to fiftysomethings doubled from 5 per cent to ten per cent. Over the same period, 16–20 year olds, Hollywood's core audience since the mid-1970s, dropped from twenty per cent to 17 per cent. In the current decade, movie attendance by 55–64 year olds is projected to increase by 14.6 per cent. Add the fact that once in the cinema, older audiences buy more cappuccinos, bottled waters and glasses of chardonnay, and the massive impact of these changes on Hollywood's income projections becomes clear.

The consequence for storytelling is obvious. If you've taken a few knocks in life, films where the characters do the same are more believable; characters who have survived bleak times are more likely to move you. The success of films like *A Beautiful Mind* (2001) and *The Road to Perdition* (2002) – both of which I disliked – is widely attributed to older audiences.

The second factor is the influence of new Asian cinema. With notable exceptions, such as *The Blair Witch Project* (1999), the Hollywood horror movie had for years been suffering from sequelitis and too much postmodern joking. Hollywood seemed to have forgotten that sobriety lies at the root of terror. Then along came a spate of Japanese horror pictures: Hideo Nakata's *Ringu/Ring* (1998) and *Honogurai mizu no soko kara/Dark Water* (2002), and Takashi Miike's *Ôdishon/Audition* (1999). These were resolutely gruesome, and their success made Hollywood horror look lightweight. So Hollywood did what it always does – steal and copy, remaking Asian films and aping their anguish.

Some of us have argued that one of the reasons Japanese, Taiwanese, Chinese and Korean filmmakers do seriousness so well is that their nations have sustained a series of traumatic shocks. The US has its own wounds, but some of them – like the humiliation and slaughter of Native Americans – did not look like wounds to the pioneering filmmakers. Others, like slavery, did, but they were borne by people who neither ran studios nor, until recently, called 'action' and 'cut' very often. Vietnam is a wound that certainly haunts American film, but it wasn't in itself cinematic, and had to be reinterpreted by mythmakers and legend-smelters like Francis Ford Coppola. The same was true of other national shocks, such as the deaths of JFK, Malcolm X and Martin Luther King.

You can see where this is going. No national event has been more cinematic, and more suited to cinematic representation, than the planes flying into the World Trade Center. They dream about 9/11, those studio executives who meet their writers in Sunset Boulevard restaurants, eat seared tuna and talk about how Anakin Skywalker, Bruce Wayne and James Bond need to go through something darker this time; 9/11 hit those execs in their solar plexus. Apart from AIDS – which was slower and stigmatised – this was the first time Hollywood saw its own kind really suffer, and the pain wouldn't go away.

So the darkness in the multiplexes these days has been caused by three changes: baby boomers in their fifties going to movies have created the audience (and market) for seriousness; Asian cinema lent an aesthetic that could incorporate psychological darkness; and 9/11 injected fear into the lives and dreams of filmmakers. Social, aesthetic and psychic factors have caused this shift to the 'battle within'.

300

Hollywood releases on average three films a week in Britain, more than 150 a year. Since the product in question is a film, which is labour-intensive and unpredictable in its income generation, it comes as no surprise that Hollywood tries to standardise as much of the production process as it can. Thus genre, stardom, story structure, themes and marketing methods are all made formulaic – frustratingly so for those of us who like surprises.

But occasionally a film comes off the conveyer belt that seems to have escaped the cookie-cutter. One such movie is *300*, which is well on its way to taking $500m at the box office. Since its release, it has been written about extensively. I intended not to add to the coverage – but then I saw it, and my jaw dropped.

Unless you gave up media for Lent, you'll know that *300* depicts the famous battle of Thermopylae in 480 BC, in which Spartan King Leonidas and three hundred of his elite guard routed Persian King Xerxes' force of 10,000, 100,000 or 170,000 (Herodotus didn't have a police helicopter, so had to guess) – for a while, at least. Not since Mel Gibson's *The Passion of the Christ* (2004) has Hollywood produced anything so rabidly, ferally frenzied. *300* feels as if Adolf Hitler has come back from the dead, got hooked on gay fisting websites, done the best digital film course in the world, then stalked into liberal-Jewish Hollywood and convinced them to give him $60m to make a movie.

Some of *300*'s bizarreness can be explained by the real events on which it is based. The military tactics of Thermopylae have, down the centuries, quickened the pulse of red-meat illiberals. The fact that the Spartans seem to have fought naked, and had sex with each other, makes the battle the site of Western ur-homoeroticism. The fact that white Hellens faced down Asian Persians means that it can be seen as the gathering storm of the clash of civilisations.

Add to this the visual route by which *300* got to the screen, and its gay Rumsfeldian surrealism starts to make more sense. The film is an adaptation of a series of graphic novels by Frank Miller. To take a comic book as your starting point is to decouple film from its original source of magic – its ability to capture the appearance of the real world. The human eye behaves roughly like a 50mm lens. Miller's drawn images look as if they were shot by a 20mm lens, on a black and white planet, where the sun is always raking. Director Zack Snyder wanted to recreate this monochrome look, so filmed on location – the real world – for just a day. He shot almost everything else in small studios. He had his actors body build for six weeks, then augmented their six-packs with body make-up and post-production compositing, thus making them look like porn stars. To work against the obvious risk of camp, he cast macho actors like Gerard Butler as King Leonidas, and had him yell throughout the film. Butler is like Sean Connery or Steve McQueen, so confident in his own skin, so rock-like on camera, that the flicker of camp, the interplay between real and fake that it enacts, didn't stand a chance.

I confess I went to *300* expecting to laugh at Butler and his gym bunnies. But the sonic overload of Snyder's picture, its seductive celebration of power and its assault of pictorial ideas about combat, landscape, sunlight, the warrior body, Europe, Asia, masculinity and heroism, meant that I did not laugh.

300's story helps explain its potency, and its filmmaking certainly does, but a third reason it packs such a punch is the uninhibitedly reactionary way it portrays Persia. King Xerxes is played by Rodrigo Santoro, but it looks like the Persians are being led by New York drag queen Ru Paul, giving it everything his make-up bag has got. His eyebrows are more arched than Marlene Dietrich's, lip-gloss is his passion, and his body is festooned with jewellery. There is, surely, hysteria in such Pierre et Gilles iconography. And then there's his army. Some are part gargoyle and, I kid you not, some appear to have flippers rather than arms. When I heard that one of President Ahmadinejad's cultural advisers had called *300* 'American psychological warfare against Iran', I thought it was more loopy talk from Tehran, but it's hard to deny that unconscious fear of Iran played a part in producing such imagery.

The key word here is, I think, 'unconscious'. For hours after I saw *300*, I puzzled over how a film industry like Hollywood's – soft, liberal and formulaic – could give birth to such a snarling, unique beast. Then I remembered Freud's 1916 lectures on parapraxis. That's what *300* is: a slip of the tongue (or camera), an inadvertent 'mistake' produced by the Hollywood system. As my article 'Film is Right' suggests, the liberal surface of American cinema overlays conflicting, strongly held impulses that are far less liberal. Films like *The Searchers* (1956), *Dirty Harry* (1971), *Apocalypse Now* (1979) and *The Passion of the Christ* are fuelled by a passionate belief in male heroism and the primacy of the loner, an excited attraction to explosive violence, a fascination with the body, deep sexual anxiety and a disgust at otherness. We get all these in spades in *300*. The fact that it is ringing the box-office bell around the world shows that it isn't only Americans who are stirred by such things.

TRUTH

Viewed from the outside, the film world seems permanently enslaved to fashion. One minute it's all romantic comedies in the multiplexes, then westerns come back, then science-fiction. But the style of movies follows technical trends too. In the 1980s, editing speeded up. In the 1990s, widescreen and shallow focus were all the rage. Today, a survey of the movie map shows that cinematic realism is in vogue.

In Cannes this year, more movies than ever were documentaries. The best-reviewed film of recent months was *L'Emploi du temps/Time Out* (2001), an understated French realist masterpiece about a man pretending that he has a job. Mexican cinema bounced back to acclaim and box-office success with the semi-improvised sex and sociology film *Y tu mamá también/And Your Mother Too* (2001). Paul Greengrass' documentary-style *Bloody Sunday* was hailed by many. The intimate character films of Eric Rohmer formed the big recent retrospective at the National Film Theatre. There is an international consensus that the most interesting place for a movie to be at the moment is close to the contours of the real world.

This is a surprise, if only because that place is a minefield. Make a film about an invented love affair in the Moulin Rouge and the sky's the limit. You have no facts to worry about, no great themes to represent, because the real world barely makes an appearance. But turn to Derry in 1972 or to the Kennedy assassinations, Watergate, apartheid or Vietnam, and politicians, activists, the military, eyewitnesses, journalists, lawyers and historians will give you a kicking for your factual errors, misrepresentations of characters, political bias or failure to tell the real story.

Movies have always whispered 'trust me, believe me' to the people sitting in the dark and until the 1960s at least the audience did what they were told. Perhaps if movies hadn't then rewritten history for their convenience, screwed around with truth so much and used the look of documentaries to spin out any old duff lies, they would now be trusted more. As it is, mainstream cinema has often let down the real world by its disinterest in it.

Take a daft example. You can't get dinosaur DNA from a bug in amber. Individual genes, yes, but the whole chain? Impossible. Nevertheless, *Jurassic Park* (1993) was made and we got the kids' dinosaur revival fad. In *All the President's Men* (1976), Alan J. Pakula's account of Watergate, the contents of *Washington Post* wastepaper baskets were shipped to California to be placed in the movie set's replicas. Full marks for this ultra – if slightly gaga – naturalism, but it didn't help the film capture reality. *All the President's Men* suggests that Bernstein's and Woodward's lives were in danger, when they weren't. It also asserts that this great upheaval in public trust was a result of the researches of two journalists. The political investigation which ensued, where the real revelations took place, was ignored. Arthur Penn's *Bonnie and Clyde* (1967) claimed that the two killers made Robin Hood-style donations to the poor. Not true. Oliver Stone's *JFK* (1991) claimed that Kennedy was planning to pull out of Vietnam. Not true. In *Mississippi Burning* (1988), the blacks are downtrodden while, in the real life events of 1964, they organised and cast freedom ballots in large numbers. These are all American examples. John Sayles in that country and Ken Loach in our own have a far better track record. But they are exceptions. In the main, few countries have fared much better in attempting to make films which bear witness to reality.

Yet audiences lap up the truth-bending fictions of cinema. Tucked into stories, brought to life by actors and suffused with feeling, untruths in cinema are mostly undetectable. If an extra wears a wristwatch in *Cleopatra* (1963), as one did, we can have a laugh at how easily it spikes Hollywood's grand plans to take us in. But factual inaccuracies in films are like chameleons adapting to the colour of the leaf they're sitting on. They bed down and wait for our scopophilic glance to scan and move on. We are too entranced to notice and, anyway, we want to believe. Producers know this, of course, especially the old timers, the mainstreamers untroubled by ethical dilemmas. Many agree with über-screenwriter William Goldman's formulation that in movies it doesn't matter what is true, what is important is what appears to be true.

David Puttnam, producer of *Chariots of Fire* (1981) and *The Killing Fields* (1984) and chairman of Columbia pictures 1986–87, recently argued in the *Guardian* that movies are shirking their moral responsibilities to deal with real subjects, to engage with the pressing issues of the day. Aware of cinema's ignoble history of tackling important subjects, he none the less called for filmmakers to walk back onto the minefield. Is he right? Should movies try again? Should we be developing scripts about Rwanda, 9/11, Le Pen and Ahmedabad? And making them accurate?

My answer is … perhaps. This is not because I am unsure. *La Battaglia di Algeri/The Battle of Algiers* and *Idi i smotri/Come and See* are models of how to capture the dynamic of the real world on film. The first, made in 1965 by Gillo Pontecorvo, portrays an anti-French terrorist cell in Algeria a decade earlier. The second, made in the Soviet Union in 1985, tells how Byelorussian townspeople are massacred by the Germans. Both are engaged films and, I trust, the sort of work of which Puttnam would approve. But my answer remains equivocal because the carcasses of rotten, well-meaning films are stacked high in that minefield of reality. Think of almost every film about Vietnam, Northern Ireland, the Cold War and the Second World War.

My problem, too, is that I do not believe that cinema should be in the service of anything, not even the need to explain the most appalling events of our age. But is there something in this intense, seeing-is-believing, big screen medium which pre-disposes it to portraying the real world? This requires a glance back at the history of ideas about the movies.

The first decent account of the evolution of cinema was written by two young Frenchmen: the poet and critic Robert Brasillach and his friend, Maurice Bardèche. Forty years from the invention of the movies, B&B's *Histoire du Cinéma*, published in 1935, defined a canon and the principles by which movies might be understood. The Museum of Modern Art (MoMA) in New York had the book translated into English, and the *cinématheque* attached to MoMA collected according to its recommendations. The B&B book had an unacknowledged thesis which is still held by many critics today. It is the formalist position; the argument that movies are like dreams or cubist paintings; that there is something fundamentally unreal about the nature of cinema.

In the first decade of the movies (1895–1905), this was not obvious. Filmmakers photographed stage plays, events occurring in front of the camera and street scenes. People marvelled at how lifelike was this 'kingdom of the shadows'. But as the medium evolved, it began to discover editing, close-up, tracking shots. In doing so, it became more formally cinematic. What was done with lenses and lights, on set and at the cutting table, was as important as what took place in front of the camera. Brasillach and Bardèche lauded the editing of D. W. Griffiths' films, the close-ups in *La Passion de Jeanne d'Arc/ The Passion of Joan of Arc* (1928), the camera angles and exaggerated design of the 1919 silent classic, *Das Cabinet des Dr Caligari/ The Cabinet of Dr Caligari*. People who argue that the shower scene in *Psycho* (1960) or the opening shot in Orson Welles' *Touch of Evil* (1958) are cinema at its most original have inherited B&B's formalism.

The art critic Clement Greenberg said the same thing about all art: it is not the job of visual media to describe the outside world so much as to generate their own worlds. He lent weight to the idea that movies were not merely a derivative of photography or theatres but that cinema was an entirely new medium with its own aesthetic principles.

Then came the Second World War and, rather awkwardly, B&B's 1943 revision of their book which contained anti-semitic references. A few years later, Brasillach was hanged for wartime collaboration and Bardèche married Brasillach's sister. The ground was opened up in France for a new theory of cinema. After years of embargo, Paris was suddenly flooded with American movies and there was something different about them. In films like John Ford's *Stagecoach* (1939), William Wyler's *The Little Foxes* (1941) and John Huston's *The Maltese Falcon* (1941) there were fewer camera moves and more concentration on what was happening in front of the camera. Two films in particular pushed these techniques to their limits. Welles' *Citizen Kane* (1941) and William Wyler's *The Best Years of Our Lives* (1946) became the focus of a principle of cinema which was diametrically opposed to B&B's.

Ironically, given the subsequent reputation of Hollywood, American cinema inspired the theory of realism. The theorist was André Bazin. He argued that the essence of cinema did not lie in technical trickery. Nothing extraneous to the action was permitted. Bazin went further, arguing that cinema must not distort or escape from reality; that cinema is at its best when it approaches the psychological realism of the nineteenth-century novel. With this in mind, his followers looked back at silent movies and discovered a new canon. Out went the high style of *The Cabinet of Dr Caligari*; in came the documentary realism of Robert Flaherty's 1922 *Nanook of the North*.

The arguments of Bazin coincided with the fact that nearly every national cinema had, in the post war years, lurched towards realism. The Italian neo-realists led the way with Roberto Rossellini's *Germania anno zero/Germany Year Zero* (1947), Vittoria De Sica's *Ladri di biciclette/Bicycle Thieves* (1948) and Luchino Visconti's *La Terra trema/The Earth Trembles* (1948). Yasujiro Ozu in Japan, and the new Indian filmmakers took their cameras out of the studios and onto the streets. Many used non-professional actors, off-the-peg costumes and natural lighting. They told stories about social devastation and recovery. They answered Jean-Paul Sartre's call for 'engaged' art. B&B formalism virtually disappeared. After the Second World War, it seemed immoral. Billy Wilder edited archive footage from Dachau and Belsen, John Huston made his extraordinary documentary *Let There Be Light* (1946), about traumatised soldiers, and even the arch-technique man Alfred Hitchcock put down his fancy equipment and made films about the war. Jean Renoir, of whom Bazin approved, was given to saying, 'you must leave a door open on the set so that reality can come in'. In the 1960s, Pier Paolo Pasolini called cinema 'the stupendous language of reality'.

By the late 1940s, the big 'nature of cinema' debate had been established. Lines were drawn between the pre-war, B&B formalists (who would have had no time for Puttnam's arguments) and the Bazinian realists (much more Puttnam's cup of tea). Very broadly, this ding-dong corresponded to the political right and left respectively.

There were some flies in the ointment, however. Two of the biggest were Michael Powell and Emeric Pressburger. In 1940s Britain, they were the banner-carriers of another kind of cinema altogether. Call it the 'personal expression' position. While Carol Reed was making masterpieces of human darkness and devastation (*Odd Man Out* (1947) and *The Third Man* (1949)), Powell and Pressburger gave us *Black Narcissus* (1947), set in a windswept convent in the Himalayas, and *The Red Shoes* (1948), about the ruinous obsession between an impresario and a ballerina. Two more stylised films it would be impossible to imagine. You might, therefore, think they fit into the B&B argument that anti-realist films are best. No. Events in their films are often pure fantasy, but they are never purely formal. The B&B

and Bazinian positions dispute the question of whether cameras and sound can capture reality, but ultimately they both take objective views of cinema as an art form. Powell and Pressburger's films, by contrast, fit neither end of this dichotomy. They grow out of the inner visions of the filmmakers rather than a sense of whether the camera is a truth teller or a styliser. The fantasies of *Black Narcissus* and *The Red Shoes* are also honest accounts of the effects of desire and jealousy.

This is the third possibility of what cinema can be: a medium of personal expression. This third way was again theorised by a Frenchman, Alexandre Astruc. His most telling idea was *le caméra-stylo*, by which he meant that a director writes with the camera, as an author does with a pen. A shot of a street is not just that, but describes how a filmmaker feels about the street. Astruc's arguments about personal filmmaking enrich the great examples of personal movies, from Eric von Stroheim's obsessive silent epics such as *Greed* (1924), through Alfred Hitchcock's films of the 1950s, to Michael Cimino's *Heaven's Gate* (1980) and the entire careers of Martin Scorsese and David Lynch.

The 'personal expression' position became the auteur theory and, many producers argued, had the cataclysmic effect of encouraging directors to think of themselves as artists. The result was the new wave of Jean-Luc Godard, François Truffaut and Eric Rohmer in France, Nagisa Oshima and Shohei Imamura in Japan, Ritwik Ghatak and Satyajit Ray in India, Ingmar Bergman in Sweden, Michelangelo Antonioni and Federico Fellini in Italy and John Cassavetes, Martin Scorsese and Francis Ford Coppola in the US. Even the mid-1990s Dogme manifesto launched by Lars von Trier and Thomas Vinterberg, which saw directors vowing not to use fancy tricks, can be traced back to Astruc.

Looking back from the twenty-first century, most experts would say that none of them – B&B nor Bazin nor Astruc – were right. Or, rather, all of them in some way expressed a truth about cinema. Their ideas form a triangle within which every film can be positioned. Just as cubism was a stage that painting had to move through in order to investigate its nature, so cinema had to undergo its own exploration. The B&B approach to film was that exploration; it established a foundation without which no film can work. Building on this foundation was Astruc's *caméra-stylo* theory. Almost no one in the film world today would deny that great films require great personalities behind them, although personal statements have to be smuggled into big-budget cinema. And, at the third point of the triangle is Bazin's idea that cinema has a gift to capture something of the real world. But cinematic realism is limited. The fact that movies have a gift for it isn't to say that it is in the nature of cinema to be real. Animation, Eisensteinian editing, Hitchcock, Bollywood, MGM musicals come as easily as, say, the Omaha Beach scene at the beginning of *Saving Private Ryan* (1998).

But there is a deeper truth, informing all the points in the triangle. This is the geometry of the triangle: film is just a language. And like a language, it can do technical, realistic or expressive things but there's nothing innately formal or realistic in it. It is reality neutral.

It is important to defend cinema's right to be reality neutral against Puttnam's echoing of Sartre that it should be engaged. A shot of a dog resembles a real dog more than the words 'dog' or 'chien' resemble one. So, yes, it has this special talent. But cinema history tells us that movies are not necessarily at their best when they use it. We must not require a shot of a dog to mean only a literal, unironic dog.

The question of what cinema can do is easily answered – almost anything. The question of what cinema *should* do depends entirely on the political or historical context. Given cinema's social penetration, the fact that it captures the individual attention of billions of people each year, if it does not engage, especially when times are tough, then it is failing. We cannot, surely, allow it entirely to flounce away from what's happening in Israel, the slums of India, religious fundamentalism, and so forth.

In the *engagé* camp you have Ken Loach, Jean Renoir and Pier Paolo Pasolini. Those for whom either formalism or personal expression are the real duties of cinema, you have David Lynch, Baz Luhrmann, Alfred Hitchcock, Brian De Palma and Martin Scorsese. Reconciling the two sides is where things get interesting.

Take something important in the real world and ask three questions. What if film-makers didn't deal with it? What if filmmakers dealt with it, but badly? And what if some filmmakers dealt with it successfully, and left other people to make other kinds of movies? Consider the gassings at Auschwitz-Birkenau between 1943 and 1945. Filmmakers didn't have to engage with these atrocities and, for obvious reasons at the time, they didn't. There isn't a single existing still or moving image of the operation of the gas chambers. This fact leads to further questions: would there be Holocaust deniers if there had been? Would there have been room for doubt? The absence of film helps fuel the case of the doubting Thomases.

On to the second scenario – where the subject was treated, but badly. In the television series *Holocaust*, the process of inserting the Zyklon B gas into the crematoria was so badly portrayed technically – a guy climbs a ladder and pops it in – that revisionists and neo-Nazis had a field day. They watched those scenes and laughed. Granted, this is mainstream television rather than cinema but the dilemma remains the same: audio-visual culture's slipshod populism led to simplifications which cheated the audience and, no matter how well intentioned, created a new postmodern vagueness around its subject.

What about the third scenario, when cinema tackles the situation and apparently gets it right? *Schindler's List* (1993) had the technical brilliance of Steven Spielberg and cinematographer Januscz Koszinski, a source novel like *Schindler's Ark*, a budget to realise their ambitions, a seriousness of tone, a largely receptive press and a credible back-up programme funded by the Shoah Foundation which is videotaping Holocaust survivor testimony on a massive scale. Still, a few aesthetic mistakes, like the girl in red and the sentimentality of the last act, makes it a flawed work. The argument to engage falls down if the form is bungled.

It is a sign of weakness when cinema goes all out to deal with the real world but then allows the message to overrun the medium. When content dominates, you can hear B&B whispering 'what about form?' Form and history are uneasy bedfellows. Form pulls away from content, runs rings around it. Puttnam's *The Killing Fields* had a big political impact; David Lynch's *Blue Velvet* (1986) seemed purely personal. Which is best? Or, a rather harder question: which is more valuable to our culture?

Here's what I think. We should take the Shoah Foundation interviews, for example, and give them to someone like David Lynch or Baz Luhrmann (who made *Moulin Rouge* (2001)) to make a film out of them, a kind of montage. To make the most valuable, engaging films, each point of the B&B/Bazin/Astruc triangle must play a part. As Truffaut argued, a film must say something about reality and about cinema. So you take the raw survivor testimony, reconceive it, connect to it personally and splash it on the big screen in a shockingly new way. No sensitive violin music, no earnest voiceover, no archive, no shots of raindrops dripping from barbed wire in the death camps. Or ask Scorsese to make a film about Rwanda. Give Jane Campion free reign on 9/11. Chantal Akerman on Le Pen. And what about the Coen brothers on Ahmedabad?

A few films which are perhaps central to this debate are nevertheless special cases. They are a small but very important breed: films which have actually changed the world. The first two were produced for television: Ken Loach's *Cathy Come Home*, made in 1965, which told the story of a young woman who loses her husband and child and becomes homeless, was part of the process that led to the setting up of Shelter. A Chinese documentary called *Heshang* (1988) was an epic telling of the history of the Yellow River civilisation, the impact of which contributed to the reform movement in the late 1980s in China and to Tiananmen Square. Finally, a film called *Monanieba/Repentance* (1984) by Tengiz Abuladze, made in the Soviet Union and (belatedly) released in 1987; its veiled account of Stalinism so affected Gorbachev and Shevardnadze that it convinced them to accelerate their reforms. If more films were like this one, I'd be with Puttnam. But there's one salient fact about *Repentance*. It was not a realist film.

HESHANG

This is the story of a film that helped change the world. It was in 1988. It had an audience of 600 million and its bold message was part of a chain reaction which led to one of the most publicised human rights violations of our times, the Tiananmen Square massacre. Yet few people outside China have heard of it. The recent book documenting the background to the violations, *The Tiananmen Papers*, doesn't mention it.

Exactly one year before the events in Beijing of June 1989, a polemical documentary was aired on Chinese television that created the greatest controversy in China's thirty-year broadcasting history. The film, *Heshang*, argued that the country's self-image of national greatness is wrong. It advocated a full-scale adoption of 'Western ideas.'

Heshang comprised six one-hour documentaries. Each episode, made by a different film-maker, looked at an aspect of the history of the 3,400-mile-long Yellow River and its impact on Chinese culture and economics. Part 1 argues that China needs to wake up and undergo a profound cultural renewal. Parts 2 and 3 argue that the country failed to capitalise on its great inventions, such as pen and ink. Parts 4 and 5 explain why the industrial revolution didn't happen in China. Part 6, the most political section, posits the bold hypothesis that world civilisation can be divided into soil-based yellow, backward cultures, and blue, sea-based, progressive cultures. China has been the former and should be the latter.

Billed as a search for a modern China and, according to one of its producers, Su Xi-aokang, conceived of as contemporary political commentary, *Heshang* argued that the Yellow River 'cradle of civilisation' had long imposed on Chinese culture a land-locked conformism, a uniform Confucian ideology, which isolated the country from global eco-nomics. The fifth episode ('Anxiety and Misery') contrasted the limitations of Yellow River civilisation with the multi-ethnicity and freedom of maritime culture (the 'Azure Blue' of episode six). Construction of the Great Wall, argued the film, had further isolated China.

Looking back it is difficult not to be nostalgic for that moment in Chinese politics when such a debate was allowable. China had a long tradition of cultural critique but, nearly ten years after the pivotal 3rd Plenum of the Chinese Communist Party (CCP) Congress in 1978, conservative reformers such as Deng Xiaoping had perhaps unwittingly created what turned out to be a temporary space for more radical reformers such as Su. Born in the year of the revolution, 1949, Su's father was a leading conservative. He studied reportage and literature, joined the CCP in 1985 and wrote books on women, intellectuals and natural disasters, arguing that in China politics were a greater tragedy than the latter. Su's co-writer and director Xia Jun studied at the Beijing Film Academy. He was just 26 when he was given the commission, by the Vice Director of Chinese state TV, which would become *Heshang*. Their recipe of influences included literature, reformist economics, comparative mythology and journalism.

Su's and Xia's methods were more Adam Curtis than Panorama. A complex mosaic montage of archive footage – most not identified, some used out of context – was accompanied by an almost non-stop ideas-led commentary. Each was remarkably dense, and made emotional as well as logical connections between observations and ideas. Seen today, it is striking how many times the camera takes to the air throughout the series. Such aerial footage not only gives an overview, a feeling of objectivity, but seems to take its leave from the soil and its culture, both of which the series lambaste. Even today it is breathtaking to see a series made by state TV call the Great Wall an isolationist and arrogant exercise in self-delusion, and portray the dragon as a slippery symbol of self-sacrifice and introversion.

The impact was extraordinary. More than half of the Chinese population saw *Heshang*. The broadcaster received thousands of letters of congratulations. All the national newspapers serialised its script, some on the front page. The film was understood by intellectuals, workers, students and peasants alike. Seven books were instantly written about it. Peoples' summer camps were organised to discuss it.

But soon signs emerged that the *Heshang* phenomenon was ruffling feathers. After its first broadcast, it was banned in Beijing. The propaganda department belatedly concluded that *Heshang* was 'unpatriotic' and 'anti-communist' and shouldn't be rerun. Zhao Ziyang, one of its few supporters in government, who appears in the film and who some felt it glorifies, was ousted after the events in Tiananmen Square. One of its producers, Wang Luxiang, was arrested. Su fled to France and then to the US. The film became a *cause célèbre* in overseas Chinese communities. Students everywhere argued over it.

Piecing together the production history of *Heshang* was not easy for those Chinese scholars who first attempted it. The filmmakers are now scattered around the world. No retrospective audience survey is possible. It was a massive phenomenon – the biggest single audience ever for a documentary film – but the clampdown has made it difficult to judge its lasting effects. Some have tried: 'Politically, it is the most significant event since the party crackdown on liberal ideas in the "anti-bourgeoisie" movement in December 1986,' wrote Tuen-yu Lau and Yuet-keung Lo in the only full account of the film available in English. 'An understanding of some of the chain reactions to *Heshang* would … shed light on the inevitable outbreak of turmoil and bloodshed in Tiananmen Square.'

Heshang obviously scared the hell out of Deng Xiaoping. Its aesthetic and historical boldness brought debate about the future of China to every street corner. Since Mao's death in 1976, a tentative civil society had emerged, where people could debate political ideas in public. But *Heshang* was a gigantic discursive advance, an assimilation of a decade of pro-Western ideas, a massive work of revisionism. It added substantially to the momentum of pro-democracy student movements. But the tanks were readying. A film had pushed too far. The idealistic minds of what Deng called 'the scum of the Chinese nation' had been too taken by its arguments.

It's hard not to see *Heshang* in Freudian terms, as a work of masochism. Certainly it is art, which is not always the case with epoch-making films. It is time to screen it, gather the filmmakers and put on record its effects.

Many thanks to Professor Natascha Genz.

BRITISH DIGITAL

A British film recently hit the jackpot at the British box office – a glimmer of hope for a crestfallen industry. The film was shot entirely on cheap digital video cameras, a first for a box office number one. Two of the biggest movie debates in this country – the viability of British cinema and the effect of the digital revolution – have been forced into focus. Some critics were sniffy about *28 Days Later*, and that is part of its fascination.

Suddenly, 'e-cinema' is mainstream. More filmmakers are shooting on video to create electronic movies, mostly in the dominant form of digital. Cheaper and more flexible than chemical film, it allows experimental directors the use of more cameras, shooting for longer from many more angles. And video cinema also has its own aesthetic properties, distinct from those of 35mm film. Pixellated digital imagery can't yet match the visual richness of its photochemical predecessor, but does permit a sketchier and freer approach.

In 1949, film studio boss Samuel Goldwyn envisaged 'large screen televisions' in movie theatres, receiving films by cable, but it wasn't until 1992 that this was first demonstrated. Computer-generated imagery went mainstream with the liquid metal effects in *Terminator 2: Judgement Day*, and the first wholly CGI feature was 1995's *Toy Story*. In 1998, British cinematographer Anthony Dod Mantle took a huge leap in the Danish film, *Festen/The Celebration*. Shot from multiple angles with pocket digital video cameras, it crafted fuzzy flickering images reminiscent of the romantic photography of 1920s cinema. The following year, the mainstream countered when George Lucas opened *The Phantom Menace* in four digital theatres. Meanwhile, several cinemas in Europe refitted for e-cinema projection. Within months came *The Blair Witch Project*, its imagery and success prefiguring *28 Days Later* (also splendidly shot by Anthony Dod Mantle).

Looking at the development of digital imagery reminds me of Richard Dawkins' genetic analogy in *The Selfish Gene*, where he proposed that just as in biology where there are genes and genetic evolution, so in culture there are memes and memetic evolution. Memes are a unit of cultural information and their replication explains, for example, why everyone suddenly begins humming a catchy tune. Many argue that biological evolution is a bad analogue for cultural change but digital imagery fits the model rather well; it has developed in wildly varied, geometric ways. It is catching on and appearing everywhere, even in the films of confirmed cinematic flat-earthers like Roman Polanksi (whose *The Pianist* (2002) uses some CGI) and David Lynch who, until recently, insisted that digital contributed nothing to the cinematic bag of tricks available to directors since the 1920s. He's since changed his tune.

28 Days Later is about how Britain is brought to a post-apocalyptic standstill by a virus called 'rage', which escapes from a lab because of well-meaning animal liberationists. The film's director Danny Boyle and producer Andrew Macdonald, who together made *Shallow Grave* (1994), *Trainspotting* (1996) and *A Life Less Ordinary* (1997), and misfired somewhat in their film of Alex Garland's *The Beach* (2000), have always been interested in intelligent genre films. Their latest echoes with references to John Christopher's book *The Death of Grass*, the old television show *Changes* and George A. Romero zombie socio-horror pictures like *Dawn of the Dead* (1978). Their track record shows that they have regularly judged audiences better than British critics. The indifference or apoplexy of some responses to *28 Days Later* indicates that newspaper critics are not up to assessing the new digital language of film.

The potential of this new language is the most interesting thing about the successful incursion of digital into British cinema. Dod Mantle's imagery in *Festen* seemed highly experimental but the same range of focus, tone and colour has now carried a film to the number one spot here. The expense of shooting 35mm meant that such cameras were regal presences on set. With the cheapness of video, time ceases to be so precious. On the first day of filming on Lars von Trier's *Dancer in the Dark* (2000), cameraman Robbie Müller shot 68 hours of tape as opposed to an average of maybe 45 minutes of film. In *28 Days Later*, multiple cameras were used.

Film critic Jonathan Romney argued a few years ago that 'we are not required as viewers to take stock of digital imagery as potential material for metaphor'. He was talking about computer-generated objects like the dinosaurs in *Jurassic Park* (1993), but in the hands of directors like von Trier, Boyle or the Russian genius Aleksandr Sokurov, digital is at least as inclined to metaphor as its silver nitrate ancestor.

Film editor and sonic theorist Walter Murch has written that the switch from film to digital is like the shift from fresco to oil painting in the Renaissance. Expensive, collaborative and prestigious work, relying on patronage, gave way to a profusion of simpler, more individual and personal modes of art. The result was a golden age.

FILMFOUR

The future of co-production between European and American film companies was the talk of Cannes this year. So was the question of whether people who make films should also sell them. The strategy of FilmFour, British filmmaker and seller, to produce bigger films with US partners had not paid off and the share price of the Franco-American Vivendi Universal was in free fall. FilmFour's experiment as a British mini-studio was based on the Hollywood model. But now both the model and its imitator are in trouble.

The very idea of making and selling movies evolved in a Euro-American *pas de deux*. The first film company to do both – to be vertically integrated – was Charles Pathé's in France at the beginning of the twentieth century. In a very French way, verticality became a moral issue: it would be wrong for local films to be handled by foreign distributors.

Then Hollywood stole France's thunder. With the establishment of Universal in 1915, Hollywood's Wall Street backers came to own sound studios, distribution companies and cinemas alike. So began the film industry.

It couldn't last. Not even in protectionist France were things so sewn up. In 1948, the US Supreme Court instructed Hollywood to divest itself of its theatres. It was the beginning of the end of vertical integration. Until the 1980s, that is. A left-field British television station called Channel 4 made *My Beautiful Laundrette* (1985) with television money and it was a hit in the cinemas; the same thing happened with *Trainspotting* (1996). As the channel distributed neither film, it lost out on the profits. The solution? Scale up production to make bigger, even more successful Trainspottings, cut out the middle men and distribute the films itself.

Thus in 1995, FilmFour moved into distribution and in a modern twist on Hollywood's own-your-own-screens idea, a dedicated digital channel also, confusingly, called FilmFour, was established, not only to screen its parent company's films but to extend the cultural context in which those films were understood.

FilmFour grew in prestige. It acquired a new poster boy, chief executive Paul Webster. It had a hit with *Little Voice* (1998), another with *East is East* (1999). It moved into US production and did a deal with Warner Bros. In the same year, 2000, it completed *Late Night Shopping*, *Crush*, *Lucky Break*, *The Warrior*, *Charlotte Gray* and *Monsoon Wedding*.

Meanwhile, France's sewage company, Vivendi, which owned Canal+, had gone to Hollywood and, in an act of amazing cultural hubris, bought that 1915 studio, Universal. Vivendi Universal's boss, Jean-Marie Messier, took an apartment on Central Park, declared that *l'exception française* was dead and insisted that the French filmmaking wing of his company got more involved with US filmmaking.

Which is what FilmFour had done. Both were banking on mainstream hits (meaning £10m-plus in Britain). None came. *Late Night Shopping* was good but underperformed; *Crush* was awful; £2m was spent selling *Lucky Break*, Peter Cattaneo's follow-up to *The Full Monty* (1997), but people stayed away; *Charlotte Gray* was the biggest movie FilmFour had made but it failed to corner the market.

FilmFour production made a profit of £500,000 in 1999, but lost £3m in 2000, and £5.4m in 2001 on a turnover of £43.1m. In July this year, Channel 4 closed the company down, folding production back into the television commissioning process, ending the make-and-sell strategy and severing ties with Hollywood. Production expenditure was slashed from £31m to £10m (less than the BBC's film spend). Webster is not re-applying for his scaled-down job.

Across the channel, things were moving in eerie parallel. Vivendi Universal's share price was down seventy per cent. Just before Cannes, it slashed its StudioCanal productions to 15 per year, the bulk of the cuts applying to its high-profile US films. Then Jean-Marie Messier was forced out.

On the historical scale, what FilmFour and Vivendi Universal are going through is another movement in the making and selling of film's *pas de deux*. Europe and America are here, as elsewhere, dancing away from each other.

Channel 4's contribution to film production is a requirement of its licence. How can it do so on just £10m per year? If FilmFour scales down production budgets by two-thirds, it might be able to make as many films as it used to by making them more cheaply, but it seems unlikely. Harvey Weinstein and British producer Steve Woolley are among many to have voiced deep concern. They point to what British filmmaking was like before Channel 4 – Derek Jarman, Terence Davies, Bill Forsyth and not much else. There is still the lottery, plus the UK Film Council and BBC Films. But when Channel 4's cuts take effect, will anyone still be able to say, as the director of the Cannes Film Festival said this year, that 'British cinema is on a roll?' Of course, we can try making different films. Maybe they should be smaller, less literary, more original. But, please, don't let there be fewer.

HOME

At the swanky dinner after the BAFTA awards recently, a ripple of excitement swept the room when Daniel Day-Lewis walked in. It wasn't only because he is handsome, which he is, or that he looks like a walking Egon Schiele drawing, which he does. Rather, as he doesn't live in London, sightings of DDL at movie blingfests are rare treats these days, so heads turned.

I don't live in London, and come from Ireland, where DDL relocated, but even I felt the allure of someone who has gone to live and think elsewhere. No other art form is better at sense of place than cinema, yet its history churns with migrations and émigrés, people making films set in places that they are just getting to know. In the studio era, location shooting was rare. No scenes in *Casablanca* (1942) were shot in Casablanca. Directors who fled the Nazis – Billy Wilder, Robert Siodmak, Michael Curtiz, and so forth – often made movies set in their adoptive home, California, but they looked at that home through shadows and scepticism.

For a while after the Second World War, realist cinema reversed this profound idea that movie places were landscapes of the mind. You had to go to where your film was set. Not to do so was shallow or old fashioned, so John Huston shot much of *The African Queen* (1951) in Congo and Uganda. Soon this hit-and-run approach to production was itself questioned: what could a filmmaker absorb about a place if she or he was only there a few months? Where a filmmaker lived was now a political and ethical issue.

In the coming decades, some of the boldest directors of their day smote such ethical worries like a gnat. The American-born, England-resident director Stanley Kubrick was disinterested in the realities of place – the Vietnam scenes in *Full Metal Jacket* (1987) were filmed outside London – yet was such a stickler for the architecture of space that, by the end of a movie like *The Shining* (1980), you almost have a site plan in your head. Lars von Trier is similarly inclined to precision tooling space with his camera whilst haughtily disregarding location verisimilitude: he's never been to America, yet has set three of his films there, all shot in Sweden or Denmark.

But lofty auteurs like Kubrick and von Trier who (sometimes) get away with floating above questions of mere realism are exceptions to the rule that residency and the fiducial feed off each other in cinema. The most revealing examples lie outside the Anglo-Saxon world. In Iran, for example, the once great Mohsen Makhmalbaf has not made a plausible film since he left the country. The Iranian authorities tried to force his contemporary, Jafaar Panahi out – they couldn't take his constant needling – yet he stayed and has remained at the height of his creative powers. When I asked Iran's most garlanded filmmaker, Abbas Kiarostami, about this, he said 'a tree grows best where it's planted'. This rule is far from universal, but it has long been a matter of concern for African cinema that a high proportion of its best francophone directors end up in Paris because that's where the money and best equipment is. It's an issue of talent retention but, also, indigeneity.

One fascinating filmmaker who's little known in the West but who's revered in Japan made residency something like a creed. In 1968, the charismatic, passionate, leftist movie obsessive Shinsuke Ogawa formed Ogawa Productions, the greatest film collective there's ever been. A stand-off had begun between peanut farmers in Shinrizuka and the Japanese government over the sighting of the new Tokyo international airport. Over the next nine years, Ogawa and his team made seven documentary films totalling 12½ hours, which charted the escalation of what, by 1971, had became a war between 30,000 police and 20,000 protestors. *Forest of Pressure: Ogawa Shinsuke and Postwar Japanese Documentary* by Abé Mark Nornes calls these films the *War and Peace* of world cinema. It's not unknown for filmmakers to follow a story for decades – look at Michael Apted's *7-Up* series – but what beggars belief about Ogawa was that he and his team moved in with the farmers.

The effect on the movies is remarkable. At first they are shot and cut conventionally, but gradually the editing rhythms become slower. As the filmmakers, mostly city people, settled in, they became absorbed in what they called 'village time', and wanted to capture it. Over nearly a decade they became part of the lives they had been depicting. This embedding is explained in part by decades of debate in Japan that raged from 1957 onwards, when anti-Stalinist critic and filmmaker Toshio Matsumoto began writing about the filmmaker's subjectivity – the *shutai*. Ogawa Productions and the great documentarist Noriaki Tsuchimoto started discussing in earnest how their own identities might become more receptive to the outside world – the *taisho* in Japanese – that they were trying to capture. Decades of Japanese militarism, then occupation and its thousands of re-education newsreels had made them sceptical of films made speedily and by 'outsiders'. They came to hate the idea of the 'outside'. Instead, as Nornes reports, they talked of 'letting the taisho enter the *shutai*', 'going with' or 'betting on' the *taisho* or becoming 'wrapped up in the *tasiho*'.

There is a radical, almost Freudian submissiveness in this idea of getting wrapped up in the real world or letting it enter you. Living in Shinrizuka was Ogawa's unique way of doing so. When he and his team finally left it, in 1977, they moved to another village, Magino, and, for another decade, made poetic, fine-grained movies about its community of rice farmers. There was no war in Magino so the focus was even more intimate. In an era when embedding means something shorter and collusive in a different way, their decade-long engagements are inspiring.

The work of Ogawa and his team is far indeed from Daniel Day-Lewis at the BAFTAs, but there are parallels between his immersive methods and belief in small communities, and theirs. Ogawa took the idea of the incoming, resident filmmaker as far as it could go. In so doing he and his collaborators created the Asian documentary sphere, the environmental film and a string of masterpieces.

RESTORATION

As a boy I always loved the bit in a cowboy movie when, after the gunfight, with the smoke from Colt .45s still in the air, the undertaker, dressed in black, would run out on to the street and measure up the bodies. Judging by the film and entertainment press in recent years, the little men in black clothes are scurrying around the corpse of cinema as we speak, measuring it up for its wooden overcoat. Box-office takings are down in many countries. Hollywood's sequelitis shows that it is running out of ideas. According to the *Guardian*, French audiences are no longer queuing up for chin-stroking art cinema. DVD and home cinema is a threat to old-fashioned moviegoing as a social activity. Writer and critic Gilbert Adair summed things up when he said that, movie-wise, 'the tube of tooth-paste is almost empty … we are squeezing out the last drops'. One of the best writers on cinema in the English language, David Thomson, says that the films of Abbas Kiarostami, celebrated by many of us as among the greatest of their time, are 'funerary art'.

I'm not convinced. Take the following. Recently a DVD of the East German fantasy film *Das Singende, klingende Baumchen/The Singing Ringing Tree* (1957) by Francesco Stefani plopped on to my doormat. Although it thrilled me as a child, it's been very hard to see since – until now. The DVD cover says the film has been digitally remastered and, sure enough, it looks and sounds gorgeous, as vivid as the moment in *The Wizard of Oz* (1939) when Dorothy steps from sepia into Technicolor. The week before, I received a seven-DVD box set of the complete films of the landmark Scottish animator Norman McLaren – 15 hours of material, including 15 documentaries on his work. Stefani's film and most of McLaren's have been dead to me for decades in the very real sense that they were very hard to see. DVD labels are bringing them back to life. They are, in a way, remastering cinema. Multiply these examples by tens of thousands and you realise that, like some filmic day of judgement, cinema's long-buried past is coming back from the grave.

But I will watch these films at home on my television, rather than seeing them at the movies, and if moviegoing dies, won't cinema stop being what it always was – collective, gigantic and overwhelming? Again, no. Just as people worship on prayer mats as well as in mosques, so the love of film does not die because it is taking place at home as well as in cinemas.

But isn't that confusing the love of film with cinema itself? Thomson, Adair and the trade press are not saying that the love of cinema is dying, but that cinema itself is. Again, I disagree. Back to my DVDs of *The Singing Ringing Tree* and McLaren's work. From the spring, 240 screens in 200 cinemas across Britain will be equipped with extremely high-quality digital projection systems. The resulting Digital Screen Network will, it is estimated, be programming an annual 165,000 extra screenings of non-mainstream films by 2011. That's nearly 500 more screenings per day of good movies. Put my new DVDs into one of these new systems and they will still project well on to a movie screen. Films that are similarly remastered, but at even higher resolutions, look as good as (some would say better than) 35mm when projected; plus, crucially, they will not scratch or collect dust. I've seen many such projections, on some of the biggest screens in the world, and they were sparkling, rich and true. The average 35mm film print costs at least £1,000; a digital copy will cost a tenth of that. The latter is the size of a shoebox, whereas the former is far bigger, so shipping costs are greatly reduced. Tot up all these benefits, and the reasons for not screening films start to disappear. Digitising is set to revive film exhibition. It is turning back the clock on film history in a way that has never happened before.

But even if this is the case, film production isn't thriving, is it? Well, if you take the broad view, it is. As I've argued before, animated film is in its best state since the heyday of Disney. Until its belated breakthrough in the mid-1990s, documentary had never really been commercially viable in the cinemas, but look at it now. And although mainstream film in English or Hindi (the two main languages of populist cinema) is a bit depressing, in the last generation, for the first time, nearly every part of the world has been making great films. Countries as varied as Iran, Mexico, Belgium, Austria, Australia, Germany, Taiwan, Spain, France, China, Russia, Japan, Senegal, Hong Kong, Thailand, Mauritania and Denmark have produced breathtakingly imaginative work. The art of film is so international now that it's hard to keep up.

Even before digitisation was having much effect, in the 1990s, new cinematic shoots were sprouting on every continent. The rebirth of film history is feeding this. The old film industry business plan may be as dead as a dodo but the art of film is far from dead. It is undergoing a renewal. Adair's tube of toothpaste is full. The wee man with the tape measure had better find other things to bury.

THE STORY OF FILM

Around 8,000 books on film history are available in English. Of these, over 200 purport to cover the whole of the subject. Some, such as those by Robert Sklar, Kristin Thompson and David Bordwell and Geoffrey Nowell-Smith, are outstanding. They cover every period and most countries and between them run to over a million words.

Eleven decades into the history of the medium, we have surely reached saturation point with such books. There are only so many times you can read about the marvel of *Citizen Kane* (1941) or the influence of Kurosawa. Bernardo Bertolucci recently reacted wearily to news of a new single volume history to be published this month: 'Another history of cinema? Something I didn't think I needed.' I'd be as sceptical as he is were it not for this fact: I wrote it.

To justify adding to the groaning bookshelves on the subject, I should at least have been revisionist. Yet at the centre of *The Story of Film* is the traditional assumption of modern film criticism, that the director is an artist. Worse still, I show little interest in accounting for cinema in economic or sociological terms. I even begin with a quotation from Lauren Bacall – 'the industry is shit, it's the medium that's great' – the position of the aesthete that has been around since at least the 1960s.

So why fell all those trees for a book which doesn't sound particularly new? Because cinema isn't how it appears in most film books. The majority misrepresent it in three ways. The first is the most obvious. They focus on entertainment cinema. This is like telling the history of art by looking to what people flocked to in the Parisian salons – splashy history works, sentimental scenes and so on. Cinema set out from the start to divert us, and some of its greatest glories have been made in the Hollywood idiom. But narrative, 'escapist' cinema is nothing of the sort. Unlike painting, theatre, music or literature, film is, as a photographic medium, inextricably linked to the real world. Directors stage and modify that world for the camera, but cinema is less good at being escapist than any other art form. For better or worse, as André Bazin argued, it is shackled to life.

From this perspective, Hollywood musicals and Bollywood love stories are not the norm, but rather a fascinatingly successful mutation from it. The thousands of such films made every year (about a quarter of a million since cinema began) do not represent the essence of cinema so much as an unstoppable spin-off, wedded to traditions of storytelling and fuelled by Freudian wish-fulfilment. Great stuff, but not central to what cinema is. A serious history of the medium needs to recognise this.

Related to cinema's dizzy Freudianism is the second area in which many film histories seem to fall short. They call the grammar of such cinema 'classical'. If classical in the proper sense means equilibrium between form and content, order, symmetry and measured expression, then the films of the great popular directors are nothing of the sort. They are utopian. They strain for emotional effect. They are romantic.

But if the works of Frank Capra, William Wyler, Nicholas Ray and Mehboob Khan are romantic, then the question arises: does cinema have a classical tradition? The answer, I would argue, is that films like *Gone with the Wind* (1939) are at one wildly emotional extreme of the expressive spectrum of cinema, and the ultra-minimalist works of Robert Bresson, Andy Warhol, Chantal Akerman and the like are at the other extreme. Somewhere at the centre is the work of filmmakers like the Japanese director Yasujiro Ozu: neither overly optimistic nor pessimistic, understated but not austere, concerned not with the peaks and troughs of the human condition, but its quotidian reality. Ozu's form, his placement of the camera and his use of space, is also ordered. This is cinema's real classicism.

The third problem with film books is an evaluative one. Most accept that there was a golden age of entertainment cinema – the 1930s and 1940s – and a new wave of innovation and modernism in the 1960s, but that it has been downhill ever since. Such pessimism does not stand up to scrutiny. The 1990s, and the years since, have been remarkably productive. Iranian directors have rethought cinema. Taiwan and Korea have produced astonishing work. Russian filmmakers have excelled. Denmark's Dogme movement revitalised film language. Latin American cinema has been innovative. Australia has had its best period since the 1970s. And America has developed a thoughtful independent filmmaking scene. Digital filming allows directors to work more personally and explains some of these advances, but its effects have not yet been fully felt. Many of the best film critics and historians came to cinema in the 1960s because, at last, there were films which were worthy of their skills. But those who deify that period at the expense of the remarkable diversity of the digital age are distorting the truth.

The treatment of these questions of entertainment, classicism, influence and perceived decline weaken many film books. Dogme, the revival of documentary, even Peter Jackson's claim at the Oscars that 'fantasy' is a dirty word in the movie world, all point to the fact that cinema has reconnected with the real world in recent years. It was time for a book to describe that fact.

MOGRABI

Israel has not produced a master filmmaker – no Sergio Leone, no Ingmar Bergman, no Alfred Hitchcock. When I was writing *The Story of Film*, I wanted to include Israeli films but ended up deciding not to, just as I didn't write about movies from my native Ireland. Neither country had contributed enough.

Over the years I'd seen decent Israeli movies about the class conflict between Ashkenazi and Sephardic Jews, about generational conflict and identity crisis. I had liked films by Assi Dayan and, in particular, veteran documentarist Amos Gitai. Many of cinema's great directors – Ernst Lubitsch, Billy Wilder, Abraham Polonsky, Steven Spielberg – have been Jewish. But not Israeli.

Why this underachievement? First, Israel is young and small. Second, its arts ministry does not seem to value film – just 5 per cent of the culture budget was allocated to this most expensive of arts in 1995. Third, the non-emergence of a Leone or Hitchcock means that talented young Israelis have had no significant role models. Lastly, perhaps, Israeli filmmakers have been hampered by feeling the insecure, harried weight of their country on their backs.

The recent Israeli film *Nekam Achat Mishtey Eynay/Avenge But One of My Two Eyes* (2005), just released on DVD, shoulders such national burdens, and if I were writing my book now I would include it and its writer-director-editor Avi Mograbi. Like many of the best Middle Eastern films, it is a documentary – its director's fifth. And like many such films, it is fuelled by a sense that Israel is committing a crime against Palestine. *Avenge But One of My Two Eyes* starts on a chilly dawn on the bleak mountain of Masada and unfolds into a brilliant cinematic essay about the causes of moral blindness.

Some scenes are familiar. A Palestinian deliveryman tries to enter a controlled zone and is forced to talk up to a watchtower; a sick woman's relatives plead with Israeli soldiers in a tank who talk back to them through a loudspeaker. Mograbi and his camermen are alert to the absurdity of such conversations, and use them to establish the mode of the whole film.

A recurring scene is Mograbi himself, late at night, at home with the television switched on, talking on the phone to his Palestinian friend, who for security reasons is revoiced by actor Shredi Jabarin. Their conversations have none of the urgency of those of the deliveryman or the sick woman's relatives, yet are compelling. The friend seems to say that, at this stage of the second *intifada*, life is hardly worth living, and is therefore easily sacrificed.

Sometimes murky camera work and crystal clear thinking combine in *Avenge But One of My Two Eyes*

The West has been convulsed by the realisation that some people in the Islamic world are prepared to kill themselves in order to be heard. The intellectual strength of Mograbi's film – its shock, if you like – is that it turns this convulsion back on Israel. It asks, 'But aren't we prepared to kill ourselves too? Isn't suicide what our myths of persecution are about?'

In the opening scene, shot with a handheld camera in cold blue morning light, birthright tourists – American teenagers and many others – are shown on top of the Masada cliffs, overlooking the Judean desert. They are told the first-century story of the 900 zealots who killed themselves there rather than submit to the Romans. The tourists are then asked what they would do – kill themselves too, or surrender?

Soon Mograbi cuts to Israeli children learning the story of Samson. His film's title is taken from Samson's entreaty to God – to let him avenge one of his eyes against the Philistines. Just as the teenagers absorb the sense that their forebears performed a heroic suicide, so now these children absorb a far older myth about killing oneself for a lofty principle. Israeli novelist David Grossman called Samson 'the first suicide-killer' in his non-fiction book *Lion's Honey*, so Mograbi's may not be an original idea. But his film has no commentary, and the point is made by showing rather than telling.

The Soviet director Sergei Eisenstein said that, in film, 1+1=3. Two ideas, when brought together, can produce a third idea – in the mind of the viewer. This is what happens in Mograbi's film, where the proposition 'death is preferable to domination' is shown to be one of the key ideas underpinning the Israeli state.

The camera work in *Avenge But One of My Two Eyes* is sometimes uncomfortably wobbly. Near the end, in an encounter with young Israeli soldiers, Mograbi loses his rag and yells at them to grow up. I was initially moved, but later wondered whether this extraordinary release of anger served the film well. It could be argued that the soldiers are rude because they have been taught that Israel's enemies are ignoble by the very suicide myths that Mograbi has been depicting. If so, then 1+1=3 again.

Right-wing Israel hated this film and some members of the Jewish diaspora are likely to accuse Mograbi of being anti-semitic. Politically he is brave. But it is also clear that, cinematically, he is innovative. *Avenge But One of My Two Eyes* is one of the great essayistic films of modern times, ranking with the work of that most thoughtful filmmaker-essayist, Chris Marker. Its people speak in Hebrew. It is subtitled in English but also, unusually, in Arabic. For a film about dialogue, this is appropriate.

GUNS

In one of the very first narrative films, *The Great Train Robbery* (1903), a cowboy in close-up shoots directly into the camera. Alfred Hitckcock's black and white film *Spellbound* (1945) has a scene with a hand holding a gun, turning towards the camera, and firing straight at the audience, producing a single frame of bright red light. Fifty years later, the people who made the *The Matrix* (1999) found a way of simulating the flight of a bullet through the air, picturing eddies behind it and distortions around it.

These are just the milestone examples of what has been a close relationship between cinema and firearms. The terms of this seem obvious at first. Movie-makers want to jolt and shock their audience, fairground style. How better to do so than with a gun? It is small, explosive, dramatic, attention-grabbing. Look how Quentin Tarantino made the very pointing of one a way of slowing down time and analysing its implications. Look how Roman Polanski elevated *China-town* (1974) to the level of tragedy just by firing one.

All art forms reflect the violent aspects of human beings but cinema's fascination with firearms is more subtle than this. The war in Iraq proves the point. How many times have we seen on television footage taken from a camera strapped to the barrel of a tank, looking along it? The rotation of the tank head makes a perfect panning shot. The wide-angle lens of the camera exaggerates the length and drama of the barrel. When it fires, the shell launches from us, dynamising the space before it, *Matrix*-like. Then, far away, a soft impact and a sensuous cloud of powder. The camera strapped to the gun has found its best, grown up buddy. Aesthetically they understand each other, a great double act. The Nietzschean aspects of war have found their perfect dancing partner.

Only a fool would deny the camera's will to power. All that speed, those distances, that g-force, swooping over valleys, aerial views of the most civilised part of the world, this is the meat and potatoes of moving imagery. The subtlety comes from the cinematic delicacy of its rendering. The green hue of videophone imagery glows like tinted silent movie footage. Night vision shots are irised as in the end of Charlie Chaplin movies. This is 'sublime' in Burke's sense, a terrifying thing, glimpsed and veiled.

Shooting with a gun, shot by a camera:
the close relationship between cinema and
firearms in *Red River*

Of course the imagery of a TV war is not enough to prove that there are complex parallels between movie cameras and guns. The language of filmmaking itself is more revealing. Right from the beginning, the opportunistic world of movie-making borrowed the robust language of combat. Filming is 'shooting', the result is a 'shot'. Directors in interviews often refer to the production process as a military campaign. Their beloved equipment has, over the years, become smaller, faster and more effective. They work in a more guerrilla style – their term – than ever before, longing for the simplicity of point and shoot. Actors talk about time stopping between action and cut, saying that their lives feel on the line. Isn't this self-aggrandising? The fey world of filmmaking has always done a bit of mirror staring, imagining itself more macho than it is, fluttering its eyebrows like a smitten coquette.

If all this is true, if movies are guns in drag, the moral implications are disturbing, aren't they? To clarity this question, consider its logical, if unlikely, conclusion: what if cameras and guns actually merged, becoming one gadget as phones and cameras have done? They have strange parallels as pieces of equipment. Each has miniaturised over the years, each is unidirectional, each is defined by the dimensions of the thing that moves through it. If cameras and guns became essentially the same thing, what kind of film would ensue?

We have answers, in a way. In Michael Powell's *Peeping Tom* (1960), the camera became central to the killing process. In this case a lowly focus puller in a film studio wants to capture on film the terror of the women he's killing so he does so by inserting a knife into a leg of the camera's tripod. Not a gun, of course, but the camera as the thing that kills nonetheless. The reviews of the film were scathing, it was called immoral, but *Peeping Tom* captured the brutality of filming, the metaphorical killing which a camera performs, its unforgiving disregard for the people in front of it. In *Dr Strangelove or: How I Learned to Stop Worrying and Love the Bomb* (1964), Stanley Kubrick looked at the same thing in a very different way. Where Powell's leading character was mad, Kubrick's murderous politicians and military men were stupid. Their cretinous lust for power and misapprehensions about its impact were mirrored in a brutally simple visual idea: put a camera on a missile. There would be an outcry if this were to happen in Iraq, of course, but ethically there is no difference between a tank barrel and a missile. The latter is just more cinematic. In Kubrick's case the dead logic of his commanders argued for a cinematic solecism: the camera on the missile did not express the sublime of war but the dumbness of its architects.

Paul Verhoeven's *Robocop* (1987) has elements of both. In it, policemen and robots have merged so we see killings through the eyes of a camera in the head of a gun-toting law enforcement officer. Where Powell used his camera to represent a deranged man and Kubrick to represent stupid men, here Verhoeven puts us in the moral position of someone who is only half a man.

None of these take us the whole way, however. The knife, missile and gun are each wielded by damaged or partial human beings. What if human agency is removed entirely? If guns and cameras have uncomfortable parallels, is it possible to imagine a film told entirely from the point of view of one? If not, why not? *Madame D* (1953) was in part told from the perspective of a pair of earrings. There have been films narrated by a knee. Filmmakers like Abel Gance in France and Martin Scorsese in America have dynamised camera work by liberating it from any particular human point of view and attaching it to inanimate things. No one, however, would have the bad taste, the amorality to make a firearm the point of view of a whole film, would they? Alan Clarke got close. In 1989 he made the 39-minute film *Elephant* in which the camera roams around Belfast. Its point of view is often that of unidentified killers' extended arms and guns. There is neither context, psychology, characterisation nor story. This is the only film I know which is centred solely on a gun. Is it the morally empty future to which cinema is headed? No. The hopeful fact is this: most people found tragedy in the very coldness of *Elephant*'s point of view. Into its central emptiness, the space derelicted by human compassion, audiences read a critique of killing. *Elephant* is the clearest evidence we have of what theorists have long argued: cinema's anthropomorphism, its innate, conventional, need to see things from a human point of view, its implication that there is a human observer behind the lens.

The BBC's static camera pointing at an uneventful road in Baghdad has represented a very different category of imagery during the war in Iraq: its Lenten, ascetic, anti-Nietzscheanism has been a relief. But even where the imagery seems to have become complicit with the killing, the lessons of cinema are that despite the parallels between shooting and shooting, one will not take the simple point of view of the other.

A camera, like a gun, has no inner life. But we give it one.

people

a gallery of heroes and rogues

POLANSKI

April 2003

Roman Polanski is making news again. The director of *Rosemary's Baby* (1968) and *China-town* (1974) surprised many when he won the Best Film and Director prizes at the BAF-TAs recently for *The Pianist* (2002). He was not in London to collect his prizes because the UK has an extradition treaty with the US, where he is wanted as a fugitive from justice. The crime was the rape, in March 1977, of a 13-year-old girl. She gave an interview last month saying that whilst she doesn't forgive him, her experience should not effect the voting of the members of the American Academy. *The Pianist* was nominated for seven Oscars and eventually won three.

It is difficult not to braid Polanski's work and life together, as this first paragraph has just done. In a tense three-hour television interview some years ago, my attempts to see one reflected in the other were derided by him as 'monkey see, monkey do'. He told me in no uncertain terms that he was far too evolved psychologically to transcribe his astonishing life into his astonishing work.

Polanski was born in Paris in 1933, to agnostic middle-class Jewish parents. In Krakow from 1936, his stern father sometimes locked him in the closet and used lie detectors on him. He was sent home from kindergarten for saying 'kiss my ass' and peed in a cinema seat because he wanted to leave and his half-sister didn't. After the occupation he, like many others, were forced by the Germans to watch films about lice-ridden, rat-like Jews. Movies, in several ways, were becoming a place of humiliation for him. By the end of the war, his mother had been killed in Auschwitz-Birkenau, he had seen six old women shot dead and had watched Poles defecate on German soldiers.

He was quickly drawn to cinema. Not the colour films or escapist musicals of the early 1950s, but two British ones, Carol Reed's *Odd Man Out* (1947) and Laurence Olivier's *Hamlet* (1948). What appealed was the articulacy of these films and, in particular, their 'studioness': both were filmed on sets, each was atmospheric and claustrophobic. He loved their spatial control and replicated it in his own work. Around this time he married Basia Kwiatkowska, who later said, 'Romek has a fire burning inside him that has always attracted people'. Of himself, he commented, 'deep down I am baroque'.

Polanski's own first feature film, *Nóz w wodzie/Knife in the Water* (1961), is one of the most claustrophobic films ever made. Amongst the first Polish films not to deal with the subject of the war, it was set and shot almost entirely on a small sailing boat. Like his subsequent movies *Cul de Sac* (1966), *Frantic* (1988), *Bitter Moon* (1992) and *Death and the Maiden* (1994), it was about the strained geometry of a sexual triangle and the humiliation of getting too close to people. It was called 'cosmopolitan' in communist Poland where Polanski's interest in jazz, style, decadence and art for art's sake did not go down well. His subject was not the society approved of by Socialist Realism, but reality itself. What lay beyond the social – fantasy, fear and desire – the stuff of Hollywood utopianism. This would remain the case throughout his career. 20th Century Fox tried to remake *Knife in the Water* with Elizabeth Taylor, Richard Burton and Warren Beatty. Polanski was already on the Hollywood radar.

The Zelig-like director arrived in London as it was starting to swing. He filmed *Cul de Sac* on Holy Island, the first of many of his films to echo *Hamlet*'s castle setting. The atmosphere on location was so tense that actor Donald Pleasance lodged a formal complaint and the crew threatened strike action. The story started to absorb some of the tension of its circumstances. Polanski had already taken the aesthetics of triangles, of strain, of isolation, further than any other director.

In 1967, he made one of his best films, a technically dazzling spoof of Hammer Horror films, *The Fearless Vampire Killers*. Again set in a castle somewhere in Jewish middle-Europe, this was cinema as a Chagall painting. Polanski himself played the lead. Opposite him his producer cast a beautiful young actress, Sharon Tate. She and Polanski dined and took LSD together, fell in love, got married and conceived a child. They set up home in the Hollywood hills just as Timothy Leary had advised to tune in, turn on and drop out. After Alfred Hitchcock turned down the script of *Rosemary's Baby*, Polanski took it on, filming with 18mm and 25mm lenses. Such was his technical knowledge that, according to cinematographer Bill Fraker, even Hollywood's famously skilled crew members learnt much from him. They were amazed at his devotion to detail and truth, using video assist for the first time, making the vegetarian Mia Farrow eat raw liver, employing Anton Le Vey, later a member of Charles Manson's church, as advisor.

On 9th August 1969, whilst in London, Polanski got a call to say that Tate and three of his friends had been murdered in their LA home. The news went around the world and froze the spine of the 1960s. Polanski was comforted by friends Jack Nicholson and Warren Beatty. The press reported that there were demonic overtones to the crime. Untrue. They hinted that Polanski's lifestyle was in some way responsible. Untrue. He joined the investigation. The murderers, it was discovered, were followers of Charles Manson. 'Sharon's death,' he said afterwards, 'reinforced my belief in the absurd … I began to take on the traits of my father – pessimism, dissatisfaction with life, a profoundly Judaic sense of guilt and a conviction that every joy has his price.' 'He was excommunicated by Hollywood,' Jack Nicholson would later say, 'because his wife had the very bad taste to be murdered by the newspapers.'

Three years later, Polanski made another castle film, about, in part, a man whose wife and child are murdered when he is away. Critics of *Macbeth* at the time and since saw Shakespeare's lines 'give sorrow words … make medicine of great revenge' as connected to Polanski's own grief process. It was his bloodiest film yet. Back in the US, the director started dating 16–19 year old women. In 1974 Nicholson sent him a script called *Chinatown*. Its writer, Robert Towne said, 'Roman was the best collaborator I ever had, the little fart.' About the rape of the Owens Valley, Towne had written an upbeat ending but Polanski reversed this, brutally killing Faye Dunaway's character at the end by having her shot through the eye. Towne called this new ending 'the tunnel at the end of the light.' Polanski had turned Hollywood Utopianism on its head. The film evinced a profoundly un-American cynicism and despair. It was about the futility of good intentions. It got eleven Oscar nominations. In 1976, he made what I think is his best film, *The Tenant*, an absurdist work about claustrophobia, transvestism and – again – the humility of intimacy.

The following year, in Nicholson's jacuzzi, Polanski drugged and had sex with the 13-year-old girl he was photographing for men's *Vogue*. Later that day he was arrested by the LAPD and charged on six counts, including rape and use of drugs. He was imprisoned for psychiatric tests for 42 days. The DA dropped 5 of the 6 charges, leaving unlawful sexual intercourse. His probation officer Irwin Gold said 'Roman Polanski expressed great remorse … great pity and compassion' for the girl. Journalists continue to write that he has never apologised. Pending further sentencing, he boarded a plane, flew to Europe and hasn't returned to the US since. He met Nastassja Kinski – then nearly 19 but reported in the papers as much younger – and together they made *Tess* (1979), a book recommended to Polanski by Tate, and dedicated to her. It is his most lyrical and golden film. When asked about this he said that since the world is absurd, it is bold to make something lyrical to add to it. Hardy's novel was, of course, about a girl who is raped by an aristocrat and rejected by rigid Victorian society. Some saw it as a further apology from Polanski. Its rape scene is one of the most tentative in his career, shot through mist, without point-of-view shots (unlike the one in *Rosemary's Baby*) and with a deliberative, zooming camera. It got eleven Oscar nominations.

It remains hard to accept Polanski's jibe that to see connections between his life and work is to believe in 'monkey see, monkey do'. *The Pianist* is his latest – and most detached – imaginative reworking of the three central crimes in which he has been involved. Where the Tate murder and the rape incident were in his adulthood, the Holocaust and the deportation of his mother were more formative. Having decided against directing *Schindler's List*, he finally chose the story of an *artist* in the Holocaust as the starting point for his own cinematic retrospection.

It is true that Polanksi has also been a man of pure cinema. *The Fearless Vampire Killers* and *The Tenant* are exquisite explorations of space and movement, fun and fear. But his human theme has often been the discomfort of closeness. His work has sailed very close indeed to the storm of his own life. The unease and claustrophobia in his films, which surpass either *Hamlet* or *Odd Man Out*, surely, in part at least, derive from this.

CONNERY

People in most parts of the world know – or think they know – who Sean Connery is. Baby boomers in the West remember his 'black Irish' sharky masculinity in *Dr No* (1962) and the other Bond movies, his grace at the *chemin de fer* table, the way he filled a Turnball and Assar shirt and drove an Aston Martin, the way he looked at Ursula Andress coming out of the sea.

In France, where the 1960s were more 1960s, intellectuals at first found him old-fashioned, a symbol of the *ancien régime*, but then they looked again and saw a stoicism, a latter-day Bogie or Gary Cooper, Sartre in a tux. In China he is 'Seen Connoll*ee*', and adored by young women. In Iran, men love his 1996 film *The Rock*, in which he plays John Mason, banged up on Alcatraz since 1963. In Britain, too, his celebrity seems to have been updated. Teens and pre-teens today are big fans because of peak-time re-runs of bond movies on ITV. In Connery's native Scotland, the tabloids have made their own photofit image of him – a tetchy, nationalist, anti-feminist, tax-exile.

It must be weird to travel around the world, or open newspapers printed in the country of your birth, and meet versions of yourself which seem to be self-sustaining and untrue. When you first meet the real Connery, it's like he has stepped down from the screen, but then you start to notice things: first, how un-klutzy he is. He does objects well, which begins to explain how easy he was in the skin of Bond – a weapons expert whom gadgety Q always seemed to be trying to outdo.

Within a few hours, you notice Connery's directness. Two years ago, a bunch of us were in an Edinburgh restaurant and the food was very late. I moaned a bit and did nothing. Connery got up, walked into the kitchen and said 'the food is late'. It arrived in haste. Ask him why he made a certain decision and he'll answer 'to get the thing done'. It's a phrase he uses quite a bit, and it reveals an approach to life, I think. Some people circle a problem and seem happy with, almost cosy in, stasis. Not Connery. He wants to get the thing done. Perhaps this is unsurprising in a person with such clout, though it's an eye-opener to see how many celebs seem paralysed by the challenge of making decisions, or agree to one thing then tell their assistant to get them out of it, pronto.

More intriguing is the third thing about Connery, which takes some time to emerge: his interest in ideas. He read James Joyce in his youth – he even had a go at *Finnegans Wake*, which daunts most of us. He is a bibliophile and, if you look carefully, you can see this in his movies. In *The Rock*, John Mason's cell is full of books. This was not in the original script, but Connery had it inserted. His character Professor Henry Jones in *Indiana Jones and the Last Crusade* (1989) is a bookworm and unworldly with it. Connery's own new book, which he is co-writing with Murray Grigor, isn't so much an autobiography as a series of ideas-led chapters on Scotland and his relationship to it.

Connery's film *Finding Forrester* (2000), in which he plays a Salinger-like reclusive writer, dramatises one of his core beliefs – that education can lift people out of disadvantage. In this case his character helps a black Bronx kid with a gift for words. The film is a key to understanding Connery because it maps some of the problems of his native Scotland – privilege, talent wasted because it is born into poverty – onto America. Connery himself came from working-class Edinburgh, so its no surprise that he is angry at such advantage. Though no New Labour fan, he is a meritocrat as they are.

My own experience gives me some small insight into this. I met Connery when I was Director of the Edinburgh International Film Festival and he was Patron. When I left the festival, I began working on TV, and started a show called *Scene by Scene*, where I would interview film people about their craft. Connery hadn't, for years, given a full career interview on TV, and hasn't since, but he agreed to do so for me, and came to my house to film it, at considerable inconvenience and for the princely sum of steak and chips at the Caledonian Hotel. Why? I think because he could see that I was (a) passionate about what I was doing and (b) hadn't got where I was because my Mum or Dad were well connected, or I had an uncle in the media.

As we talked in that interview, I realised that Connery's distrust of the military was another passion, another driving force. He joined the Navy aged 16 and had to leave because of a stomach ulcer, but the privilege he saw there, the unfair treatment, seems to have marked him. *The Hill*, which he made for Sidney Lumet for almost no fee in 1965, was about the absurdity of punishment meted out to ordinary Second World War soldiers by Staff Sergeants in Libya. Even the plot of *The Rock*, made two decades later, turns on a General's anger at seeing soldiers and their families maltreated.

Connery's directness, or ideasiness, his interest in education and the military, are the sort of things that you notice at the table, or over a drink or a drive somewhere. But there's something less obvious that took me ages to pin down. Queer Studies theorists use the phrase 'the performed self' to describe the way that gay, lesbian, bisexual and transgender people 'pass' in a heterosexual world that is sometimes hostile to them. I have always liked the phrase because it is true to the fact that many people – not just queer ones – present surfaces. Working-class people, for example, when they migrate into middle-class worlds.

Connery migrated in this way, from the working class into show business, the ultimate industry of the performed self, yet here's the real surprise about him: he seems to have no performed self. Little things clue you into this. When you deal with him, it is not through layers of assistants and managers – all symbols of, or moats around, the performed self. There is genuinely no sense when you talk to him that he has manufactured personas, modes of table talk, routines to deal with autograph hunters or, more psychoanalytically, versions of himself that even he believes in, to deal with the fear or emptiness that international celebrity must surely make you feel.

This explains why on-screen there's no flicker in him between confidence and doubt as there is in, for example, Marilyn Monroe.

But what of Connery on-screen? Where does he stand? Neither of his contemporaries Steve McQueen or James Coburn flickered either. His solidity on-screen from the 1960s to the 1990s, his lack of neurosis, was like a rock against which more unravelled actors such as Robert De Niro and Al Pacino lashed. They reflected recent social change in the West. He drew from more archetypal men like Henry Fonda and Gary Cooper and was the continuity candidate. That's why movies seemed to fit around him, rather than vice versa.

KAUFMAN May 2004

The old joke about the starlet who was so dumb she slept with the screenwriter captures both the cynicism of Hollywood and the lowly status of its scribes. Not all screenwriters are powerless, but the exceptions have been few and far between. Ben Hecht, Robert Towne and William Goldman in their different ways had leverage beyond the norms of their profession, but none achieved the unique *éclat* of the man behind one of the most talked about films of the moment, *Eternal Sunshine of the Spotless Mind*.

Charlie Kaufman's status in Hollywood is a singular one. When *Premiere* magazine compiled its movie 'Power 100', there was only one screenwriter on the list – Kaufman (at number 100). George Clooney, who directed *Confessions of a Dangerous Mind*, one of three movies penned by the writer in 2002, said: 'One of these days, the term Kaufmanesque will be just as familiar as Mametspeak.' Cameron Diaz, who was unrecognisable in *Being John Malkovich* (1999), Kaufman's debut screenplay, said of it: 'They say in Hollywood that there are only 14 screenplays. Well, this is number 15.' Both *Being John Malkovich* and his second script, *Adaptation* (2002) – about Kaufman and his fictional brother trying and failing to adapt a book for the screen – were nominated for Oscars. In the press, Kaufman is often given possessory credits for these films despite the fact that they were directed by Michel Gondry, Clooney and Spike Jonze. Kaufman, it seems, has achieved that rarest of things: recognition as an auteur screenwriter.

His Lynchian eccentricities haven't hindered the process. He sometimes doesn't eat lunch because, as he puts it, 'the thought of getting food stuck in my beard is almost unbearable' (rather like David Lynch telling me once that he wears three ties 'for protection'). A recent *Esquire* profile of Kaufman, commenting on his move to LA in 1991, had to make do with sentences like this: 'He may or may not have brought his wife, who may or may not be called Denise.' His résumé claims that he was born 'between three and five decades ago'. The enigma notwithstanding, his life story is unexceptional. Kaufman was born in 1958 and brought up in a Long Island Jewish family. He acted at school and studied film at NYU. His taste in culture was comic-surreal: the films of Lynch and Woody Allen; the writing of Franz Kafka, Samuel Beckett and Flannery O'Connor. After his move to LA, he wrote for television sitcoms and comedy shows and began drafting a spec screenplay about a puppeteer who works on the 7½th floor of an office building and finds a tunnel which leads into the mind of John Malkovich. Kaufman didn't expect to get the result made, but Malkovich read and liked it and got it to studio execs, many of whom thought it was too weird, until Michael Stipe's company bought it. Spike Jonze directed and an all-star cast signed up for parts.

Being John Malkovich was critically acclaimed and, as a result, even bigger stars – Nicolas Cage and Meryl Streep – were cast in *Adaptation*. After the dreamlike promise of the first film, Kaufman's static account of a split personality paralysed with anxiety and indecision seemed like marginalia. It looked as if the curse of the auteur had already kicked in: acquire a reputation for genius and no matter what you write, it will get made.

Thankfully, *Eternal Sunshine of the Spotless Mind* is a far more vital work. Its main character's oscillations are not about how to turn a book into a film, but whether to forget a love affair. Kaufman's science fiction conceit is that the woman in the story, beautifully played by Kate Winslet, has had her memories of the relationship wiped and the man – Jim Carrey – begins to undergo the same process, and then has doubts. As with *Adaptation*, the film is not about how people change – the traditional character arc in US cinema – but how the flickering nature of the human mind makes them too indecisive to change. Kaufman appears more obsessed by breakdown than love in the film, and there are times when its fragmentation seems pointless, but by the end it has achieved honesty.

Does Kaufman deserve the accolade of American cinema's only auteur screenwriter? He is certainly consistently un-Hollywood in his concerns. No other screenwriter today has shown such an interest in the activity of human consciousness. Most write classically-structured screenplays about characters who speak externally and whose experiences form the story of the film. Such an approach renders the screenwriter invisible. Kaufman produces an admixture of memory, fantasy and mental association. Dennis Potter did this, and so did Paul Mayersberg (*The Man Who Fell to Earth* (1976), *Merry Christmas, Mr Lawrence* (1983)) and what is striking is that they too were considered auteurs: no matter who directed their work, it was considered Potterian and Mayersbergian.

Such work is distinctive because it is about interiority and inaction, and, crucially, it requires the imagery to be unreal. It – the writing – directs the image track and the timeline of the film. But Kaufman's position is ambiguous. Fawned over by a film industry starved of new voices, he is also indulged by that industry and worn as its badge of prestige. There's not much room for more films such as his in the multiplexes, but perhaps his success will inspire more ambitious writing in the future.

WILDER

I wonder if, before he died in March, Billy Wilder's life flashed before his eyes like some Hollywood biopic? If so, did it occur to him that no one life could really contain so much, that perhaps the memory banks of some latter-day Zelig had accidentally shorted with his own?

He was named Billy after Buffalo Bill, on whom his mother had developed a crush. Aged ten, he saw Archduke Franz Josef's funeral; Otto Von Hapsburg was in the cortège. Decades later, Wilder would give the ageing Hapsburg a tour around Paramount Studios.

In Vienna during the First World War, he stood in line for twenty hours for three potatoes. His sense of the unreality of Hollywood was sparked off by Douglas Fairbanks offering to buy Austria during the hyper-inflation. Unsurprisingly, he claimed that he was a cynic by the age of 12. A stint as a crime writer in early adulthood toughened him more.

It was only the beginning. He interviewed Ferenc Molnar, Sigmund Freud and Richard Strauss, wrote songs and sold one to his US jazz hero Paul Whiteman. He moved to Berlin, which at the time had 120 newspapers, forty theatres and 360 movie houses, and became a gigolo. He advised Erich Maria Remarque not to write *All Quiet on the Western Front* and in the late 1920s wrote outlines for over 200 films, for which he received no credit. He was a 25-year-old hedonist with an apartment full of Mies van der Rohe furniture.

In 1933, as the Reichstag burned, he left Berlin with $100 in his hat band. He spent a year in Paris, cabled Columbia Studios with an idea and sailed to America in 1934. Five years later, by which time he was friends with James M. Cain, Dorothy Parker and Dore Schary, he swore the oath of allegiance.

On the studio lot, the newly Americanised Wilder saw fading star Gloria Swanson and, years later, made *Sunset Blvd.* (1950) with her, the film that begat the musical which is still playing around the world. At Paramount, Wilder learned the tricks of screwball comedy – outrageous coincidence and intricate construction. Tone was everything in this most Europeanised of studios, but here they quoted George Kaufman: 'satire is what closes Saturday night.'

At the end of the war, Wilder edited raw footage from the death camps where his mother had been murdered. In 1947, his hero, director Ernst Lubitsch, died. Wilder had a sign on his office wall: 'How would Lubitsch do it?' The Lubitsch trick was to top a punch line with another, unexpected gag and hide your plot points.

In 1945, Wilder made *The Lost Weekend*, which Woody Allen says is the best film ever made. In 1951 he did *Ace in the Hole*, which Spike Lee paid tribute to in *Malcolm X* (1992). His *Sabrina* (1954) was recently remade (in 1995). *The Seven Year Itch* (1955) didn't work, he said, because it needed a shot of one of Marilyn Monroe's hairpins in Tom Ewell's bed. Then 1959 brought *Some Like it Hot*. The 1960s ('I didn't even know they were the sixties', he cracked) heralded *The Apartment*, for which he won three Oscars, as writer, producer and director.

Wilder made fewer films in the 1970s. He used to say that *Bronenosets Potyomkin/ Battleship Potemkin* (1925) was his favourite movie, but that was before *Schindler's List*, which he himself wanted to direct. In 1993, the winner of the Oscar for best foreign film said 'I don't believe in God, so I'd like to thank Billy Wilder.'

He was a very great man, perhaps Hollywood's best narrative director. *The Apartment* is the film I've watched more than any other. So it is with reluctance that I offer the following opinion: Billy Wilder never made a masterpiece. Like many of my generation and the generation before (the so-called 'movie brats' who started making films in the 1970s) I saw the great Wilders on television. There, they are masterpieces. *The Apartment* is balanced, beautiful and wise on the small screen. *Some Like it Hot* is an annual delight. *Sunset Blvd.* has for years made Saturday afternoons gothic. Families are rare in Wilder films but they are part of our domestic lives.

In order to write an introduction to the screenplay of *The Apartment*, published a few years ago, I watched Wilder films on the big screen. It was an extremely unsettling experience. I knew that *The Apartment* was made in widescreen Panavision, but the acres of space around Jack Lemmon's and Shirley MacLaine's heads robbed the film of clarity and intimacy. With more films, I noticed something worse. Wilder's movies are so beautifully structured and preconceived that there is nothing in them that is abstract: no pauses, no excess, nothing purely formal or expressive. It's all reducible to words; nothing is pure cinema.

I also saw films by Wilder's fellow 1950s Hollywood directors: Nicholas Ray, Vincente Minnelli and Douglas Sirk. On television, I thought they misfired, lacking Wilder's more evolved sense of shot and cut. In the cinema, the tables are turned. Ray's hysteria, Minnelli's choreography, Sirk's repressed desire were each more interesting than Wilder's Lubitsch-inspired storytelling. Wilder is indeed a god, but for a television generation of film lovers and the classicists. Truly great cinema does something else, something unscriptable that you can only catch projected across space and painted onto a huge canvas.

INGMAR

February 2003

See, also, Antonioni

In nearly twenty years of programming films – at university, in film festivals, on television – I have never shown a single work by Ingmar Bergman. This is the first time I have written about him. Of all the art movie *auteurs* who emerged in the 1950s and 1960s – Federico Fellini, Michelangelo Antonioni, Luchino Visconti, Luis Buñuel, Jean-Luc Godard, Ousmane Sembène, Satyajit Ray, Pier Paolo Pasolini, Robert Bresson, François Truffaut, Nagisa Oshima, Shohei Imamura and so on – Bergman is the only one I have virtually ignored. I have seen all his famous films but to many critics of my generation (born in the 1960s) he was the most overrated of these directors. We dismissed Bergman as a passionless patrician even when, in 1983, he re-imagined one of our favourite films, *Meet Me in St Louis* (1944), as the grand and gorgeous family saga, *Fanny and Alexander*. But, as the National Film Theatre mounts a retrospective of his film work and his production of Ibsen's *Ghosts* appears on the London stage, Bergman's disappearance from the canon of post-1960s film criticism is due for reappraisal.

He was born in Uppsala to the sternest of parents in a year, 1918, when Swedish cinema was booming. His Lutheran father, a pastor to the Swedish royal family, disciplined his theatre-obsessed son by locking him in dark cupboards. Bergman became a screenwriter in 1944, directed his first film in 1945 and in 1955 had his first international success with *Sommarnattens leende/Smiles of a Summer Night* (1955), a grand country-house comedy, set in the 1900s, about the infidelities of middle-aged couples. Derived from Jean Renoir, it in turn was the basis for Stephen Sondheim's *A Little Night Music* and Woody Allen's *A Midsummer Night's Sex Comedy* (1982). By 1957, with *Det Sjunde inselet/The Seventh Seal*, Bergman's tone had darkened. A medieval allegory about a knight returning from the crusades who is challenged to a game of chess by Death himself, it drew even more attention than *Smiles of a Summer Night*, won prizes at Cannes and led to the first retrospective of Bergman in London.

I hated *The Seventh Seal* when I saw it in 1982. High on Orson Welles, Alfred Hitchcock, Pasolini and Godard, I found it stolid and academic. Why had older critics been so blind to its dreary aesthetic calculations? They saw Bergman as the messiah of new art

114   widescreen

cinema, a godsend after decades of Hollywood brainlessness. The 1950s were the high wa-
termark years for his reputation but by 1960, when Godard had refreshed movie language,
Bergman's sober, middle-class metaphysics seemed, even to some of his supporters, dated
and losing relevance.

In 1966 he made *Persona*, a film about an actress who becomes mute and is treated by
a nurse, whose identity she absorbs. Gone was the obsession with religion and marriage.
This was an intense, modernist work full of unexplained images. Its six-minute pre-title
sequence is startling – we see the death of a sheep, its guts, a nail going into a hand, a tap
dripping, a phone ringing, a boy lying on a slab. Robert Altman, Woody Allen, John Sayles
and Martin Scorsese admired the mastery of such sequences and the film marked a shift
to the theme of female hysteria which would become central to Bergman. *Persona* was as
iconic as Picasso's *Les Demoiselles d'Avignon*, but how does it stand up today? Where is
the simplicity, joy or adventure of Godard and Truffaut, the rage of Pasolini, the excess of
Fellini? *Persona* is structure, refinement, mannerism and symbolism.

In 1969, shifts in film theory left Bergman high and dry. The idea of 'Third Cinema'
emerged, neither industrial (like Hollywood, the 'First Cinema') nor auteurist (like Bergman, the 'Second'), but oppositional and politically engaged. Pasolini filmed among peasants, Buñuel explored the disruptions of desire, even the aristocratic Visconti was a Marx-
ist. Bergman, by contrast, looked haughty and, some said, misogynistic.

In 1976, he was arrested for tax fraud and had a nervous breakdown; he moved to
Munich, where he worked in theatre and television. When the charges were dropped, he
returned to Sweden and directed *Fanny and Alexander*, which won four Oscars. He then
announced his retirement and became a semi-recluse on the island of Fårö. In Sweden his
mystique grew, like Garbo's, with every interview refusal.

Then the critical tide turned back in his favour. The disdain some of us used to feel
started to seem as cold and lofty as his films. In the late 1990s, the NFT embarked on a
reassessment of the art cinema of the 1950s and 1960s which it was initially so instrumen-
tal in canonising. Second Cinema was under the spotlight. When Visconti's films are explored later this year (however much you love *Rocco e i suoi fratelli/Rocco and his Brothers*
(1960)), it might reveal the leadenness of his erotic imagination.

But now that it is Bergman's turn, I think it will show that he is better than my generation thought. We read him too politically. We ousted him because his middle-class,
middle-aged themes didn't appeal to us. Now that we are middle-aged ourselves, and have
seen the tragic side of love, his films seem more alive.

But the retrospective will also show that Bergman is not as good as his early advocates
believed. He opened cinema up to theories of mind and theology, but there was something
of the pedagogue in him. Cinema has benefited from the iconoclasm which pitched him
from his pedestal; Bergman's talent, rather than a false image of genius, is what remains.

JLG

If you were born before 1945, were brought up in a city, had a good education and were a moviegoer, there is a good chance that a certain Swiss cineaste shook you up. You probably started seeing films in the 1950s when the movie theatres were swamped with stories and ideas from the America of Eisenhower. You may have noticed that some of these apparently conformist films were inclined to hysteria, aesthetic excess and rage, and that they were directed by Nicholas Ray, Vincente Minnelli and Sam Fuller.

The Swiss man saw these films too. He wrote about them in highbrow magazines in Paris, his adopted home. He wrote about them as Baudelaire did of the Boulevards, in the idiom of Huysmans or Walter Pater.

And then this Swiss man took up a camera and, either because of an extraordinary intellectual confidence developed in his cinephile magazine world, or because he was instinctively disruptive, or because it was crystal clear to him that a certain tendency in film language had died, he synthesised the little shocks that avant-garde cinema had been delivering into a film called *À bout de souffle/Breathless* (1960). It made waves. It was his only box-office success.

He went on to direct more than sixty films including *Le Mépris/Contempt* (1963) with Brigitte Bardot and Fritz Lang; *Bande à part/The Outsiders* (1964), after which Quentin Tarantino named his production company; the overrated sci-fi film *Alphaville* (1965); *Deux ou trois choses que je sais d'elle/Two or Three Things I Know About Her* (1966), which Scorsese pays tribute to in *Taxi Driver* (1976); *La Chinoise* (1967) with *nouvelle vague* icons Anne Wiazemsky and Jean-Pierre Léaud; *Je vous salue Marie* (1983), which had Catholics in uproar; a mad *King Lear* (1987) featuring Norman Mailer, and with Woody Allen as the fool; and *Eloge de l'amour/In Praise of Love* which played at Cannes this year and takes pot shots at the director's *bête noire*, Steven Spielberg.

Forty-one years after the release of *À bout de souffle*, a season of his films is showing in the UK. It is a whopper: 205 film and tape screenings in London, a selection repeated in other arts cinemas, and a four-day symposium at the Tate Modern, with fifty academic speakers. The only notable absences will be the man himself and *Eloge de l'amour*.

I was born in 1965, not 1945, at the end of the baby boom and on the cusp of generation X. We weren't around when the Swiss director turned the movie world upside down, so this season is aimed at us. How brave of the organisers. Don't they know that our cinemagoing started around 1980, a movie time as conservative as the 1950s? We queued for *Jaws* (1975), *Grease* (1978), *Porky's* (1982) and *Top Gun* (1986). Don't they know that Gen-Xers are always looking back and questioning what the fuss was about? We do this because we have a sense of being in the slipstream of great things, because we've been told the parade's gone by, and we're not sure it was all that good in the first place.

As if to provoke our proud amnesia, the organisers of the retrospective have called their season 'Forever'. Who do they think they are? Don't they know that we don't believe in forever? It's as if they are trying to establish as an absolute truth that this man's work is timeless. Ho ho ho, how we laugh. How we mock the longing in their title for a time when movies were audacious.

And yet, I have a confession. Over the years, I've gone out of my way to see almost everything in the season. I've smuggled into my BBC2 film programme extracts from *À bout de souffle*, *Une femme mariée* (1964) and *Bande à part*. *La Chinoise* and *Deux ou trois choses que je sais d'elle* (her being the woman and the city) are amongst my favourite films. I never go to the Cannes press conferences, but this year I went to his.

I'm as reluctant as my peers to accept unchallenged the evaluations of those who went before. The writers who will attend the symposium (in spirit or in fact) – Serge Daney, Raymond Bellour, Laura Mulvey, Thomas Elsaesser, Peter Wollen – are the people who interpreted cinema for me when I only partially spoke its language. They told me that this director was in a class of his own. Looking for myself, I've accepted their judgement. François Truffaut said that anyone who rejects Nicholas Ray's film *Johnny Guitar* (1954) 'should never go to the movies again. Such people will never recognise poetic intuition, a good film, or even cinema itself.' Insert *Deux ou trois choses que je sais d'elle* instead of *Johnny Guitar*, and the same is true.

Until the mid-1950s a shot in cinema was, in general, a piece of action – someone entering a room, firing a gun, falling from a horse, doing a dance. For the Swiss director, a shot was something more. He didn't cut when the action was complete because that subordinated the shot to the action. You can let the person walk through the door and then hold and not cut. The issue becomes time rather than action. A shot becomes a new thing, closer to a thought than a gesture. Avant garde artists and filmmakers of the 1920s prefigured the cinema revolution of 1959/60. But one director merits particular credit for vitalising the movie image. His name is Jean-Luc Godard.

SOKUROV

I first came across the name Aleksandr Sokurov in an almost empty cinema in wintry Berlin in 1995. I had turned up to see a five-hour documentary called *Spiritual Voices*, shot on the battle front of the Tajikistan civil war over one and a half years. The lights went down and a trance-like elegy for dead and dying soldiers unspooled. Not one of the clichés of war appeared on-screen. Instead I saw a film with the intensity of silent cinema and a nineteenth-century sensibility. Shots lasted for minutes. The dust of the desert seemed to enter the camera.

Others were on to the Sokurov secret before me. Russia's master of transcendental cinema, Andrei Tarkovsky, a great curmudgeon who was impressed by nothing, said that the Irkutsk-born director was 'a cinematic genius'. Susan Sontag called his 1992 film *Kamen/Stone*, about a museum custodian who talked to the ghost of Chekhov, which she saw in a retrospective later in the decade, one of the best films of the 1990s.

The year after my Berlin revelation, Sokurov released an almost unimaginable thing: an even better film. *Mat i syn/Mother and Son* was a 73-minute chamber piece about the last weeks, days or moments of a frail old woman and her attentive offspring, who feeds her with a bottle and carries her into the fields so that she can see the swollen sky. Filmed and acted in slow-motion, shot with glass and mirrors in front of and around the lens, some of which were painted on with a fine Chinese brush, it led Paul Schrader, writer of *Taxi Driver* (1976) and *Raging Bull* (1980), to write that it is '73 heart-aching, luminescent minutes of pure cinema. His films,' Schrader added, 'define a new form of spiritual cinema.' The musician Nick Cave saw it in London and later described what happened: 'Ten minutes in, I started crying and continued to do so for the continuation of the film. I can't remember crying so hard, without a pause.' When the son carries her outside, the mother gasps for air, looks to the swollen skies, hears a thunderclap and says, 'Is there anyone up there?' When she dies, a butterfly lands on her Dürer-like hands. *Mother and Son* captured the fading spiritual light of painter Caspar David Friedrich, whom Sokurov much admires, and also the glowing pantheism of one of the greatest soviet films, *Earth*, made by Alexander Dovzhenko in 1930, of which critic James Agate wrote, 'A picture for filmgoers who are prepared to take their cinema as seriously as Tolstoy took the novel.'

He could have been talking about Sokurov's next film *Molokh*/*Moloch* (1999), about Hitler and his coterie at Berchtesgarten. Shot as if through pea soup, it features an inane Hitler moaning about his health, about peas and soup and a twittery Eva Braun. This is the pathetic Führer of Norman Stone, the banal evil of Hannah Arendt. Once again at its Cannes premiere there was something of the flickering intensity of silent cinema: the screen seemed small and dim. *Moloch* was aesthetically astonishing, but I nonetheless felt it unforgivable that Sokurov makes his main character apparently unaware of the existence of the gas chambers.

The following year's *Taurus*, a parallel portrait of a dying Lenin, was again a film from another world. In another greeny-blue monotone we see the dying of the light of an out of touch idealist. *Taurus* was a tender Chekhovian study of the year 1923 and conveyed an overwhelming sense of a coming storm, especially when Stalin visits the old man. It confirmed what we already knew, that Sokurov was something astonishing from beyond planet cinema. A flood of retrospectives ensued at MoMA in New York, in Ohio and Ontario. Almost no Sokurov films had been shown in North America before this date. Sontag upped her support, calling the director, 'perhaps the most ambitious and original serious filmmaker of his generation working anywhere in the world'. Martin Scorsese added his name to the admirers. In 2001, Vladimir Putin congratulated the director, whose films were once banned by the Soviets, on his 51st birthday.

In Cannes last month, programmed on the ninth day, was Aleksandr Sokurov's latest film *Russkiy kovcheg*/*Russian Ark*. Only in the days before the press screening did the rumour go around that the movie was filmed in one single shot.

Things are so hazy in Cannes, so exhausting and intense, that there wasn't really time to anticipate this. Instead, we were simply keen to see 'the new Sokurov', whatever it was. We got to the cinema at 1pm – no lunch as usual – and the lights went down. As the opening credits finished, the film broke. A groan from the assembled journos. A few minutes later, the light went down and we saw … a film far better than *Spiritual Voices*, *Mother and Son* or *Taurus*. We saw the best film in Cannes in ten years. We saw a milestone in film history.

Russian Ark is about the Hermitage Museum in Sokurov's adopted city of St Petersburg. It is ninety minutes long and, indeed, comprises one shot, 'one single breath', as the director calls it. Those who know about filming know this is impossible. Not any more. Throughout the history of cinema, filmmakers have dreamed of making a film without any editing, but the limited duration of a film magazine made this impossible. In *Rope* (1948) Alfred Hitchcock simulated a single-shot film by filming swathes of choreographed action then tracking behind a wall or a person, changing film magazines, then tracking on as if there had been no pause. Latterly, directors opposed to what they see as the commodification of Western entertainment cinema have experimented with longer, more meditative ways of filming, but even the most modern of digital betacam videotapes can store only 46 minutes or so of complex audiovisual material.

Sokurov's solution, in collaboration with a German company Egoli Tossell Film and Kopp Media, was to store his 'single breath' neither on film nor tape but on an uncompressed hard disc, which could hold up to 100 minutes. He wanted one choreographed movement to take us through 1,300 metres of the Hermitage's rooms, including the winter palace where the October Revolution took place, and through four epochs of Russian history. Travelling with the camera would be a European stranger (played by Sergey Dreiden), a civilised minstrel. He would argue with the camera and the off-screen, half awake, half dreaming voice of Russia itself. On their journey through history they would encounter Catherine the Great, Nicholases the First and Second, cavaliers, museum officials, spies, great balls and portents of the horrors to come. This could have been a bit *Blue Peter* but is in fact so vivid and delicate that anyone who has ever been interested in nineteenth-century Russia, or indeed Pasternak or Akhmatova, is likely to be profoundly affected.

Planning began, on an almost unimaginable scale. Six months of rehearsal; 867 actors and extras; three live orchestras; 22 assistant directors; 33 galleries containing Rembrandts and da Vincis had to be lit to allow 360-degree camera movements. For various reasons, filming had to take place on 23rd December. There are only four hours of daylight in St Petersburg at that time of year. The single shot would take one and a half of those hours. Worse then this, the hard disc 100-minute system was not wipable and start againable.

Imagine the tension as Sokurov and cameraman Tilman Buttner (who shot some of *Lola rennt/Run Lola Run* (1998)) began their take. Nearly a thousand people had to hit their marks. For ninety minutes there had be no technical or human faults.

Five minutes into the filming, something went wrong. They had to restart. Only 95 minutes left. Five minutes into the restart, something else went wrong. Only ninety minutes of disc time remained, for a ninety-minute film. They started their third take and an hour and a half later, cinema history had been made. Like Sontag, Schrader and Cave before me, I cried.

JEANNE MOREAU

One of the first pronouncements made by the young François Truffaut when he started directing films was that he would never work with two of the great ladies of French cinema, Danielle Darrieux and Michelle Morgan. At the time, the late 1950s, this seemed astonishingly arrogant, like a snotty Guy Ritchie-type banishing Judi Dench from the films he might yet make. While the French film establishment's response to Truffaut may well have been 'he should be so lucky', in retrospect, his lofty exclusion of Darrieux and Morgan seems like one of the great decisions in modern cinema. Truffaut burnt his bridges and, for a time, the new wave followed him.

Truffaut's reason for ruling out these two postwar *grandes dames* has always dazzled me. He said that their faces 'influence too much the *mise-en-scène*'. Their looks dictated the composition and the movements of the camera. So, instead, Truffaut cast Jeanne Moreau, who went on to make 110 films and counting. Orson Welles called her the 'greatest actress in the world'. In a few short years in the early 1960s, she so rose to embody the new, liberated international style of filmmaking that, forty years later, the BBC's brainy arts channel BBC4 launched with a season of her films.

Jeanne Moreau had read Racine by the age of ten, devoured Molière when the literary fashion was for the Left Bank, joined the Comédie Française and became a minor star in more than twenty movies of the 1950s, wearing make-up trowelled on, because that's how it was done in those days and because she was considered unphotogenic. Then a young director, Louis Malle, who had worked with Jacques Cousteau, cast her in his debut feature *Ascenseur pour L'échafaud/Lift to the Scaffold* (1958) and asked his cinematographer Henri Decaë to film her without make-up and lit only by ambient light. The result was a revelation. Moreau looked beautiful and real, the film was like a documentary about her face. The new wave had found its intellectual muse.

Directors couldn't get enough of her. Truffaut made *Jules et Jim* (1962) 'of and for her'. Welles cast her five times. Luis Buñuel gave her the title role in *Le Journal d'une femme de chambre/The Diary of a Chambermaid* (1964). Antonioni fetishised her walk in *La Notte/ The Night* (1961). She became Marguerite Duras' representative on-screen by acting in the film version of *Moderato Cantabile* (1960), being directed by Duras in *Nathalie Granger* (1972) and playing Duras in the recent *Cet amour-là* (2001). Kazan, Fassbinder, Angelopoulos and Wenders also joined her list of auteur admirers.

Why is Moreau's career more interesting than Deneuve's, more lasting than Bardot's? In Britain, Julie Christie looked as if she might last like her French role model, but didn't. In the US, Jane Fonda had the attitude, but her ideas were too specific. Moreau was harder to pin down and the auteurs loved this. They pointed their cameras at her and their shots became more like thoughts than feelings. When she spoke the dialogue of Duras or Jean Claude Carrière, she made the smart talk that helped movie-making grow up.

She was good, in the Freudian sense, at forgetting. Moreau on-screen doesn't harbour bad thoughts or useless desires. Her charm in *Jules et Jim*, the Welles films, and Malle's *Les Amants/The Lovers* (1959) was her ability to jettison the past, to live in the rapturous present. Despite Racine and Molière, despite her relative disinterest in the events of 1968, she has always looked and sounded of the moment. She once said that her greatest achievement has been 'to live without protection.'

Add forgetting to braininess and you get the bracing, edgy freedom of her best work. A quintet of films, *Les Amants*, *Moderato Cantabile*, *La Notte*, *Jules et Jim* and *Eva* (1962) explore this theme. In the first three, Moreau plays an upper middle-class woman who feels trapped by marriage. In *Les Amants*, she has a night of passion with another man, is transformed and walks out on her life and her child. In the second, the situation is identical, though in Duras' more pessimistic universe escape is not possible. In *La Notte* she ends the relationship. Neither Catherine in *Jules et Jim* nor the prostitute Eva could for a moment live like these three trapped women. Catherine is a Baudelairean *flâneuse*, so free she tests everything to the limits; Eva is so unattached that she cannot feel the pain of others. Taken together, these five films, made in three short years, establish Moreau as the Simone de Beauvoir of cinema. Not since silent cinema star Louise Brooks had an actress so expressed the ideal of physical and emotional freedom.

I met Moreau recently in a restaurant near the Arc de Triomphe, to do an interview to accompany the BBC4 season. At dinner, she told me that we were allowed to talk neither about cinema nor herself. I had sent her a postcard months before and she remembered precisely what it said. She is the first person I've interviewed who knew exactly the aims and format of my programme.

A few days later she arrived to talk. I showed her extracts of her 'freedom quintet'. She spoke in detail for well over two hours, yet insisted on the mystery of acting. Talking to Moreau was like running through those fields in *Jules et Jim*, trying to pin her down, when that's impossible.

ALMODÓVAR AND CRUZ October 2006

As I write, Britain's art-house cinemas are *muy contentos*. Since its May premiere at Cannes, they have been licking their chops at the prospect of showing Pedro Almodóvar's new movie, *Volver*, about a woman whose mother returns from the dead. Art-house cinemas need quality hit films to subsidise their education and repertory programming, and *Volver* had 'hit' written all over it.

Almodóvar's following has grown over the years, and his style has matured as he has reduced the amount of gay sex in his films and increased the range of feeling, the harmonics of his mode of melodrama. He has become the closest that beleaguered art-house programmers have got to a dead cert. This following alone does not explain *Volver*'s success, however. The film's most memorable imagery is that of its star, Penélope Cruz, at a chopping board as Almodóvar's overhead camera looks down into her breasts; or her getting out of a car; or looking straight to camera in close-up. The most memorable sound is the exaggerated kissy noise that the women in the film make when they embrace each other.

Cruz is gorgeous, of course, yet she's been in 14 American films without being nearly as memorable. What did *Volver* do to her? How did Almodóvar render her so indelible? Part of the answer has been all over the tabloids. Almodóvar gave Cruz curves. The imagery of women in American cinema derives from the cult of thinness in southern Californian culture – think of Nicole Kidman. Almodóvar, by contrast, had in mind the sort of women he knew in La Mancha. 'I put on three kilos,' Cruz told journalists, 'and Pedro asked me to stay at that weight level during the filming.' The reverse is usually the case in Hollywood, and weight reduction is often written into the contract. Almodóvar has said that Cruz's breasts are 'one of the visual virtues of cinema', but it was her bottom that he had padded so that it 'represents a glorious maternity'. According to Cruz, 'he said a big bottom would push me down closer to the earth'.

Yet Cruz's Raimunda isn't only memorable for her curves. The kohl-blackness of her hair and eyes are etched on to the screen. America's most iconic movie women – Marilyn Monroe and Doris Day – were both luminous blondes. Cruz, like Sophia Loren and Anna Magnani (to both of whom she is regularly compared) seems in *Volver* to drink in light rather than burnish it. Where Monroe and Day sometimes dissolve into a scrim of soft focus, Cruz's contours are rock hard – back to the earth again. Cruz is grounded in Almodóvar's film. She visibly comes from this place. She makes you think of Iranian director Abbas Kiarostami's point that a tree grows best where it's planted.

A further reason why *Volver* is so memorable is that it is all about women in a year in which – once again – the best films are about men. The key movies this year have been, for me, Michael Mann's *Miami Vice*, Bruno Dumont's *Flandres/Flanders*, Ken Loach's *The Wind that Shakes the Barley*, Douglas Gordon and Philippe Parreno's *Zidane: Un portrait du 21st siècle/Zidane: A 21st Century Portrait*, Rafi Pitt's brilliant Iranian film *It's Winter*, and Laura Poitras' Iraqi documentary *My Country, My Country*. All are centred on men to the exclusion of almost everything else. Almodóvar's is the reverse, a portrait of women to the exclusion of almost everything else.

Almodóvar's homosexuality has been used to explain his affinity with women in general and the observational fine grain of *Volver* in particular, but it is difficult to find any kind of firm equation between the sexuality of a director and the way he or she portrays women on-screen. Gay American director George Cukor's key leading lady was Katharine Hepburn, all stalky brio; straight director Howard Hawks went for a similar type. Cult gay director John Waters treated the characters and contours of women as if they were cartoons, as did hetero Italian Federico Fellini. Among the best movies I know about women – the most honest, the least sentimental – are those by heterosexual director Shohei Imamura. So perhaps the sexuality factor is overplayed.

What is certainly underplayed in Almodóvar's work, and one of its most interesting elements, is the influence on it of the Spanish theatre aesthetic *esperpento*, a combination of realism and irony not seen much elsewhere. Says Almodóvar, 'In the 1950s and 1960s, Spain experienced a kind of neo-realism which was far less sentimental than the Italian brand and far more ferocious and amusing. I'm talking about the films of Fernan Gomez … and *The Wheelchair*.' Watched now, *The Wheelchair* (directed by Marco Ferreri, 1960) seems to have been a wellspring for Almodóvar – its story of a widower who, in trying to buy a motorised wheelchair, inadvertently ends up killing his whole family, prefigures Almodóvar's admixture of tears and absurdity. This too is a reason why Cruz's face burns on-screen. Behind her eyes, puissant human forces are at play. Raimunda's life and experiences are both absurd and deeply moving. She sees her dead mother – how could we not be moved? – and yet the events which allow her to do so seem to mock the feelings we have. The mix is Spanish and Almodóvarian. It is his face, too, that we see on-screen.

CHAHINE

I am in Egypt, interviewing the director Youssef Chahine for the documentary version of my book *The Story of Film*. Now in his 80th year, Chahine is one of the few cinema pioneers still alive. His were the first great Arab and African films. Chatting to him in his office in hot and dusty Cairo in December, it's difficult to believe that he's something like the continent's D. W. Griffith.

Yet Chahine is almost invisible in the Anglo-Saxon world. He had a retrospective at the NFT in London a few years ago, but he's not talked about here. No filmmakers and only one critic mentioned his work in *Sight and Sound*'s 2002 poll of the best films ever made. His groundbreaking film *Bab el hadid/Cairo Station* (1958) is not available on DVD or VHS. His movies are never shown on British television.

This sequestration reveals much about Western cinema. Try the following thought experiment. You are a European film critic contemplating the movies of the 1950s. You think first of *Rebel Without a Cause* (1955) and the Marlon Brando films; then *Rear Window* (1954) and *Vertigo* (1958); then CinemaScope films like *The Robe* (1953) and *Ben-Hur* (1959). Moving beyond America, you jot down the early films of Fellini and Bergman, the austere work of Robert Bresson and, in Britain, the Free Cinema of Lindsay Anderson and Karel Reisz. Mindful of the mid-decade breakthrough of Asian cinema in the west, you include on your list Ozu's *Tôkyô Story/Tokyo Story* (1953), Kurosawa's *Shichinin no samurai/The Seven Samurai* (1954) and Satyajit Ray's *Pather Panchali* (1955).

This is as far as most diligent critics would go, but it's exactly the point at which things get interesting. Do you notice that there are no African films on your list? If not, if you have never even considered it, then you are, at least, guilty of a lack of curiosity.

Let's assume, however, that Africa does cross your mind. What then? You perhaps assume either a) if there had been great African films of the 1950s you'd have heard of them, or b) there may have been nascent talents there but that they were hampered by primitive equipment. The first is naïve about distribution – do we really think that the best is naturally made available to us? The second is more excusable, but equally untrue. There was a sophisticated film studio in Egypt from 1935.

Which leaves a third position: that although you've seen no great 1950s African films, you should use Karl Popper's principle of demonstrating that your assumptions are right by trying to prove them wrong. Do so and you will discover the career of Chahine. He's a Christian Alexandrian Arab who studied film in Pasadena, where he fell in love with the musicals of Fred Astaire, Ginger Rogers and Gene Kelly. He began making movies in the early 1950s and in his sixth film discovered Omar Sharif. *Cairo Station*, his twelfth, was the first great movie made by an African. Set during one day in the Egyptian capital's main transport hub, it anticipates Alfred Hitchcock's *Psycho* (1960) in its depiction of the murderous consequences of sexual repression. Its main character, Kenawi, a crippled newspaper-seller in love with a voluptuous lemonade vendor, was played by Chahine himself in a performance, like Anthony Perkins' Norman Bates, which is remarkable in its detail and understatement. The film combines a Nasserian belief in Arab socialism, a Reichian view of sexuality and an Italian neo-realist focus on the everyday. Stylistically, it manages to be realist, musical and expressionist all at once, and its images are robustly composed, like an Eisenstein film. 'I believe in no boundaries – sexual or social,' Chahine tells me, 47 years later, drawing on an Egyptian cigarette and tapping his toe as if 'Dancing Cheek to Cheek' were on the radio.

Such idealism has often been tested. Chahine was spat on when *Cairo Station* was released, for daring to deal with such *outré* sexual themes. In his subsequent career, *al-Asfour/The Sparrow* (1972) brilliantly confronted the Arab world with its defeat in the Six Day War and Nasser's resignation. *al-Massir/Destiny* (1996) attacked Islamic fundamentalism by dramatising the life of the moderate medieval scholar Averroës. Chahine was pilloried. As a result of such outspokenness, and despite being famous in his own country, the director is no longer allowed to appear live on national television. He has criticised Mubarak too many times. His eyes glint as he says this. I've interviewed hundreds of film people but none – not Dennis Hopper or Roman Polanski – is more rebellious.

Chahine is underrated in the Anglo-Saxon world (though not France, where he won a lifetime achievement award at Cannes in 1997) because our film writers are incurious or worse. In the era of DVD and Arab film websites, there is no excuse. And the blame lies not only with writers but programmers, film magazine editors and television and radio commissioners. To survey 1950s cinema without Chahine (never mind the great Indian directors like Guru Dutt and Mehboob, or South Americans Leopoldo Torre Nilsson and Glauber Rocha, or the Russian Sergei Gerasimov or the Chinese Xie Jin) is complacent and ignorant.

At a press conference for the Cairo International Film Festival in December, Morgan Freeman said that cinema can help with international communication and 'combat the clash of civilisations'. If he's even partially right, then the Anglo-Saxon world's ongoing cinematic narcissism is a disgrace.

GHATAK

About fifty years ago, Indian cinema changed fundamentally. The first Bombay International Film Festival showed a selection of Italian neo-realist films and the effect was immediate. The dominant musical and mythical aesthetics of Hindi cinema was knocked off course. Within two years, Bimal Roy's *Do Bigha Zamin/Two Measures of Land* (1953) was released and the history of Indian realist cinema had begun.

No national cinema at the time, not even vanquished Germany's, needed to turn its face towards reality more than India's. The trauma of partition had taken place just a few years before, as had the assassination of Gandhi; landlord exploitation was rife; the caste system was clashing with the modernising politics of the new Indian government. The art of place, cinema, had work to do.

The seed planted by the Italian screenings in 1951 thrived particularly in Bengal, on the opposite side of the country to Bombay, where the problems were most acute. The film society movement of the 1940s had prepared the ground and the West Bengal state government lent initial support to filmmakers but, within a few years and a few hundred miles of Calcutta, the founding father of modern Indian cinema, Satyajit Ray, emerged. His *Pather Panchali* was the toast of Cannes in 1955 and his subsequent films were distributed around the world. He was to western taste. His approach was novelletish, psychological, realist, measured. He was Strindberg behind the camera.

In the rush to discover and acclaim Ray, a fellow Bengali was overlooked. Where Ray graced the festival circuit, the other filmmaker grumbled at home. He left work unfinished, bartered film rights for booze, hated his producers, raged against the partition of his beloved Bengal and spent time in a sanitarium. Temperamentally, he was the Sam Peckinpah of Indian cinema. Aesthetically and politically, he was its Pasolini. Ray himself called him one of the greatest Indians to handle a camera. His name was Ritwik Ghatak.

Ghatak was born in Dhaka, 100 miles east of Calcutta, in 1925. He ran away from home at 14 and became involved with politics in 1943 and, later, in the Indian People's Theatre Association. He translated Brecht into Bengali. His brother, who had worked on English documentaries in the 1930s, introduced him to filmmakers. Ghatak liked the reach of this new medium and, in Eisenstein and the Soviets, found a radical film language which he made his own.

Then came partition, the explicit or implicit theme of most of his nine features. The loose trilogy, *Meghe Dhaka Tara/The Cloud-Capped Sky* (1960), *Kamal Goudhar/E-Flat* (1961) and *Subarnarekha/The Golden Thread* (1965), portray it as a wretched, impoverishing event and are among the most expressive Indian documents of partition's effects. In the first, a woman called Nita sacrifices her life to rebuild her family, which has been shattered by national events. At the end of the third, the main character, Sita, cuts her throat. Ghatak said that they pictured a 'deceived age', India's 'original sin'. In his view, the Muslim League and the Congress Party had torn the country apart by accepting 'a destructive independence'.

I recently saw these three films again at the Mumbai (Bombay) Film Festival, half a century after Vittorio De Sica's *Ladri di biciclette/Bicycle Thieves* (1948) was first shown here. They are fresh and vivid, at least as good as anything by Ray. *The Cloud-Capped Sky* is a masterpiece.

Now Ghatak is all the rage. Cornell University held a tribute to him, so did the New York Film Festival. UCLA did a retrospective, as did Ahmedabad and the Cinematheque Ontario. *Rows and Rows of Fences*, the first Ghatak monograph in English, appeared last year.

So why such a flurry of interest and why now? There's a rush to revise the evaluation of Ray in the 1950s and a muted *mea culpa* from those who found him more palatable; there's the glamour of the self-destructive alcoholic whose schizophrenia mirrored that of Bengal; and there's the life cut short (Ghatak died at 51). One US critic at the time of the New York screenings wrote that in the 1960s Ghatak's rage embarrassed Indians and Westerners determined to pretend that partition had worked. Televised 'partitions' and ethnic cleansings in the 1990s, the same writer argued, have made Ghatak relevant again.

Perhaps. My own view is that Ghatak has made a comeback because his filmmaking isn't lazy. You can imagine him drunk and growling in the edit suite, like Peckinpah or Welles, working through the night. His choice of lenses, especially in his final film, the autobiographical *Yukti Takko Ar Gappo/Reason, Debate and a Story* (1974) in which Ghatak himself plays an alcoholic intellectual, is as experimental as a work by Godard, a filmmaker who is also back *à la mode*. Certainly, seeing Ghatak films now in wretched Bombay, his rage seems appropriate to the problems.

Ritwik Ghatak died in 1976, during Indira Gandhi's state of emergency. The separation of Bangladesh from Pakistan in 1971, during which almost a million people died, was too much for him. India's first political filmmaker drank permanently thereafter. He always insisted that cinema wasn't an art, yet produced some of the greatest of it.

ANTONIONI

August 2007

With the double deaths, on the same day, of Ingmar Bergman and Michelangelo Antonioni, the Golden Age of European art cinema became past tense. I'm currently making a
documentary series on the history of world cinema, so both directors were near the top of
my interviewee wish list. As I strike them off I notice that almost no one remains to talk
about the emergence of European art cinema in the 1950s and 1960s. The wall between it
and us feels sealed, now, which is sad.

The avalanche of media coverage of their coinciding deaths has complicated the sadness. Bergman and Antonioni were intellectual musts in the 1960s and 1970s, when most
newspaper editors today were educated, so their passings were given full page obits and
some of the front page. On *Newsnight Review*, Toby Young did his now standard oik revisionism (Bergman was for bores). Writing in 2003 (see 'Bergman' in this volume) I, too,
tried to describe why my generation (born in the mid-1960s) took Bergman down a peg or
two, but ended by saying that he was growing on me.

He continued to grow, and one of the most electrifying experiences I've had in the cinema in the last five years was seeing his *Viskningar och rop/Cries and Whispers* (1972) on
the big screen; but back to that media coverage for a moment. Mixed in with the sadness,
and the joy that Antonioni and Bergman were front page news, was truculence at their
column inches compared to the relatively scant attention paid to the deaths of Senegal's
Ousmane Sembène or Japan's Shohei Imamura, figures of equal significance for world cinema. The anglophone media felt their loss far less because their films are hardly known in
the UK. The African and Asian worlds they invented seemed less relevant to the European
Narcissus of the 1960s and since.

Though Bergman and Antonioni tripped off the same tongues in the 1950s and 1960s,
and their self-evident seriousness and aesthetic confidence forced film culture finally to
accept that it was an art, and that modernity was the new game in town, *so be there or
be square*, they were profoundly different artists. The best way to see this, I think, is to
think of how it feels watching, on the one hand, *Det Sjunde inseglet/The Seventh Seal*
(1957), *Smultronstället/Wild Strawberries* (1957) and *Persona* (1966) and, on the other

Unhappy human beings with no proscenium:
Monica Vitti in *L'Eclisse*

hand, Antonioni's trilogy *L'Avventura/The Adventure* (1960), *La Notte/The Night* (1961) and *L'Eclisse/The Eclipse* (1962). As I do so I can imagine myself stepping into the worlds of the latter but not the former. I want to be the characters in Antonioni films but it wouldn't occur to me to be Bergman's. Antonioni's films feel like open structures, whereas Bergman's are closed.

What do I mean by these generalisations? I've long argued that the three great directors of European art cinema that emerged in the 1950s – Bresson, Fellini and Bergman – were each masters of closed worlds. Bresson's central metaphor in his work was life as a prison. Fellini's was life as a circus. Bergman's was life as a theatre. In every Bergman film I've seen, the characters feel as if they are on stage. They have symbolic status conferred on them at the very moment of their conception by Bergman and there's an invisible proscenium between them and us. Not only are his worlds physically microcosms – bourgeois homes, islands, etc – the human themes he addresses are distillations. We do not go to Bergman films to see the transient fashions or the passing scene of European or Scandinavian life. He is concerned with essences, distillates. His films feel as they are about the first human beings, Adam and Eve, Tristan and Isolde or Abelard and Heloise.

The opening abstract montage in *Persona* is a brilliantly modern as the films of Jean-Luc Godard, and when I think of *Cries and Whispers* I see a blood-red painting by Mark Rothko, but in general in Bergman's films, imagery is in service to psychology and ideas.

Compare this to Antonioni. His human beings are as unhappy as Bergman's, and as far from paradise, but there's no proscenium. Settings are contemporary. Space is photographed as an architect might photograph it, as if it's a real thing that is inviting us in. Antonioni 'got' urbanism, he was entranced by space as a thing in itself. There is no back wall in his films, no stage left or right, just infinite possibilities for wandering. When you watch Antonioni, you think of Le Corbusier or de Chirico.

The realness of the spaces in his films not only makes them 'open' structures, it effects the characters and how they behave. Whereas Bergman's people circle each other, spiralling inwards, honing in on the knot of the matter that discomforts or separates them, in Antonioni they lose themselves. In the famous ending of *L'Eclisse*, Monica Vitti walks out of an apartment, onto a street, pauses in a doorway, we see an empty street corner, other people, the occasional passing vehicle, and modern buildings. Minutes pass. We expect her to return but slowly it dawns on us that she's fled the movie. She's dissolved into the world of the story. In *The Passenger* (1975), we follow the meandering of Jack Nicholson's character but, in a famous shot at the end of the picture, the imagery continues to wander without him. When it finally returns to him we discover that during its independent drifting through space, he has died.

Blow-Up (1966) is about the investigation of an event that in the end bypasses human agency and moves into the realm of photographic grain. Even during the shoots, Antonioni films did not feel as if they were about human beings. When I interviewed Jeanne Moreau, three decades after she starred in *La Notte*, she could still hardly contain her irritation at how uninterested Antonioni was in what she, as an actress, could bring to the part.

Much of the media coverage of the deaths of Bergman and Antonioni noted that they both loved actresses and had bleak worldviews, which is true as far as it goes. But their differences were far more profound. More than any other director before him, Bergman insisted that cinema would look inside human being forensically. That was his great gift to film history. In looking he found an irreducible core, a knot. Antonioni looked at human beings just as intensely, but as he did, they dissolved before his eyes, the opposite of Bergman. This dissolution of the self had never been attempted before in film history. This was his great significance.

In the last week I've argued this point with friends and colleagues. Few dispute the contrast but many argue that Bergman's probing of the inner self is more valuable, more humane, more of a contribution to the culture of Kant, of Hegel, of Hume. I disagree. Antonioni's sense of what a human being is – a figure that can disperse – is in a line that stretches back to ancient myth, or Buddhism, or Socrates, or Thomas Aquinas, to name a motley crew. For me, personally, this is a truer portrait of human nature and so, in the end, I love Antonioni films more.

DANNY BOYLE

June 2007

I went to see Danny's Boyle's sci-fi film *Sunshine* last month, and was immediately back on planet Boyle. One of Sunshine's very first images is a very wide, canted, off-angle close-up of a white T-shirt and sideways lips. It tracks leftwards and upwards to dark glasses, reflecting an intense orange light. It thus introduces us to the character, and the world of the story in a fresh way. Previews of *Sunshine* had said that it was derivative of other sci-fi films but here on-screen from the opening frames, before questions of genre or story started to kick in, was a new image. As I watched, I could feel Boyle's passion for pictorial novelty, his belief in the articulacy of imagery. No British director of his generation has held such a kaleidoscope up to life.

Boyle has always done so. *Shallow Grave* (1994) was influenced by the Coen Brothers' *Blood Simple* (1984) but, even so, its ending with Ewan McGregor's corpse smiling, Kerry Fox in hysterics, Andy Williams singing 'It's My Happy Heart You Hear' and that tracking shot down through the floor to reveal the hidden money, the cause of the mayhem, took my breath away. The Lou Reed 'Perfect Day' heroin scene in Boyle's next film, *Trainspotting* (1996), also featured Ewan McGregor lying on his back, out of his box or, rather, into his box because the floor opens and he sinks into it as if it is a soft, welcoming coffin or grave. Steven Spielberg spoke for many entertainment filmmakers when he once said that he didn't want photographic grain to show in his imagery, yet Boyle's zombie movie *28 Days Later* (2002) looked like it was photographed through a scrim of grain and videolines. It broke Spielberg's cardinal visual rule, went kerching at the box office, and influenced the look of entertainment cinema thereafter.

Boyle doesn't work alone, of course, so his producer Andrew Macdonald, his writers John Hodge, Alex Garland and Frank Cottrell Boyce, the wielders of the kaleidoscope – his cinematographers Brian Tufano, Anthony Dod Mantle and Alwin Kuchler – and his designers Kave Quinn and Mark Tildesly, should all take a bow. Together they have created the visuality of Boyle films but also their second characteristic – their rapture. In interview after interview, Boyle has said that he's interested in cinematic vivacity more than realism and this can be seen in the movies. They always want to swirl or take off into the air. They are structured like musicals in that they build up to scenes of choreographed expressivity. Parts of *A Life Less Ordinary* (1997) take place in heaven, like *A Matter of Life and Death* (1946), which its producer Andrew Macdonald's grandfather Emeric Pressburger co-wrote, co-produced and co-directed. *A Life Less Ordinary* is full of those alchemical moments in musicals when reality melts away and life becomes a song – the rapture of a 1950s MGM musical. It looked like a mere soufflé to many critics, a film with a dated sense of joy, and there was something in this (though I loved it). In contrast, *Sunshine*'s rapture is more modern. In one scene the space crew, on its way to restart the sun because Earth is freezing, is seated in the spaceship's huge, cinematic observational window. One of them says, 'ladies and gentlemen, Mercury...'. They watch, in awe, hypnotised as the small planet crosses the massive burning orb of the sun. The music is trippy. The emotion is, in part, ecological. *Sunshine*'s rapture is a post-1990s one, the bliss of the Ecstasy generation.

So if Britain has directors as markedly cinematic as Boyle, where does that leave the old canard that Britain's movies aren't very cinematic? None of Boyle's films have, as far as I know, been invited to art cinema's top table, the Cannes Film Festival. François Truffaut once asked if cinema and Britain are contradictions in terms. Many on these shores – especially liberals, perhaps influenced by Reformation and Enlightenment ideas – are suspicious of images; they see them as redolent of surface or shallowness, disposable and inferior to words. Yet consider where Boyle fits into British cinematic tradition, the company he keeps, and you discover the richness of UK film and his unexpected place within it.

Born in 1956 and brought up in Manchester, Boyle first made his name as Artistic Director of the Royal Court Theatre Upstairs between 1982 and 1985. One of Britain's greatest film directors, Lindsay Anderson, set that place alight in the 1960s but, *Trainspotting* notwithstanding, Boyle hasn't Anderson's electrifying, scabrous misanthropy. From the Court Boyle went, like many of the UK's best directors, to the BBC, where he directed four dramas in the 'Screenplay' strand and produced Alan Clarke's remarkable film about Northern Ireland, *Elephant* (1989). Time at the BBC often turns filmmakers into passionate realists and being young, Northern and creative at the time of Thatcher meant that Boyle could hardly be other than on the left, but he stands apart from the realistic filmic tradition that leads from John Grierson to Ken Loach and Paul Greengrass, who made *United 93* (2006). Like his fellow Lancastrian Michael Winterbottom, Boyle also worked for ITV (directing *Inspector Morse* where Winterbottom did *Cracker*) but has been far less prolific in his film work than Winterbottom. One of the latter's big themes is the distance between human beings – sexual, social, etc – where Boyle's worldview is warmer. Groups and communities start close in his movies and it takes a force of repulsion like money or greed to separate them. *The Beach* (2000), Boyle's dud, and *Shallow Grave* were about such fissures.

Visuality, trippy rapture and anti-Thatcherism together are the elements of Boyle's 1990s romanticism, but this doesn't make him similar to England's arch-romantic director Michael Powell. Powell's films are aristocratic in tone; Boyle's are the opposite. Nor do they have the fine grain or state-of-the-nation quality as the movies of Stephen Frears, the UK's great movie classicist. And though Boyle and Shane Meadows are equally interested in young people, particularly those outside London, Meadows is less of a colourist and his work is laced with scepticism about human nature. Finally, when you watch a Boyle film you do not encounter the powerful sense of self as you do in British auteur directors like Terence Davies, Derek Jarman, Nicolas Roeg, Bill Douglas or Lynne Ramsay.

So does that mean that Boyle is unique in British cinema? No. His instinct to heightened drama and his taste for stylised dialogue have touches of Mike Leigh about them. Leigh is often considered a realist and lumped with Loach, but this has always seemed wrong. Boyle's earliest films were built upon some of the vivacity and Scottish surrealism of Bill Forsyth's work, such as *Gregory's Girl* (1981). But it's another Scottish director, Alexander Mackendrick, whom he most closely resembles. Mackendrick debuted with *Whiskey Galore* in 1949 and Boyle's moonshine can be glimpsed in it, but it's in *The Man in the White Suit* (1951), *The Ladykillers* (1955) and *The Sweet Smell of Success* (1957) where the ancestry of Boyle's cinema lies. The first has the magic quality that Boyle modernises. The second is deliciously sharp about the eccentricity and almost theatricality of friendship – which chimes with *Trainspotting*. And *Shallow Grave*'s astringent presentation of yuppie-dom in all its vainglory is like *The Sweet Smell of Success*. As with Boyle, when you think of Mackendrick movies you think of imagery – Alec Guinness's white suit, the gothic house in *The Ladykillers*, the whiskey strewn harbour in *Whiskey Galore*. There's a quaintness in Mackendrick which seems miles away from Boyle, but pare away the dancy 1990s layers in Danny Boyle films – their humming, electronic, Leftfield soundtracks, one of the things I like about them most – and you find something like the worldview of Mackendrick. And the comparison works in industry terms too. At the age of forty, both Boyle and Mackendrick began working for the US studios. Hollywood has always seen the 'cinematic' UK directors, the ones least discomforted by Hollywood optimism and least inclined to social realism, as like-minded entertainers with a UK accent. Boyle and Mackendrick both had to negotiate the degree to which they would use that accent.

Which brings us to the question of the endings of the films that Boyle has made. In *Sunshine*'s third act, a deranged character boards the spaceship and starts to kill the crew. As a story device it's as old as the hills, but that shouldn't mean it doesn't work and yet, in my view, it doesn't. *Shallow Grave* was about how greed kills friendship, so the mayhem of its ending was appropriate, but *Sunshine* is about a group of people facing death. It should have ended like an Ingmar Bergman movie, in a grace note, with the remains of the crew in conversation, facing death, in that golden, glowing observation platform, taking drugs perhaps, unified by the sombre, magnificent, existential fact of their oblivion. Instead, storywise, it went for a bloody climax.

And then, when you think about it, *28 Days Later* seemed to bottle out too. The infected zombies begin to die, the main characters retire to a farmhouse and their rescue seems imminent. After the initial release of the film, it became clear that a less happy finale had also been shot. The 'happy' one features on a website called ruinedendings.com.

The dynamic frame and digital contrast of *28 Days Later*

Why haven't Boyle and his writers always cracked endings and third acts? Hollywood often gets endings wrong because, for commercial reasons, it wants to leave people on a note of high action or optimism, and this factor probably comes into play with Boyle and his collaborators, though they have far more talent and integrity than most studio movies. Less obvious, perhaps, is the question of how to resolve a story that is structured around a series of tent poles. If Boyle films deliver excitement, self-loss, or rapture along the way, how do he and his collaborators top this, or withdraw convincingly from it? The answer, I think, is to use grace notes, and more philosophical endings. Contemplation, when it follows sensation, is not necessarily a letdown. It's fitting, believable and satisfying. Boyle is an optimist, his films are big hearted. How do optimists end anything? How do trips end? There has to be a downturn and Boyle and his collaborators are hesitant about such downturns. They seem to have swallowed a bit too much the conventional wisdom – leave them smiling or go out with a bang.

I wrote the above yesterday. Last night I bought *Millions* (2004), the one Boyle film I haven't seen, and watched it this morning at dawn. What was it like? *E. T.* seen through a kaleidoscope. Once again I was on planet Boyle. The opening shots are of two boys on their bikes whizzing through blurry fields of yellow rapeseed. The cutting is fast, the angle is high, trains whip across the screen, the camera sweeps, the music sweeps. Though I say it's like *E. T.* – money falls into the lives of two kids and they have to keep it a secret just as ET comes into the lives of two kids and they have to keep him a secret – it has none of the rigorous control of point of view of Spielberg's film. Where the latter is shot mostly from one height and told from Eliot's perspective, *Millions'* shots (by Anthony Dod Mantle, the brilliant DP of *Festen/The Celebration* (1998), *28 Days Later*, *Dogville* (2003) and *The Last King of Scotland* (2006)) are on cranes, soaring and plunging, with frames within frames. Sometimes we see real things, often fantasy things. This makes *Millions* frenetic and less moving. But it has the magic that Boyle likes, and unashamed human tenderness and rapturous moments where the boys lie on their backs, and a catholic, baroque exuberance of colour and movement – all Boyle signatures. Its tone has some of the whimsy of *A Life Less Ordinary* but *Millions* disproves my point about endings because in its final section (the script is by Frank Cottrell Boyce) it comes together. The movie finds seriousness and significance in its last reel in that it shows how each boy is grieving for his dead mother. At the end of the story, truth emerges rather than departs, as it did in *28 Days Later* and *Sunshine*.

One other thing. As it is a story about a windfall, a miraculous arrival (in this case, of money) that changes people's lives, it is like a re-incarnation of *Whiskey Galore*, directed by Alexander Mackendrick.

LATE WORK

In the couple of months around publication of this article, the following film events will have taken place. Francis Ford Coppola's presentation at Cannes of a longer version of *Apocalypse Now*. The paperback publication of Michael Powell's autobiography. The re-release of Nicolas Roeg's *Don't Look Now* (1973). A South Bank Show profile of Ken Russell.

A common note sounds through all these retrospective celebrations which is rather embarrassing for cinema. Paul Schrader got it right a few years ago. 'Looking back at my movies is a lose-lose situation,' he said. 'If they seem bad, you think "my God, I had no talent"; if they seem good, you think "my God, where has my talent gone?"'

What Coppola, Powell, Roeg and Russell have in common is that their talents seemed to diminish long before their time was up. Now, when Coppola makes a film like *Jack* (1996), it is as anodyne as *Apocalypse Now* (1979) was grand. Powell's *Age of Consent* (1969) was as execrable as his wartime collaborations with Emeric Pressburger had been glorious. Roeg's decline started with *Insignificance* (1985), which came after a string of masterpieces such as *Don't Look Now* and *Bad Timing* (1980). Ken Russell's late work must surely have been directed by a talentless acolyte of the man who once made *Women in Love* (1969).

In all these directors there is a falling-off. It is replicated throughout the history of cinema. You can see it in the careers of – to take a random sample – Hitchcock, Antonioni, Welles, Lang, Wenders, Cukor, Minnelli, Peckinpah and Polanski. It is hard to think of an important director in world cinema whose late work is his or her best. Eric Rohmer and Bergman come close, but Luis Buñuel and Sergio Leone are the only true exceptions. Why don't filmmakers conform to the principles of creative evolution?

Artists should mature, develop and intensify their own personal style. It happens with writers and painters. Poussin's late mythological landscapes are a striking advance; late Caravaggio dares to be more austere; the elderly Monet created his water lily screens. James Joyce's experimental energy went into top gear at the end. Dostoyevsky's three greatest novels came in his last 15 years. Of course there are exceptions but in the arts the ideal is that late work comes as a culmination born of greater knowledge and self-knowledge. Beethoven composed the late string quartets when he was aged and deaf.

Great architects usually produce their best work after the age of fifty. The same should apply to film directors.

So why doesn't it? To start with, movie-making is physically demanding. A day on set or on location when you're seventy is more of a grind than a day at the typewriter or easel. Then there's the argument that the language of cinema moves on and leaves the old behind. Cinema has undergone at least four technological revolutions (sound, colour, stereo sound, computer imaging) in a little over a hundred years; and while Ridley Scott at 63 wasn't put off using computers to recreate Rome for *Gladiator* (2000), what if he'd been ten years older?

Yet neither of these points explain the problem. Look again at the quartet of Coppola, Powell, Roeg and Russell. All four treated the camera as a pen, as Astruc put it, and created a signature style. None, as he got older, was daunted by the technology of cinema. They were not 'left behind' aesthetically, nor was it a matter of external factors shifting while they remained constant. Instead an internal sense of what constituted their voices diminished and they began to resemble the conservatives whom they once despised.

Roeg, Russell and Powell/Pressburger were great iconoclasts and explorers of the erotic imagination. In late middle age, they and others seem to fall into clichés about gender (Roeg, Powell), horror (Russell) and power (Coppola). The commercial imperative of the movie industry requires even older filmmakers to make films about young people – people the age of moviegoers. A gap in empathy and understanding opens up. They no longer see themselves in their characters. Their themes become those of resentment, of the best times being in the past.

So the industry tends to arrest the creative development of its filmmakers by refusing to let them move on to middle-aged themes and characters. Something happens socially, too. Successful movie people, more than other artists, rocket up the class ladder. They often become very rich, begin to see the world through tinted limousine glass, travel the globe for filming or publicity and isolate themselves in swanky houses. Martin Scorsese is perhaps an example. His films were about the wise guys on the streets of Lower East Side Manhattan, but he can't continue to draw on his receding childhood forever. Success has removed some of his material problems, while perhaps creating – or revealing – existential ones. Watching him search for new themes and settings is fascinating.

Artists have always found that search difficult. But Paul Schrader's pain on looking back on his work is a pain which filmmakers know particularly well.

LYNCH AND BARNEY

This is the story of a lost film, but to care about its loss you first need to know what happened in 1976. Back then, a thirty-year-old Montanan painter called David Lynch completed his first feature after five years of shooting and editing. Nihilistic and Freudian, *Eraserhead* was about a character whose detached head is taken over by a mutant baby, and who exists in rooms vacated by the mysterious 'woman in the radiator'. The film was a revelation of textures. For visual inspiration, Lynch had dissected a cat, seeing an abstract beauty in its membranes, hair and skin which he translated into the glistening, fleshy imagery of the film. Variety called it a 'dismal exercise in gore … commercial prospects nil.'

But an alternative New York distributor, Libra Films, which had screened the psycho-western *El Topo/The Mole* (1970) for over a year in the city, bought *Eraserhead* and ran it in a single cinema for as long as *El Topo*. Lynch described the process by which such experiments gain recognition: 'First, the real weirdos will see it; they'll see anything if it's running at midnight. If it clicks with them it'll enter the next phase, which is a slightly bigger group of people. All these transitional areas are critical. You can't tell how long it will take for word to spread.'

Stanley Kubrick admired *Eraserhead*, though Lynch wouldn't tell him how he filmed the mutant baby. *Sounds*, the British rock magazine, raved about the film. Its soundscapes influenced metal-industrial noise bands like Throbbing Gristle and Test Dept. David Bowie claimed that all he wanted to see in the twenty-first century with was a videotape of it.

Eraserhead is now a staple of student film societies, and considered a work of high surrealism. Its additional interest, for those of us who care about the relationship between the avant-garde and what we still call the mainstream, is that it also provides a model of how to cross over. If it hadn't been for Libra Films and the midnight weirdos, Lynch's textural, allegorical masterpiece would have disappeared.

This is the fate facing a new film which has much in common with *Eraserhead*. Like Lynch's film, the experimental epic *Cremaster 3* (2002) was directed by an artist; it too is a textural nightmare (in this case the texture is that of solid and melting Vaseline), featuring deformed human beings. The film's soundtrack is as layered with low-frequency feral and cavernous noises as Lynch's. Yet whereas the reputation of *Eraserhead* grew and grew, *Cremaster 3* has been dropped from the British release schedule.

Director Matthew Barney is already an acclaimed figure in the art world; the *New York Times* has called him the most important artist alive today. Overall he has made five *Cremaster* films, a quintet of metaphorical investigations into the nature of sexual differentiation, named after the muscle that lowers the human testicle. (The films were created out of order between 1994 and 2002; *Cremaster 3* is the final one.) Together, they are as physically astonishing as great silent epic films such as *Ben Hur* (1907) or *Cabiria* (1914), and have attracted some US public sector arts funding (as did *Eraserhead*). All five films have played in film festivals in Britain. This, however, is where the good news ends. Although *Cremaster 3* is even more of what the *New Yorker* critic Pauline Kael called a 'head' experience than *Eraserhead*, and is even more original and considered, the cancellation of its British distribution means that only hardcore cinephiles will see it.

So what accounts for the reversed fortunes of epic avant-garde cinema since 1976? Well, people are taking different drugs for a start. And DVD and home cinema have taken many of the more obsessive film fans off the streets. But there can't be fewer of those edgy weirdos who took a risk on way out films, can there? If anything, opposition to the mass consumption of formulaic Western culture is greater today than it was 28 years ago. The most likely answer has been put forward by film historian Chris Rodley: 'It would be virtually impossible to deliver [*Eraserhead*] to an audience now, because that underground circuit barely exists. Theatrical venues and distributors rarely take risks today.'

The picture isn't all bleak. New experimental film clubs are being formed in some of Britain's major cities, but these usually screen on 8mm and 16mm, not the 35mm widescreen format which *Cremaster 3* needs. A more encouraging development is planned at Edinburgh's Filmhouse, which is launching 'Secret Cinema' in March, a new regular commitment to midnight alternative screenings. More cinemas should follow this innovation, and if necessary share prints and find a way of distributing Matthew Barney's masterwork themselves. This is not only because the film is valuable in itself, but also because, just as Lynch's avant-garde *Eraserhead* made possible *Blue Velvet* (1986), the TV series *Twin Peaks* (1990) and the film version *Twin Peaks: Fire Walk With Me* (1992), *Lost Highway* (1997) and *Mulholland Dr.* (2001), so a filmmaker of Barney's talents might also contribute much to the art of future cinema. In order to do so, *Cremaster 3* must enter the mainstream. If it does, our film culture will be healthy. If not, and if other edgy films are blocked too, then the horizons of British cinema will be that much lower.

CRONENBERG

December 2007

In Woody Allen's movie *Match Point* two years ago, Londoners saw the London Eye, Tower Bridge and the Houses of Parliament – their city as tourist metonym. In their tuxes dressed down with Converses a few weeks ago for the glitzy premiere of *Eastern Promises*, David Cronenberg's latest movie that opened the London Film Festival, a very different city stared back: dank alleyways, a nondescript hospital and service entrances instead of front door, monumental urbanism.

It's tempting to see the former as fake and the latter as real, but as you watch Cronenberg's world unfold scene by scene, you realise that *Eastern Promises* is not any kind of a response to Woody Allen's blindness to the particularities of twenty-first-century London. Cronenberg's film isn't interested in the specifics of place at all, but then again neither was the *Kammerspiel* of *The Fly* (1986) nor the vehicular world of *Crash* (1996). Cronenberg's films could be set almost anywhere. Excise from them the markers of individual cities and they work better as universal nightmares.

But this is not to say that physical reality is of little interest to him. Far from it. Alongside David Lynch, he is the North American director most interested in texture. Though *Eastern Promises* is not his most distinctive film, he nonetheless appeals to our senses through the blonde softness of Naomi Watts's character, a midwife who investigates the death of a Russian teenage girl, and her contrast to the black hardness and muscularity of the Russian chauffeur who is connected to her murderers. In one signature scene the chauffeur, played by Viggo Mortensen, asks for a hair-dryer to defrost a frozen human body so that he can peel open its jacket and remove a wallet. We can sense Cronenberg's relish at the involuntary way we imagine the feel of marble-hard flesh as it softens, and smell its decay.

Add this relish to the textural quality of Cronenberg movies and his refusal of the social specifics of location and you realise that whilst his movies are full of wrongdoing, he isn't interested in the *wrongness* of wronging, but its repulsiveness. In person Cronenberg is a liberal Canadian but in his movies he takes the wrongness of murder or gangsterism as read and, instead, is intrigued at how nice, blonde, decent, liberal people like Naomi Watts's midwife, or we the audience, react to it as material. Cronenberg's career is about the form of evil rather than its content.

Plonk this distinction into movie history and things light up. Moralists as varied as Ken Loach, Oliver Stone, Woody Allen, John Grierson and Claude Lanzmann censure with content. Loach at his best, for example, does so in a wholly integrated way – story, theme, characters and social world unite to deliver a compelling truth about injustice. The cycle of American gangster movies of the 1930s – *Little Caesar* (1931), *Scarface* (1932), *The Roaring Twenties* (1939), etc – were often less integrated, telling a thrilling story of the rise of Chicago hoodlums in acts one and two, then delivering the sort of comeuppance society required by showing their fall in act three.

Compare this to those filmmakers who denounce with style. In their different ways Douglas Sirk, Luchino Visconti and Brian De Palma, in films like *All that Heaven Allows* (1955), *La Caduta degli dei/The Damned* (1969) and the remake of *Scarface* (1983) starring Al Pacino, conjured monstrous human beings in superficially beautiful and opulent movie worlds, the very excess of which, like gilded cages, served to suggest the characters' inner emptiness and the directors' disdain. No homily at the end was needed. The stench, as it were, came from the excess of style.

Then there are those directors who don't censure wrongdoing at all, either because they see little to disapprove of in their characters' behaviour (mid-period Clint Eastwood, most of Michael Winner, etc), or because they are brave enough, or society is temporarily tolerant enough, to allow the wrongdoers to go unpunished. Hence the furore over *Bonnie and Clyde* (1967) and *The Godfather* (1972), which were like the 1930s gangster movies but with the moral improvement lopped off the end.

Cronenberg is certainly brave in this way. He doesn't denounce but, more than most, loves to cup the form of moral transgression in his hands and, in a sense, rub it against our cheek (or elsewhere). Hence the distinctiveness of his movies. He's interested in the cheek being rubbed, i.e. the person who is repelled by slit throats, dead bodies, gynaecological instruments (*Dead Ringers* (1988)) or rubber and metal sex (*Crash*). We remember his movies because they are sensory screeches rather than intellectual sermons. Most interesting of all, I think, they have a moths-to-a-flame structure. Naomi Watts keeps going back to the gangster underworld for more. Geena Davis is repelled by Jeff Goldblum's scientist in *The Fly* but then fascination and attraction take over and she goes back again and looks at him again, as he turns into a fly or vomits on his food. Cronenberg's movies are structured in such loops. Their stories zoom in on dark, fascinating, 'hot' places, get singed and then flee outwards to the cool air of liberalism. But they aren't out in that air long before the heat, the form of wrongdoing, begins to compel once more.

The cool Canadian has come to a hot place, London, and partially, only partially, captured its heat.

MAGGIE CHEUNG April 2007

I have just spent a week with Maggie Cheung. If you have heard of her, please feel free to swoon. If not, let me explain. Her ex-husband, the French filmmaker Olivier Assayas, said that until he met her he no longer believed that cinema made movie stars with auras. Since the late 1990s and, in particular, since Wong Kar-wai's elegant *Fa yeung nin wa/In the Mood for Love* (2000), critics have acclaimed Cheung as 'an icon of modernity' and 'the most fascinating woman in modern cinema'. When, for the first time in its history, the Cannes Film Festival used a photographic image of a real actress on its poster, that actress was Maggie Cheung. She turned down the chance to be a Bond girl, was a woman warrior in the most commercially successful Chinese film of all time, *Ying xiong/Hero* (2002), is the most famous woman in Hong Kong and one of the most famous in Asia. She came to Edinburgh, where I live, to talk about Chinese films and hang out.

I invited her because I am co-director of a festival called Cinema China, which is touring Britain. Where most festivals now have a film industry marketplace, ours has a series of lectures on Chinese history, society and aesthetics, presented by the University of Edinburgh. I think that's why Cheung came. We needed a major figure in contemporary Chinese film as our guest of honour, someone whose work would be a lens through which to view that nation's cinema and, we hoped, China and its people too.

What a lens Cheung turned out to be. One of the first things we talked about in her masterclass was the astonishing work rate of Hong Kong cinema. Cheung has been in eighty films since 1985, regularly making a dozen or more in a year. Some were cheap and forgettable, but many, like *San lung moon haak chan/Dragon Inn* (1992), are complexly engineered action films using thousands of shots, balletic choreography and gravity-defying pugilism. When asked how so many fine-tooled films could be made in such a short period, Cheung answered, 'because Chinese people work harder than Europeans'. As if to prove the point, the Chinese state television crew that was in Britain making a documentary about Cinema China kept filming well into the evening, long after the rest of us had conked out.

The second thing that Cheung's career tells us about China – particularly the south – is the role that migration and emigration play in people's lives. In *Ke tu qiu hen/Song*

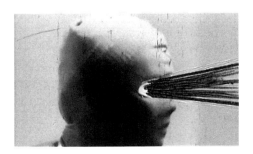

The ending of *Irma Vep*: scribbles on Maggie Cheung's eyesight

of Exile (1990), she is a young woman pushed towards Europe and modern life by her grandfather, but pulled back to Asia and tradition by her mother. In *A zai bie xiang de ji jie/Farewell China* (1990), she starts a new life in America and becomes schizophrenic. In *Tian mi mi/ Comrades: Almost a Love Story* (1996), she is a mainlander trying to live a chic, modern entrepreneurial life in Hong Kong. In *In the Mood for Love*, she is a Shanghainese in Hong Kong, living in a tenement so crowded that she must slalom past her handsome neighbour when they cross in the corridor or on the stairs. Few film cultures – and certainly not those of Britain, America or France – deal with the longing of exile, its problems of jobs or living space, humiliation or romance, as insistently as China's does.

The third insight is a cinematic one. Maggie Cheung has been in five films by Hong Kong art-house maestro Wong Kar-wai, and is often called his muse. In fact, as she said on stage: 'I am not Kar-wai's muse; William Chang is.' Chang's name will be new even to hardcore film buffs, but look up his credits and you find that he not only edited *In the Mood for Love* but was its production and costume designer and associate producer. Those who have seen the film will remember that it takes its audience through a sultry nighttime world that has no temporal bearings, no sense of the next day arriving. Except that Cheung changes her *cheongsam* dresses – high-necked, slim-fitting, popular in cosmopolitan China since the 1920s – each day. Only by clocking the new dress do we know that the story has moved on. The dresses, Cheung's extraordinary hairdo and the film's dreamy musical rhythms all came from William Chang. He has worked on all Wong's films and, it appears, confers on them much of their pictorial and rhythmic distinction. Chang has clearly been overlooked as one of the central figures in international art cinema.

Finally, compare Cheung in *Hero* to Angelina Jolie in Hollywood's *Lara Croft: Tomb Raider*, released around the same time. Both play women warriors, but where Jolie's film is kickass turbo feminism and she seems to exist on just one psychological plane, Cheung in *Hero* goes from meditative to mysterious, gnomic to supernaturally airborne, at rest to spinning through arabesques. I have argued often that such differences are partially explained by the influence of Buddhist aesthetics on Eastern action cinema, but in this case they are emphasised by the contrast between Cheung and Jolie themselves. Both are beautiful and athletic, but Cheung's mastery of body language and sense of emotional containment make her a far more intriguing presence.

In real life, Maggie Cheung is also fun: we walked up Edinburgh's Royal Mile singing Bay City Rollers songs, if you please.

WENDERS

January 2008

I have just spent an afternoon and the next morning with the German filmmaker and writer Wim Wenders. A retrospective of his movies is in London and Edinburgh and two of them – *Alice in den Städten/Alice in the Cities* (1974) and *Land of Plenty* (2005) – are being released here. Spending time with him has sent me on a train of thought about his cinema and my life.

I first saw a Wenders film, *Alice in the Cities*, a road movie about a German man hooking up with a nine-year-old girl, as a student in 1983. I still remember the opening sequence. The camera cranes down from a wooden walkway to actor Rüdiger Vogler sitting below it, alone, on a beach, singing 'Under the Boardwalk'. I'd known the Drifters' version from boyhood, of course, but only in that scene did I click what a boardwalk actually was. I hadn't travelled much at that stage or, rather, I'd done so only through the proxy of cinema. Like most Westerners born in the era of mass culture, American clothes, slang, songs, imagery, attitudes, movies, food, buildings and ideas were absolutely familiar to me but perhaps, like boardwalks, in an empty way.

I adored *Alice in the Cities* in 1983. At one point Vogler, who's driving around America, staying in cheap hotels, snapping everything with a Polaroid camera, says that he takes photographs not to speak, but to listen. Though I was only eighteen back then, I loved the daring idea that art – even if it was just a Polaroid – might not be about self-expression, but about paying attention. Soon afterwards I saw Wenders' *Im Lauf der Zeit/Kings of the Road* (1976), another road movie starring Vogler, and was shocked when one of the characters squats by the roadside and defecates, in full view of the camera. I'd never seen that before, in life or the movies. Its European insolence punctured the decorum of entertainment cinema.

The following year I saw *Paris, Texas* (1984), fell in love with Nastassja Kinski (especially her back) and realised that Wenders' films were all about what he now calls the 'triple As' – alienation, angst and America. Thereafter, when I graduated, my own work took off. The adrenalin of early adulthood did not stop pumping for long enough for me to notice how much I missed the stillness and open spaces of Wenders movies. Looking back it's tempting to think of them as 1990s slacker movies *avant la lettre*, but slacker cinema was slighter and less spiritual than Wenders' work.

By 1987's *Der Himmel über Berlin/Wings of Desire*, Wenders' poetics had become more *outré*. I loved the film, but somewhat less so than my friends. Two years later, in October 1989, I found myself working in Berlin, where *Wings of Desire* was set, as the wall came down. For the first time in my life, I was having experiences more intense than cinema. The traveller in me had overtaken the traveller in it, cinema. In the years since, film's wanderlust and my own have criss-crossed often, like the ending of *Kings of the Road*, in which the two men, one in a van, one on a train, criss-cross each other's tracks. I really fell for Iranian cinema after I'd been there, for example, yet I am passionate about Senegalese movies without ever having visited the country itself.

From *Wings of Desire* onwards, I felt that Wenders had started talking rather than listening. His 1990s movies, including *Bis as Ende der Welt/Until the End of the World* (1991), *In Weiter Ferne, so nah!/Faraway, So Close* (1993) and *The End of Violence* (1997) were full of heart but, also, sounded to me like a waterfall of words and, anyway, I was too busy planting the seeds of my own angst to give them the benefit of the doubt. Wenders was more in focus for me in documentaries such as *Tokyo-Ga* (1985), *Aufzeichnungen zu Kleidern und Städten/Notebook on Cities and Clothes* (1989) and *Buena Vista Social Club* (1999). The latter's huge success helped make the ne'er do well genre of non-fiction film, which had become the way I earned my crust, commercially successful in cinemas for the first time since the birth of the movies.

In 2000, under the influence of Wenders' road movies, I bought a campervan and drove to India via Iran. Then, flash forward to yesterday, when he walked into the green room of the BFI Southbank, sporting a ponytail. His spoke slowly, almost in a whisper. We filmed him, fly-on-the-wall style, as he talked to students and was interviewed by Sky TV. Last night, in my hotel room, to prepare to interview him this morning, I watched *Alice in the Cities* for the first time in perhaps fifteen years. Not a frame of it seemed wrong to me. The film industry in which I now work is obsessed by the idea of 'back story' for its characters. Vogler has almost none in the film, yet is entrancing. *Alice in the Cities* is passionately committed to capturing the present tense, what Geoff Dyer called 'the ongoing moment'. It isn't driven by story as much as itinerary. In the opening scene, when Vogler sang 'Under the Boardwalk', I cried.

Then, this morning, I sat down in one of London's poshest new hotels to interview the cineaste with the pony tale. His voice had become even quieter. I felt that we were intruding. Then, through the reticence, I thought I glimpsed something like idealism. This started when he said that for Europeans of his age, America was utopia until you went there. I asked him if it had ever made him cry. Yes, when he last visited Monument Valley, where John Ford shot some of his famous westerns, to discover that it has become a theme park. I asked about the relationship between Vogler and the nine-year-old girl in

Alice, played by Yella Rottlander. Even when he is in the bath and she's on the toilet, it is completely without the taint of paedophilia and, what's more interesting is how immediate and equal the relationship is. Neither Wenders nor Vogler were fathers when they made the film, but that isn't quite the point either. Wenders said that he works with young people in the hope that some of their idealism will rub off on him. Whilst shooting *Alice*, he gave Rottlander the right to say 'cut' if she didn't like the scene. This is almost unique and helps explain his commitment to teaching and, perhaps, his long-running presidency of the European Film Academy.

We wrapped our interview at 1pm today. Afterwards, I walked across London for five hours because I had things on my mind and, also, as a daft tribute to Wenders. In his hotel room he told me that he didn't know what a boardwalk was until he saw the one that he filmed in *Alice*. Places tell stories, he said. There's a close link, as Herr Wenders knows better than any filmmaker who has ever lived, between motion and emotion.

elsewhere

films around the globe

OPEN ROAD

I've just driven 1,200 miles around the West Coast of Ireland in my VW campervan. Though I didn't see a film for the whole fortnight, the trip felt cinematic. A windscreen is exactly the same shape as a movie screen, so driving is like one long travelling shot. Hollywood calls its blockbusters 'rollercoaster rides' to suggest thrilling emotional peaks and troughs but also, in part, because to sit in a rollercoaster car is to see an oncoming vista, like watching a crane shot.

But my trip was cinematic for more than visual reasons. As I had my bed in the back of the van, and had no fixed route, the structure of my holiday was open. On the Dingle peninsula, I saw a sign for an ancient oratory, so decided to head for it. In Galway the sun came out, so I drove to a beach I'd glimpsed on the horizon. Those who have read anything about screenwriting will think such capriciousness unfilmic. Movies are all about structured stories, we're told. Screenwriters say the hardest bit is engineering the narrative, establishing personal, social and existential dilemmas in the system of characters and incidents in acts one and two that will afford complex and satisfying revelations in act three. The editorial in this week's film industry magazine *Screen International* couldn't agree more, and calls for the re-introduction of the Best Story Oscar that was awarded between 1940 and 1957.

I don't disagree. The recent German film *Das Leben der Anderen/The Lives of Others* (2006) moved me deeply because its plot built to tragic climaxes layered with irony and regret. But in the majority of films, narrative operates with far less richness. Its purpose is to provide new challenges for its characters. You can hear its whirr, the clunk and clang of its cam shaft. When a film is slow or when I feel I'm *ahead* of it, it's not a matter of editing speed, but story sputter or languor. One of Britain's best producers told me, years ago, that the secret of a successful film is lots and lots of plot.

Narrative, then, is in part, a newness machine. Unless it is *deus ex machina*, story from on high, it generates novelty from within the world of the story. But as my idyllic drive showed, newness can come from outside the world of the story – a sign to an oratory, a glimpsed beach. Great road movies like Arthur Penn's *Bonnie and Clyde* (1967), Wim

Wenders' *Alice in den Städten/Alice in the Cities* (1974) and *Im Lauf der Zeit/Kings of the Road* (1976), Terrence Malick's *Badlands* (1973), David Lynch's *The Straight Story* (1999), Dennis Hopper's *Easy Rider* (1969), Shinji Ayoyama's *Eri Eri rema sabakutani/My God My God Why Have You Forsaken Me?* (2005), Alfonso Cuarón's *Y tu mamá también/And Your Mother Too* (2001), Federico Fellini's *La Strada/The Road* (1954), John Ford's *The Grapes of Wrath* (1940) or *The Searchers* (1956), Stanley Donen's *Two for the Road* (1967), Soulymane Cissé's *Yeelen* (1987) and Nicholas Ray's *They Live by Night* (1948) start with characters who have a social or psychological reason to leave town, or set off on a quest, but often, perhaps when the landscape they're travelling through opens out into a vista, or there's a fork in the road, the story goes down a gear and you can feel the movie undergo a kind of self-loss. Narrative drive slackens. The protagonists go more with the flow. Urgency is replaced by alertness to incident and atmosphere. These films continue to have newness – lots of it – but the flow of incident, call it picaresque, further slows the movie's motor. Unlike, say, the films of Roman Polanski, which are usually set in one place and become tighter as they progress, there's an opening unto the fields and to the sky in the road movie genre (and its sister, the western) which, to my mind, gets close to the essence of cinema. Just like my holiday, they combine forward movement with freedom to choose and dissolution of self.

That the picaresque is cinematic is widely misunderstood. I am co-producing a feature film based on Alan Warner's great novel *The Man Who Walks*, which is a man hunt full of digressions and set pieces. When we submitted it to the UK Film Council for funding, one of its main executives wrote back saying that it didn't have a strong enough narrative. I replied, arguing that strong narrative is exactly what road movies shouldn't have, mentioning some of the best and elaborating my point, and offered to publish his letter and my reply as he was a key funder of British film. He phoned me and we resolved the matter, but the point is clear. Yes, films (like novels and all sequential culture), need to introduce newness along their timeline, but that newness need not come from within the narrative in the classical sense, nor need it have significance further along that time line. It can drift in, engage the protagonist, create its own world or micro-story, then sashay out again. As in life.

So why does most conventional wisdom about cinema not accept this? My list of great road movies above is long and contains some obscure films because I disagree with those film historians who argue that the road movie is an essentially American genre. America's immigrant populations, the novels of John Steinbeck, the later ones of Jack Kerouac and the construction of the US's main freeway network from 1940 onwards, are precursers that created the road movie, they argue. But Germany's autobahns came before freeways and interstates, Homer and Cervantes rather pre-date Steinbeck and Kerouac, and the idea of the unsettled self going out into the world is as old as myth, as Joseph Campbell has shown. It's no surprise therefore, that the films mentioned above are from Germany, Mexico, Mali, Japan and Italy as well as the US.

Perhaps our sense that films should be driven by plots derives from our over-awareness of American cinema's brilliant best, our sense that it is *cinema nostrum*. Road movies and westerns show that structured stories in films are fabulous affectations, but not crucial.

ASIA

At the end of last month a Chinese film, *Ying xiong/Hero* (2002), topped the US box-office chart, despite the fact that it was already available on DVD. A lush action film in the manner of *Wo hu cang long/Crouching Tiger, Hidden Dragon* (2000), it was directed by former cinematographer Zhang Yimou. *Screen International* called it 'one of the most eagerly awaited films in Asian film history'. By the end of August 16% of all tickets sold in America were for it. It also went to number one in France and cut a swathe through the box office in many Asian countries.

This is unheard of, yet Zhang's follow-up, the even more beautiful *Shi mian mai fu/The House of Flying Daggers*, looks set to follow *Hero*'s extraordinary breakthrough. Shot partly in the rust-red forests of Ukraine, it has already broken box-office records in China itself.

Something remarkable is happening in Asian cinema, and Hollywood has cottoned on. 'Check out the latest US movie production slate and it is hard to escape the conclusion that Hollywood is turning Japanese. And Korean. With a dash of Thai and Hong Kong thrown in', reported the *Guardian*. No less than seven new versions of box-office hits from the other side of the world are preparing to go before Western cameras. Tom Cruise is developing a remake of the Hong-Kong/Thai horror picture *Gin gwan/The Eye* (2002); Martin Scorsese's prepping a new version of the smash hit Hong Kong policier *Mou gaan dou/Infernal Affairs* (2002); a creepy Japanese thriller, *Honogurai mizu no soko kara/Dark Water* (2002), is being reworked for Jennifer Connelly; the British director Gurinder Chadha is remaking the Korean feminist crime comedy *Jopog manura/My Wife is a Gangster* (2001).

This is not the first time that Hollywood's imitation of Asian cinema has seemed like flattery. *Star Wars* (1977) borrowed from Kurosawa and the *Matrix* films (1999–2003) use Hong Kong fight techniques, but Western film industries have never before to the same degree banked on the East. Virtually every Hollywood studio has optioned an Asian project. Their interest in the continent's movies has become a groundswell. Part of this is the usual tinsel town faddiness – let's adapt classical epics, let's shoot on grainy video, let's remake Asian box-office smashes – but that misses the point. *Dark Water*, *The Eye* and the *Ring* films – also being updated in the US – unnerved Hollywood because they beat it at its own game. They found new, subtle, inventive ways of doing what producers in Southern

California have spent a century perfecting: jangling audiences' nervous systems. From *Frankenstein* (1931) through *Jaws* (1975) and *The Blair Witch Project* (1999) Western cinema has prided itself on being able to electrify film-goers with novel terrors. All of a sudden, it seems, Japan and Korea have stolen their thunder. Directors from these countries are using the power of sug-

An Asian director making the magic box his own: *Onna ga kaidan wo agaru toki/When a Woman Ascends the Stairs* (Mikio Naruse, 1960)

gestion, the brooding way in which cinema can gently turn the screw of tension, to scare audiences more profoundly. They build up tension more slowly, hint at unseen horrors, use sound more evocatively. Highly productive systems, such as the American studio one, are always on the verge of depletion. They constantly search for new material and ideas. In the last few years, Asia has been Western cinema's new source of ideas.

The mentality of the world's premier entertainment industry is always worth observing, but Asian cinema doesn't merit our attention at the moment only because it has captured Hollywood's. Yes there is a wave of remakes on its way, and those of us who've seen the originals will have a good moan if they are crap, but way beyond the world of horror cinema, contemporary Asian directors are onto something remarkable. Despite the brouhaha caused by Michael Moore's *Fahrenheit 9/11* in Cannes this year, the lasting impression of the festival was the overwhelming beauty of a quartet of films from China, Japan, Hong Kong and Thailand. I have been going to Cannes for well over a decade but I have never before seen audiences applaud the visual magnificence of an individual scene, as they did with *The House of Flying Daggers* which *Screen International* called 'beyond doubt the most visually ravishing film on offer this year'; Hirokazu Kore-eda's *Dare mo shiranai/ Nobody Knows* was one of the greatest works of observation that cinema has produced; at the end of an exhausting day, I had to stand throughout Wong Kar-wai's two-hour *2046*, yet the world it created was so ravishing that I continued to see it for the rest of the evening; and Apichatpong Weerasethakul's *Sud pralad/Tropical Malady* delivered the festival's greatest coup. Hollywood is rightly ransacking Asian horror cinema to renew its own techniques, bit it is unlikely to be able to replicate the pulchritude of this quartet.

The reasons why this is so lie deep within the history of Asian cinema. There has always been a sense in which America and Europe owned film. They invented it at the end of the nineteenth century in unfashionable places like New Jersey, Leeds and the suburbs of Lyons. They tinkered at their clumsy new camera-projectors and at first saw them merely as more profitable versions of Victorian lantern shows.

Then the best of the inventors looked beyond the mechanical and fairground properties of cinema. They started to expand its potential. Pioneering, and now mostly forgotten, directors saw that the flickering new medium was more than just a Victorian *divertisse-ment*. This crass commercial invention began to cross the rubicon to art. D. W. Griffith in California glimpsed its grace, German directors used it as an analogue for the human mind and the modernising city, Soviets emphasised its agitational and intellectual proper-ties and the Italians reconfigured it on an operatic scale.

So heady were these first decades of cinema that America and Europe can be forgiven for assuming that they were the only game in town. They were self-absorbed, but under-standably so. In less than twenty years Western cinema had escalated from nickelodeon to vast rococo picture palace; its nobodies became the most famous people on the planet; it helped define the erotic and aspirational for audiences and, in the process, made mil-lions. It didn't occur to its Wall Street backers, its canny producers, visionary directors or publicity hanger-oners that another continent might borrow their magic box and make it its own.

Yet this is what happened. In making the magic box their own, Asian filmmakers es-tablished distinctive visual and production methods which explain the fascination of *Hero* and the Cannes quartet. Film industries emerged in Tokyo, Shanghai, Hong Kong, Delhi and Bombay, some of which would dwarf those in the West. India made its first feature around 1912 and was producing more than two hundred films a year by 1930; Chinese production began at the same time and managed four hundred between 1928 and 1931 alone; and Japan was quicker off the mark – four production companies were established by 1908, four years before Hollywood became a production centre – and by the end of the 1920s, it was releasing four hundred films a year. Vast production factories were built. On sound stages as grand as anything in Hollywood or Rome, huge sets recreated scenes from Asian history.

In some ways the film industries of the East mirrored their Western forbears. Just like scandal-ridden Hollywood, the Eastern film world killed the thing it loved, its movie stars. The Chinese actress Ruan Lingyu was as famous and enigmatic as Greta Garbo yet the Shanghai tabloids hounded her and when she took a fatal overdose in 1935 (aged 25), her funeral procession was three miles long, three women committed suicide at it and the *New York Times*' front page called it 'the most spectacular funeral of the century'. Despite her key role in Chinese cinema in its heyday, she appears in almost no Western film en-cyclopaedias. She was better known in America and Europe than almost any other figure from Asian cinema, yet her fame did not introduce Eastern to Western cinema in any meaningful way.

By the time of Ruan's death, Europe and America's disinterest in Asian cinema was starting to seem less excusable. The Western film world was still a heady place, of course. Film industries there had refitted for sound and new genres like musicals and gangster pictures had come along but, on the other side of the world, something startling had hap-pened. Those who had borrowed the football had started to do dazzling things with it. The film industries of China and Japan were undergoing golden ages. Tokyo and Shanghai had become the centres of movie innovation as much as Southern California. And Hollywood hadn't yet noticed.

In the five years before Ruan's death, her country had produced more than five hundred films, mostly conventionally made in studios in Shanghai, without soundtracks. Its best directors – Bu Wancang and Yuan Muzhi – had begun to introduce elements of realism into their stories, making them more observationally alive than almost any of the decade. As a result, *Tao hua qi xue ji/The Peach Girl* (1931) and *Malu tianshi/Street Angel* (1937) respectively are regularly voted amongst the best ever made in the country. Both directors, and most of their colleagues, opposed both the Japanese invasion and the emergent nationalism of Chiang Kai-shek. After 1937, Yuan Muzhi went to Yen'an to work with Mao's Communists, and in 1938 the Chinese film industry moved from Shanghai to Hong Kong. There, directors like Wang Weiyi and Zhu Shilin paved the way for the explosion of Hong Kong cinema in the 1950s and again in the 1970s.

India set a different course. Whereas in the West the coming of talking movies gave birth to one genre in particular – the musical – in India, with just two exceptions and astonishing as it may seem to Westerners, every one of the 5,000 films made between 1931 and the mid-1950s had musical interludes. The effects of this were far reaching. Movie performers had to be able to dance. There were two parallel star systems – that of actors and that of playback singers. The films were stylistically more wide-ranging than Western movies, encompassing realism, escapist dance and sentiment within individual sequences, and they were often three hours long rather than Hollywood's ninety minutes.

The cost of such productions, as well as the new national reformism of the Congress Party, together resulted in a distinctive national style of Indian cinema. Performed in Hindi rather than any of the numerous regional languages and addressing social and peasant themes in an optimistic and romantic way, 'All India' films represented just under half the continent's annual output of around 260 movies throughout the 1940s and 1950s. They were often made in Bombay and were the mainstay of what is now known as Bollywood. By the 1970s production in India would reach five hundred films a year and a decade later it would double once more. All India films, as well as some of the more radical work inspired by the cultural impact of the Indian Communist Party, found audiences in markets such as the Middle East, Africa and the Soviet Union. By the late 1980s the centre of gravity had moved away from Hindi production in Bombay. Madras was producing a remarkable ten films a week, more than Los Angeles, and there were around 140 productions per year in the languages of Telugu, Tamil and Malayalam.

In Japan, the story was rather different. The film industry no longer rivalled India's in size but was distinctive in two significant ways. Until the 1930s, commentators called *benshis* attended every screening, standing in front of the audience, clarifying the action and describing characters. Directors did not need to show every aspect of their tale, therefore, and tended to produce more tableau-like visuals. Even more unusually, Japan's was a director-led system. Whereas in Hollywood, the producer was the central figure who chose the stories, and hired the director and actors, in Tokyo and the other production centres, the director did this. The model was that of an artist and his or her studio of apprentices. Employed by a studio as an assistant, a future director worked with senior figures, learned the craft, gained authority, became promoted to director status him or herself and then had the power to select screenplays and performers.

These radical digressions from the norms of industrial cinema are in part explained by Japan's psychological retreat from twentieth-century Westernism. Its chauvinistic belief in Asian superiority led to its invasion of Manchuria in 1931 and China in 1937, to catastrophic effect. Hollywood's self-obsession seems trivial in comparison but the uncomfortable fact is that it was wrong to ignore Japan in the 1930s and 1940s, because no national cinema anywhere was more artistically accomplished. The directors had considerable freedom, their nation was (over)confident and somehow the result was cinema of the highest order.

The films of Yasujiro Ozu, Kenji Mizoguchi and Mikio Naruse were the greatest amongst these. Mizoguchi's were usually set in the nineteenth century and unpicked the social norms which impeded the liberties of the female characters which he chose as his focus. From *Naniwa erejî/Osaka Elegy* (1936) to *Ugetsu Monogatari* (1953) and beyond he evolved a sinuous way of gracefully moving his camera in and around a scene, advancing towards significant details but often retreating at moments of dramatic confrontation or when his women express emotion. No one before had used the camera with such gliding finesse. Great Western directors like Vincente Minnelli and Bernardo Bertolucci would in later decades borrow his techniques.

In the 1930s, the West was oblivious to the innovations of Asian cinema: *I Was Born, But...*

Perhaps significantly given the political climate, Naruse's best films were also beautifully controlled accounts of women's lives. Even more important for film history, however, is the work of the great Ozu. Born in Tokyo in 1903, he rebelled at school, watched lots of American film comedies in the 1920s and imported their boisterous irreverence into his own work. By 1932, however, he had rejected much of their physicality and from *Otona no miru ehon – Umarete wa mita keredo/I Was Born, But...* embarked on a string of domestic films about middle-class parents and children and the quiet dilemmas of marriage and aging which are the most poised and resigned in world cinema. Brilliantly cast and judged, Ozu's films – the most famous is *Tôkyô Monogatari/Tokyo Story* (1953) – went further than Mizoguchi's emotional reserve. Where Hollywood cranked up drama, Ozu avoided it. His camera seldom moved. It nestled at seated height, framing people square-on, listening quietly to their articulations. This sounds boring but the effect is the opposite. The families we see are bracingly alive. Their hard-earned wisdom is deeply moving.

The human elements of the Ozu films would have been enough to endear him to many of those in future generations – Wim Wenders in Germany, Hou Hsiao-hsien in Taiwan and Abbas Kiarostami in Iran – who have called him the greatest of film directors, but then there was his technique. Ozu rejected the spatial conventions of editing, cutting not on action but for visual balance. His films analyse the space in which his characters move rather like the cubist paintings of Picasso and Braque – rigorously and from many angles. Even more strikingly, Ozu regularly cut away from his action to a shot of a tree or a kettle or clouds, not to establish a new location but as a moment of repose. Many historians now compare such 'pillow shots' to the Buddhist idea that *mu* – empty space or nothing – is itself a compositional element.

By the beginning of the 1950s then, and despite the ravages of nationalism, war and independence struggles, the three great Asian nations had national cinemas of real distinction. The medium was pliant. Influenced by Western directors, those in the East nevertheless musicalised and rethought it spatially, making it rapturous or rigorous, according to their own sensibilities.

And Western directors *still* took no notice. They had new darlings by this stage – directors like Orson Welles, Alfred Hitchcock and Marcel Carné for example, and actors like Ingrid Bergman, Judy Garland, Bob Hope and Humphrey Bogart – but their blindness to Asian cinema was now chronic. And then something remarkable happened. A film festival in Venice, started by Mussolini's cronies in 1932, awarded its top prize, the Golden Lion, to a Japanese film in 1951. Floodgates opened. The film was Akira Kurosawa's *Rashômon*. Audiences on the Lido couldn't work out what they loved more, the film's ravishing cinematography or its philosophical disquisition on relativism. Other Japanese films had been shown in the West, but none with this impact. *Rashômon* went on to be shown in cosmopolitan cities throughout the West and won the Best Foreign Film Oscar, a prize that Japan would again win in 1954 and 1955. Kurosawa had been crowned and Lucas and Coppola would soon pay attention.

Within no time, other festival directors wanted a piece of the Venice kudos and suddenly Japanese cinema was being pored over for new discoveries. Kurosawa's *Shichinin no samurai/The Seven Samurai* was feted in 1955 and remade in Hollywood in 1960 as *The Magnificent Seven*, more than four decades before the current spate of ransackings. The irony was that Kurosawa had been deeply influenced by Hollywood's John Ford, but at least the flow was now two-way. The year before *The Seven Samurai*, Venice again made the running by programming Mizoguchi's *Ugetsu Monogatari*. Audiences were bowled over. What sinuous tracking shots! What an extraordinarily depiction of a ghost! What a serene ending! No matter that Mizoguchi had been making films for three decades. The film won the festival's Silver Lion.

India too found the limelight. A new master director, Mehboob Khan, gained international acclaim – and an Oscar nomination – for his *Mother India* (1957), an epic often compared to *Gone with the Wind* (1939). In their belated rush to raid the treasures of the East it was inevitable that even Japan's least showy director, Ozu, would finally find favour amongst the Western cognoscenti. He did, but it took a while. By the late 1950s, despite festival screenings of his work and having six of his films named 'best film of the year', in Japan, few abroad recognised his talents. Eventually, the British Film Institute would say that he was 'one of the greatest artists of the twentieth century in any medium, in any country'. Wim Wenders would call him 'a sacred treasure of the cinema'. An over-compensation for the years of neglect, perhaps, but praise indeed.

The evolution, and retarded recognition, of Asian cinema in the 1950s is bang up to date relevant because of what is about to happen. Half a century after *Rashômon* and *Ugetsu Monogatari*, a new Asian aesthetic is once again hitting Western cinema. As Hollywood's current remake-itis shows, Japanese and Korean directors have a way with fear, but watching the Asian films in Cannes this year was like being in Venice in 1951 or 1954. There was an overwhelming sense not of 'how can they scare me so deeply?', but 'how can they make images so beautiful?' The sheer loveliness of the breakthrough films of fifty years ago was somehow feminine – certainly delicate, rich, soft, and shallow-focused. Each of the new wave of Asian films is highly decorated, tapestry-like, with an emphasis on detail, visual surface, shallow focus, costume, colour and patterning and centred on a woman, or feminised men.

It comes as no surprise, for example, that Zhang's *The House of Flying Daggers*, is so beautiful. His *Da hong deng long gao gao fua/Raise the Red Lantern* (1991) was visually striking and he started as a cinematographer on the breakthrough work of modern Chinese cinema, *Huang tu di/Yellow Earth* (1984). In *The House of Flying Daggers*, Zhang Ziyi plays Mei, a blind dancer in the year 859 who is sympathetic to a group of revolutionaries threatening the power of the Tang dynasty. An early sequence takes place in a large pavilion entirely decorated by peonies. A local captain suspects that Mei is a subversive and sets her a test. In the pavilion's central space, he surrounds her with vertically-mounted drums. She stands in the middle, dressed in a coat of gold silk, embroidered with cerise and turquoise chrysanthemums and peonies. Her face is entirely passive, her body completely still. Presented with dishes of dry beans, the captain flicks one at a drum. The camera follows it though space. As it strikes the taught surface, Mei spins and flicks the enormously long sleeve of her coat in the direction of the sound. It travels as the bean did and strikes the drum in a rococo flourish. Then the Captain flicks another bean, and Mei spins and flicks again. Then another. Then a small handful, which scatter around the circle of drums. Mei responds to the percussive effect, her sleeves darting and soaring, her face still serene and expressionless, at the centre of the vortex. The bean shots are computer-generated – the most satisfying use of CGI yet – and the combination of such cinematic modernity with martial arts choreography, production design influenced by Chinese art, photographic splendour and, central to it all, Zhang's enigmatic performance, makes this scene an instant classic.

If anything, Hong Kong director Wong Kar-wai's *2046* goes even further. It too is a widescreen film of seductively shallow focus, stillness, surface patterning, chromatic intensity and feminine beauty. It again stars Zhang Ziyi, this time joined by Gong Li and Maggie Cheung. Like Wong's previous film, *Fa yeung nin wa/In the Mood for Love* (2000), it is an evocative exercise in mood and music, set in Hong Kong in the 1960s. Tony Leung plays a brilliantined writer caught in a destructive web of relationships. Wong and his cinematographers take the colours and lighting of Edward Hopper but reconfigure them into wide, flat scroll-like images where sometimes only eye-lashes or lips are in focus, where everything has a melancholic sheen, where women move in slow-motion and where their stilettos click in night-time alleyways. To this Wong adds a futuristic element. A dazzling bullet train rockets forward through time to a cerise world or cat-walk poses and Matthew Barney vaginal spaces, where robotic people symbolise the empty state of love. The year 2046 seems to represent for the writer the place he travels to in his mind when he falls for a woman, the place from which, he says, few men return.

At first glance the Japanese director Kore-eda's film *Nobody Knows*, is very different from the aesthetic worlds of Zhang and Wong. Set in present-day Japan, it tells a true story of a neglectful mother who rents an apartment with one of her children and, when she moves in, opens her suitcases to reveal two more. In his way, however, the former documentary director is equally interested in stillness, in shallow focus and in production design. The mother leaves her children but instead of a *Lord of the Flies* decline into chaos, the children subtly transform their apartment into a world suitable for them: scruffy certainly, but full of play and adventure. *Nobody Knows* is as much a tapestry film as *The House of Flying Daggers*. Shots of children's feet, of drawings, of plants grown from seeds, of looks and smiles, but most of all of the timeless way in which kids can amuse themselves, are woven into a complex portrait of their lives.

Thai director Apichatpong Weerasethakul's *Tropical Malady* is more enigmatic still. In its first half, a soldier befriends a young guy who lives in the country. The men drift around, sit talking, go to the movies and grow fond of each other. In one scene the soldier puts his head in his friend's lap, in another the latter urinates and the soldier licks his hand. As their growing eroticism looks as if it might become more explicit, the peasant man walks into the jungle. Then the screen goes black. No sound, no picture, as if the film has broken. Then a second film begins. The actors are the same but their situation is more fable-like. A monkey talks to one of the characters, the other is the spirit of a tiger running naked through the jungle.

Tropical Malady is likely to be seen as one of the most experimental films of its time, but what is again striking in this context is its gentleness and stasis. Though made in re-markably different countries, Weerasethakul's film shares with Zhang's, Wong's and Ko-re-eda's, certain ideas about human beings and about art. *Tropical Malady* in particular invites philosophical speculation, but just as the work of Ozu can only be fully understood by balancing its psychological aspects with more abstract, Buddhist questions of space and stillness, so the influence of Buddhism can be seen in these new films. To generalise about this is not to simplify. Despite the range of Western cinema today, most of it derives from the assumption that movies are narrative chains of cause and effect, that the characters in movies have fears and desires and that we follow the film by understanding these fears and desires. The new films of Zhang, Wong, Kore-eda and Weerasethakul make similar assumptions but are less driven by them and balance questions of selfhood with Zen ideas about negation and equilibrium. This makes their beauty hard to replicate in the West.

But Buddhism is not the whole picture. Another Asian philosophy explains the gender and space of these films. Unlike Maoism which pictured a clear moral opposition between the good, victimised workers and the bad exploitative managers, and unlike Confucism in which masculinity is an ideal and femininity is less so, Taoism is philosophically more rela-tive and less clear cut. Morally, it sees good within bad and vice versa. For it the feminine is a virtue as, crucially for artists, is emptiness.

Every one of the great Asian films in the pipeline (the non-Taoist Indian cinema, which continues to be economically successful, is at the moment much less innovative) evinces such Taoist ideas of sex and space. In none of them is gender polarised. In all of them, space is crucial. And the influence is not only speculative. Zhang, for example, has talked about how Chinese painting has affected his work. His shots are often very wide. The body is frequently de-centred. Space and landscape weigh as heavily within the frame as the human elements. Art historians have long discussed the Taoist component of such paintings.

As the art form most swayed by money and market, cinema would appear to be too busy to bother with questions of philosophy. This is not the case. Just as deep ideas about individual freedom have led to the bracingly-driven aspirational cinema of Hollywood these last hundred years, so Buddhism and Taoism explains the distinctiveness of Asian cinema at its best. In Venice in 1951 and Cannes in 2004, audiences left the cinemas with heads full of dazzling images. But the greatness of *Rashômon, Ugetsu Monogatari, 2046* or *The House of Flying Daggers* is, in the end, not to do with imagery at all. Yes they are pictorially distinctive, but it is their different sense of what a person is and what space and action are which makes them unique.

CANNES 1

The big story in world cinema is that Asia is on a roll. It's hard not to notice. A Chinese film, *Ying xiong/Hero* (2002), went to number one at the US box office the year before last. There's hardly an action movie made anywhere in the world now that doesn't nick the balletic 'wire-fu' combat techniques which originated in Hong Kong. In certain genres such as horror, Hollywood might as well put up its hands and say to Eastern filmmakers, 'OK, you won.'

Asia is winning because it has found a more satisfying balance between cinematic action and repose. Yes, its movies can be as kinetic and violent as Hollywood's, but the non-macho and equilibrium ideas in Buddhist and Taoist philosophy keep the violence in check in the best Asian films. Stasis is a real compositional element in Eastern aesthetics and the recent movies of Zhang Yimou, Wong Kar-wai, Hideo Nakata, Takashi Miike and Hirokazu Kore-eda, and many others, are better as a result.

The story of Asian surefootedness continued in Cannes this year. The best film, shown right at the end of the festival, was the Taiwanese director Hou Hsiao-hsien's masterly *Zui hao de shi guang / Three Times*, in which the same couple is seen to meet, flirt and communicate by letters and then texts in the 1960s, 1911 and the present day. A symphonic structure. The 1911 section is particularly fine, its characters unaware of Taiwan's complex future. In a real *coup de cinéma*, Hou presents this section as a silent movie, complete with inter-titles.

Hou's film is not at all violent. Its moments of quiescence, like those in Zhang's and Wong's recent movies, and like those of Hou's master, Yasujiro Ozu, help explain its breathtaking beauty. But unlike last year's Cannes, 2005 was not dominated by such beauty. The festival's annual snapshot of world cinema told a new tale. The buzz films were European and Anglo-Saxon. Western filmmakers were back in form. Canada's David Cronenberg, Austria's Michael Haneke, Belgium's Dardenne brothers, America's Jim Jarmusch, Denmark's Lars von Trier and America's Gus Van Sant all presented work of the highest standard. One of these, Jim Jarmusch, openly acknowledged the Asian influence, pointedly saying 'Hou Hsiao-hsien, I am your student' in his acceptance speech for the Grand Prix for his film *Broken Flowers* (Hou's film won nothing). But the really meaty issue in Cannes this year was how Western directors are accepting that they, too, must think more deeply about the violent instincts in human beings.

Take Cronenberg's thriller, *A History of Violence*, in which Viggo Mortensen plays Tom Stall, a placid small-towner who shoots two thieves when they try to rob his diner. He is acclaimed as an all-American hero, a defender of private property, but his facility with a gun discomforts his family, as does the brutality of the shooting. Stall is not what he seems. His wife comes to realise that she is living with a killer. Hollywood westerns are full of men who have apparently laid their violent pasts to rest. Cronenberg's film shares with them an Old-Testament belief that it is not possible to do so, and that savagery lies below the surface of liberal assumptions about human decency and reform. A familiar theme, of course, but seldom more cogently depicted.

If a Canadian auteur is selling the very un-Canadian idea of innate fury, what of Denmark's greatest director? Those who have seen *Breaking the Waves* (1996) or *Dogville* (2003) would expect Lars von Trier to find little to dispute in Cronenberg's vision. They'd be right. His new movie, *Manderlay*, spurns Scandinavian humanism even more than Cronenberg does Canada's. Provocation being von Trier's mode, he chooses a 1930s slave plantation in America as the setting for his story, numbers his black characters and calls them 'niggers'. Most filmmakers see slavery in morally clear-cut terms yet von Trier has his liberated African-Americans volunteer for re-captivity and even suggest that they themselves wrote the rule-book which governs their servitude.

American critics in Cannes once again accused von Trier of being an unreliable, self-appointed professor of American history, but *Manderlay*'s scope is universal. Like Cronenberg, von Trier's point is an introverted one. If the victims of violence will continue to choose it rather than the uncertainties of freedom, he seems to be saying, then how can we ever hope to make brutality a stranger to us?

Cronenberg and von Trier's shared view that human nature is like a cake in which a top layer of civility covers deeper, volcanic instincts, shaped their films. Each was a story of erosion, a wearing away of the top layer of life. Like much of Western drama they started with worlds that we initially took to be true but discovered, as we peeled away at their surfaces, that the real stuff was underneath. They were, thus, suspenseful. We were waiting for the explosion.

Which was certainly the case with *Caché/Hidden*. No film in Cannes this year got people talking more than Michael Haneke's latest. It begins with a couple, Georges and Anne, played by Daniel Auteuil and Juliette Binoche, watching video footage of themselves leaving their ordinary Parisian home. Someone has filmed them. He is a TV presenter, so it could be a stalker. Then another video arrives, then one showing an office block and a specific door in that block. Georges goes to the door and knocks it. Majid, an Algerian man his age opens it. It turns out that they knew each other in childhood; Majid's parents were Georges' family's servants. He reminds Georges that the latter forced him to do something terrible. The videotapes, we assume, are his long-gestated revenge.

But no. Another video arrives and its shows that the Majid-Georges conversation was filmed. Who could have done that? Who could have set up a camera in the Algerian's apartment, secretly, and laid in wait for the encounter? This is where the director of *Benny's Video* (1992), *Funny Games* (1997), *Code inconnu/Code Unknown* (2000) and *La Pianiste/The Piano Teacher* (2001) comes into his own. We are scared now, but by what? A videotape? No. Rather, by the implications of the filming – its pre-mediation, its cold stare, the fact that the perpetrator was so close to his victim, Georges, that he could almost have touched him.

Then, the biggest shock of the film and the festival. Georges visits Majid again and this time, suddenly, the latter slits his throat. The weight of the event, all those years ago, makes him take his life. How then, must it weigh on Georges' mind? An encounter forces an answer. Majid has a son, who is angry. He visits Georges and, of course, he and we assume that the son is the menacing videographer. But still no. Explaining his visit he says, simply, 'I wanted to see what a guilty conscience looks like.' At this point Haneke's central metaphor comes into view – Georges represents France's African misdeeds. But we still don't have an answer to who is sending the tapes.

Hidden was by some way the best of the European and Anglo-Saxon films dealing with violence this year, and it establishes Haneke – if we didn't already know this – as the best European filmmaker of his generation. The final significance of his film is that imagery itself was the cause of its terror. If Cronenberg and von Trier were being introspective, Haneke was too, even more so because he was pointing the finger not only at his own society, but his own medium. More than any film I've seen, *Hidden* catches the icy inhumanity of moving imagery. The video footage that caused Georges and Anne such distress was almost always static, carried no pounding music and indulged in none of the clichés of the horror genre, yet it froze their spines.

Taken together, Cronenberg's, von Trier's and Haneke's films seem to me to be part of what could be called the *Kill Bill* effect. Just as *Natural Born Killers* in 1994 shocked the film world, waking it up to the medium's effortless facility with amoral violence so, I think, the *Kill Bill* films did the same recently. I've heard many in the film industry (mostly on the creative side) express something like revulsion at their lack of consciousness. The *Kill Bill* circus made movies look formally omnipotent but clueless and amoral, dangerously close to the problems in society.

Cannes 2005 showed serious filmmakers in the West reacting against such formalism. They did so in a way that is very much their own, very unlike how Hou would. Great, and more please.

The final irony in this story is, of course, that the *Kill Bill* films were very influenced by Asian cinema in the first place.

EASTERN WESTERN

If the main theme of film history these last eleven decades has been the growing artistic rivalry between Hollywood and Asian cinema, then that rivalry has seldom been in sharper focus.

One morning recently I went to see *Memoirs of a Geisha*, Columbia Pictures and American director Rob Marshall's account of the education of a young girl who becomes one of the figures in Eastern life that most fascinates the West – a *geisha*. As the end credits rolled, I walked to an adjacent screen and watched *Brokeback Mountain* (2005), Taiwanese director Ang Lee's portrait of the lives of the figures in Western cinema who most fascinate Eastern directors – cowboys. Each is a ventriloquism of sorts, or a stealing of the rival's clothes. Seen back to back, it feels as if Marshall is photographing Lee who is photographing him in return.

Memoirs of a Geisha and *Brokeback Mountain* have several things in common. Both were made by American production companies – though, to add to the hall of mirrors effect, *Memoirs of a Geisha*'s backer, Columbia, is owned by the Japanese company Sony. Both films are about sex. Marshall's has the girl slowly realise that the beautifully dressed, Dionysian women who surround her sell a sophisticated form of sex. Lee's film takes the most prevalent male archetype in American cinema and – as American critics say – queers him, positing eros in a relationship between frontiersmen where we are not supposed to have seen it before.

The techniques of the films – their ambition, language and tone – could not be more different, however. From the off, *Memoirs of a Geisha*'s business is mythmaking. The opening commentary mentions a 'forbidden, fragile' world full of 'mysteries'. The camera is always craning and gliding, attempting to make us feel awe at the places in which we are being immersed, as if they are the settings of a fairytale. Image after image is veiled by slats, shadows, smoke or the hub-bub of on-set action. The lighting is stylised throughout, as it was in Marshall's last film, the musical *Chicago* (2002). The aesthetic strategy is smoke and mirrors: to conjure a cultural and sexual elsewhere through visual uncertainty, glimpsing and feeling.

Lee's film is from another universe. His camera hardly moves. Almost everything is seen in crisp, clear and naturalistic light. Shots are held a long time. There is little or no filtration. Camera tricks are almost non-existent – just three small dissolves in the whole movie. This is filmmaking as cold hard stare. If Lee and his screenwriters Larry McMurtry, Diana Ossana and E. Annie Proulx (who wrote the *New Yorker* short story to which the film is faithful) intend something like an introduction of the explicitly erotic into an already homosocial genre which has nonetheless ignored or tiptoed around sex, they could not have chosen a better approach. They have taken America's greatest fairytale and reintroduced it to the real world. Others have tried to do so but their observations were mostly social. *Brokeback Mountain* goes deeper. Its fine-grained account of the disruptive power of eros makes us feel as if we are seeing a western for the first time. By contrast, Marshall's film about sex and myth is tedious and repetitive. It tries to get us excited about something that we've seen in movies a hundred times before, always in the same way, so we are ahead of his film from the start and he never catches up.

The triumph of *Brokeback Mountain* and the failure of *Memoirs of a Geisha* are suggestive in a number of ways. First, Hollywood seems to be completely indecisive about whether it wants to stoke the fire of myth or pour water on it. From the 1930s to the 1950s it did the former; in the 1970s it did the latter. Today it does both, hesitantly, with one eye on Asia. It knows that 'reality' sells like never before, but cannot shake its atavistic dreaming.

Secondly, Eastern directors like Ang Lee use stasis more convincingly and to greater effect than Western directors like Rob Marshall use action and movement. The cutting rate of Hollywood films increased from once every ten seconds to once every six seconds during the 1980s – forty per cent faster – and remained at that rate from the 1990s onwards. *Memoirs of a Geisha* suffers from such cutting norms. Accelerated cutting has become a cul-de-sac for mainstream American cinema.

Films should show something new or say something new. They should, as Jean Renoir advised, try to remove cliché from the world. *Brokeback Mountain* does. *Memoirs of a Geisha* piles cliché on cliché. With East and West borrowing each other's tricks so readily, orientalism should have been a dead duck long ago. Filmmakers from Jean-Luc Godard to Kenji Mizoguchi, Sergio Leone to Orson Welles and Billy Wilder have long been fascinated by the figure of the prostitute. Marshall's film is too, but he has nothing new to say on the subject.

It would be wrong to read too much into one bout, of course, but in this case of Hollywood versus Asia, the East wins on a knockout. Luckily, however, Hollywood is a world unencumbered by pride. Rightly, it steals from the best. It ransacked Europe in the 1920s, 1930s and 1940s, then again in the 1970s. Now it is doing so with Asia.

How will it learn? The answer is, certainly at the level of personnel. Not only Ang Lee but John Woo, Michelle Yeoh and many others have taken trans-Pacific flights after offers from Hollywood. They have stayed and enriched film culture there. And as Sony's ownership of Columbia shows, there are no barriers at the corporate level either. Seeing *Memoirs of a Geisha* and *Brokeback Mountain* back to back shows that it is at the level of form and philosophy that the estrangement continues. The clash, and engagement, between Hollywood and Asian cinema is proving to be one of the great cultural contests of this or any other time.

ORIENTALISM

On hearing that I am to co-curate a British festival of Chinese cinema, a colleague warns against the dangers of orientalism. When I made my series on Iranian cinema for Channel 4 last year, people also questioned whether I was being orientalist. A popular topic for PhD film students these days is how Chinese breakthrough films like Zhang Yimou's *Ying xiong/Hero* (2002) and *Shi mian mai fu/The House of Flying Daggers*, are 'pandering' to the West. In Iran, director Abbas Kiarostami is often accused of the same thing. At the Mexico City Film Festival this year, local films featuring peasants or agricultural workers were often called 'folkloric'. In Scotland, where I live and work, the pitfalls of kitsch and tartanry have led directors and screenwriters in the opposite direction, towards social realism.

The fear of fake in cinema is everywhere. This is understandable. For fifty years, the world's two largest film industries – Hollywood and Bollywood – have kitschified every corner of the globe. Edward Said's influential book *Orientalism* arrived in 1978, just as America was shaking off its 1970s flirtation with seriousness and inventing the blockbuster and the multiplex, so Said's arguments seemed bang up to date. Mainstream cinema today, with its Arab terrorists and exotic *geishas*, would still enrage him, but in general, the fear of fake – call it kitschophobia – is damaging global film.

Nearly every aspect of cinema is globalised these days; pirate DVDs of even *Brokeback Mountain* (2005) are on sale outside mosques in Cairo. The exchanges of imagery, eroticism, narrative and myth between the Middle East and the West are no longer, as Said envisaged, simply based on colonial power and updated by nineteenth-century grand tourists enthralled by ill-informed views of the Arab world.

Take the charge of pandering levelled against Kiarostami and Zhang. Just as Said accused some Arab intellectuals of internalising colonial power structures and so parroting orientalist ideas, so these filmmakers are seen as equally masochistic, hurting their own culture by 'stripteasing' it for the gratification of the onlooker. Nonsense. If anything, Zhang's recent films could be criticised for sucking up to China's ongoing reconstruction of its national pride, certainly not grovelling to the West. And if Kiarostami is making things we want so much, why do his films make so little money in the West, and why is there such a black market for them – untainted as they are by *mullah* discourse – in Iran?

The career of Alfred Hitchcock sheds an interesting light on the orientalist/pandering complaint. Unlike fellow émigré Billy Wilder, when Hitchcock upped sticks and started making films in America, he showed no interest in the realities of his adoptive country. There is almost no social content in Hitchcock. His middle-class American businessmen have none of the economic anxieties of, say, Jack Lemmon's character in Wilder's *The Apartment* (1960). Instead, America is a Freudian stage on which Hitchcock presents, for our gratification, his scenarios of sex and escape. Yet *Vertigo* (1958) and *North by Northwest* (1959) are acclaimed around the world. They gut a complex country of its social complexity and, as a result, float untethered above the civic, easily absorbed by libidinous dreamers anywhere in the world. This untethered quality of Hitchcock films is not necessarily kitsch and is not necessarily to be feared. Rather, it is part of the essence of cinema and, you could argue, an accurate reflection of the nature of existence.

Wong Kar-wai's films float like no others. *Fa yeung nin wa/In the Mood for Love* (2000), for example, is about Hong Kong in the 1960s, when the music was all cover versions of Latin American songs and Nat King Cole. The clothes were Hollywood, via hit parade chic. The mood of the title is not love but drifting, renting a new place in an anonymous apartment block, passing time in noodle bars. Made in 2000, it was difficult not to see the film as a reaction to the handover of Hong Kong – its identity slippage.

A good way of understanding cinema in transnational times is to consider Homer's story of the oar and the winnowing fan. In it, Odysseus is instructed by Tiresias to take an oar from his ship and walk from the shore with it until he comes to an agricultural place where the locals consider the oar to be a winnowing fan. The truth is that objects change when they travel. Cinema is just such an object. At the recent Cannes Film Festival I encountered filmmakers from Kazakhstan and Peru, Nigeria, America, Europe and Korea, all carrying their oars, many of which I will have seen as winnowing fans. This is the nature of modern life. We live in intermediate zones where ideas have travelled. Yes, we risk misunderstanding them if their formative circumstances get too lost on the journey, but if they – ideas, films – are well made, they will transcribe their native places in readable ways.

The charge of orientalism is that I am ethnically unable to make such readings. The assumption is that those with authority should read and the rest of us should merely listen. No way. We are all in that place where oars morph into winnowing fans.

BRITAIN

It looks like self-hatred, but when the press performs its ritual denunciation of British cinema, it is more like self-love thwarted. The reporting of unanalysed but apparently disastrous box-office figures is a seasonal event. The revival of British cinema is once again declared a sad joke. Lessons, we are told, have not been learned.

The latest omen of doom is Peter Cattaneo's *Lucky Break*, his follow-up to *The Full Monty* (1997), which has shown tiny returns for its sizeable advertising budget (otherwise known as 'hype'). Never mind that a surprise hit has merely been succeeded by a not-so-surprising disappointment. Other flops will be lined up, whatever their target audience or marketing budgets were, and shown to represent the demise of British film. The *Independent* recently exposed a movie called *Another Life* for taking only £11,300 at the British box office and Steve Coogan's *The Parole Officer* for taking a 'mere' £2.6m by the end of August. The term 'flop' clearly covers a great deal of territory – from genuine dud to 'might have done a bit better'.

You have to be blinded by Hollywood financial ratios to imagine that an initial £2.6m (now risen to well over £3m) at the British box office is a disaster. *The Parole Officer* might not have won the £18m jackpot of last year's *Billy Elliot*, but the latter was a runaway hit. If it is box office that ultimately counts, then *Kevin and Perry Go Large* (2000), which took £10m, or *Chicken Run* (2000) (£30m) should be paragons of British cinema.

How many times since the mid-1980s, when British cinema rose like Lazarus, has newsprint tolled its grave bell? Of course, the same papers, even the same journalists, will happily stretch a point in the opposite direction every time a *Full Monty* or a *Trainspotting* (1996) captures a slice of the international imagination. But that's the love/hate pathology. They imagine British cinema has turned a corner. They want it to be so. They look for trends in an industry they don't quite understand. They flush hot, and then they flush cold.

Not since the late 1940s, and the collapse of the studio system which made and distributed films within each country (the US, France, Britain, Japan), have movies played a game of modest stakes. Then, if a film made at the Gainsborough studios was released on, say, a Wednesday, played a week or two, and was taken off the screen, it would break even or maybe return ten per cent above costs. Nowadays, movies are either famine or feast. They make a lot or lose a lot. There is nothing unusual in that; it is the same in every Western film economy. I am writing this in Italy, where the native industry's hit rate is about the same as Britain's. Ditto Germany. France performs better, but that's because for two generations now movies have been taken as seriously as books.

We don't see the German flops; or the Italian ones. Once a year or so their journalists wring their hands, as ours do, about embarrassing local pictures, but they are as wrong as ours to do so.

The economics of film are famously slippery. *Citizen Kane* (1941) and *It's a Wonderful Life* (1946) were flops of their time (as the newspapers duly reported), yet that is no indication of what they came to be worth. And even for run-of-the-mill releases that won't be vindicated by history, the measure of commercial success cannot be gauged merely from initial box-office figures. You need to account for every territory in which a film is released on its first run. You have to add up its total sales to terrestrial and the various satellite television channels – either as an individual film or, as is often the case, in a package. Then you need to tally its video and DVD rentals and, finally, evaluate its worth as part of a catalogue of rights that will be saleable in future dispersal situations such as video on demand.

Media correspondents have become blinded by box-office figures, but they are not alone. At many multiplexes, ticket sales are pasted on the walls (often US takings, which is a perverse inducement to see a film in Britain). On American tabloid television the weekend take of films is often top of the agenda. Moviegoers in the US, and increasingly so in Britain, are aware of these figures. But how is their pleasure or appreciation related to the number of people who have passed that way before?

Assumptions about the sorry state of British cinema, based on a few 'flops', are as phoney as the contrary presumption that, since admissions in the first half of 2000 were the highest in 26 years, British cinema must be on the verge of a new golden era.

The real issue is that we – moviegoers, cultural journalists – aren't asking far more interesting questions. Why, for instance, after fifty years' hiatus, are *Rank*-style comedies suddenly in the cinemas again? Why are even the serious newspapers so concerned with the budget and the box-office take, instead of the themes and pleasures, stories and ideas in British cinema? A paper like *Libération* is full of such talk about cinema. There is some good British stuff, but it is increasingly depressing to read the narrow prognoses for cinema in Britain from those who have recently discovered the box-office page in *Variety* magazine.

THE ENGLISH CHARACTER March 2006

Three Oscar-nominated films this year attempt a portrait of England. The concurrence of Stephen Frears' *Mrs Henderson Presents*, Woody Allen's *Match Point* and Terrence Malick's *The New World* is a surprise because, beyond travelogue, England hasn't been a subject for cinema in some time.

Back in the 1950s, the Ealing studio made a series of comedies that seemed bent on capturing something of the English national character. And in the 1980s, the idea of England was used as a starting-point for Merchant Ivory, *My Beautiful Laundrette* (1985) and Derek Jarman's experimental *The Last of England* (1988). But that idea seems to have fallen from movie favour in the last decade. Ken Loach has set most of his recent films in Scotland or the Hispanic world. The prolific Michael Winterbottom seems driven by international stories and by genre. Even Mike Leigh's work seems to start with the idea of character rather than nation. America has John Sayles, but England seems to have no equivalent state-of-the-nation filmmaker.

This can't be because the idea of Englishness is of no interest. There has been a steady drip-feed of articles on the subject since Scottish and Welsh devolution at least. If these had all been by the political right, this might explain the left-leaning world of film's silence. But they haven't. A more plausible explanation is the fact that previous films that attempted to capture the character of Albion now seem dated. The popular but now mostly forgotten 1940s films with actors Arthur Askey, Jessie Matthews and Gracie Fields suggested that cheeriness was at the root of Englishness – as, in their very different way, did the *Carry On* films. Ealing's *Passport to Pimlico* (1949) and *The Man in the White Suit* (1951) put eccentricity at the heart of the nation. Michael Powell and Emeric Pressburger's *The Life and Death of Colonel Blimp* (1943) seemed to say that tolerance – a refusal to fall for ideologies such as fascism or communism – was to be cherished in the English. And reliability was at the core of movies like Noel Coward's and David Lean's *In Which We Serve* (1942).

Cheery-eccentric-tolerant-reliable was a decent enough stab at a national portrait, but it was a portrait in response to war. By the late 1950s, it was being queried. The most influential dissenter was Scottish director Lindsay Anderson who spent his childhood in India, where he saw the Raj at close quarters. Together with the Royal Court theatre, where he was a central figure, he blasted a hole in cheery-eccentric-tolerant-reliable. In *This Sporting Life* (1963), England was dirt poor and sexually repressed. His later films *If...* (1968) and *Britannia Hospital* (1982) made no attempt to hide his hatred for what he saw as the timidity, inertia and conservatism of his adoptive nation.

Anderson begat Derek Jarman's equally enraged denunciations of what he saw as an English garden defiled by Thatcherism. Both were master directors, but in hindsight, this timid-inert-conservative 'essentialism' was an equal, though opposite, counterpart to the cheery-eccentric-tolerant-reliable brigade. That's why Hanif Kureishi and Stephen Frears' film *My Beautiful Laundrette* was such a breath of fresh air. There had been other 1970s and 1980s films about class and race (such as the work of the Amber Collective in Newcastle and *Handsworth Songs* (1986)), but *My Beautiful Laundrette* was a new standard-bearer which showed that there was nothing at the root of England at all. The country was a mosaic of new Pakistanis, Thatcherite entrepreneurs, gays and neo-Nazis having fun and games as a rump white middle-class sat at home and fumed. The state of the nation was multiple. For a generation – until 9/11 or the recent debate about multiculturalism, perhaps – this view held.

Does it now? What is the England we see in the Oscar films? Woody Allen's England is the least interesting. Visually it is a tourists' view, the London landmarks serving as backdrops to the story. Like *Crimes and Misdemeanors* (1989), *Match Point* is morally intricate and needed to be set in a world where a rich elite is detached from the rest of society. The problem is Allen's own detachment. He fails to capture the way these people talk or their codes of behaviour. He's interested in ethics but his film is socially empty which makes it lopsided. If anything this is a reminder of how disinterested Allen has always been in transcultural issues. His central joke, after all, is that in mid-town Manhattan, you find the whole world, which is funny but untrue.

Compare this national blankness to Frears' *Mrs Henderson Presents*, scripted by American playwright Martin Sherman, which is more interested in England than perhaps any film I can remember since *My Beautiful Laundrette*. And in a similar way, the nation is seen as a collage of energised performers and entrepreneurs. Judi Dench's theatre owner Laura Henderson gets things done not by going through official routes but because she takes afternoon tea with the Lord Chamberlain: the blue-blood way. Bob Hoskins' Vivian Van Damm is the theatre's decent impresario, whose conservative Jewishness is as quintessentially English as Dench's Henderson. Will Young plays a gay choreographer. Out of this braid of aristocracy, Judaism and homosexuality, England is portrayed as vibrant and multiple, even in the 1930s. The enjoyable truth of the film comes from the fact that Dench's character is the most radical of the three.

If *Mrs Henderson Presents* is ideasy, Terrence Malick's *The New World* is overwhelmingly so. A retelling of the settlement of America and the John Smith/Pocahontas romance, you'd expect it to be only secondarily about England, and at first glance this is the case. Much of the glorious first half of the film is like a prayer to the swamplands of Virginia. But in the second half the story follows Pocahontas and her husband John Rolfe to the English court of James I. England is portrayed as a world of gateways. Nearly every scene is framed by one, or features a character passing through one. For Malick and his creative team, England is obsessed by the idea of home, of arriving, of framing nature as something to be seen from inside looking out. The relationship between the human world and the natural one in England is that of Capability Brown. Some of the film was shot in Hampton Court Palace, where Brown was Head Gardener.

This is an art and garden historian's view of England, and it works brilliantly in *The New World*. But it's not only the English bits of this film which seem to say something about England. The film looks and sounds as if it was conceived by Percy Bysshe Shelley. It is the most romantic film I have ever seen, constantly externalising mental states, enraptured by the rush of feeling caused by nature and by love, intoxicated by sensation. It is not in any way a state of the nation film, at least not of the English nation. But it is a masterpiece nevertheless, one of the most thoughtful films ever made, and many of its thoughts derive from England.

ESFAHAN

It is exhilarating to have such ambiguous political bearings. In Esfahan a few days ago, Iran's spiritual leader Ayatollah Khamenei spoke to a crowd of tens of thousands on Emam Khomeini Square. Our hotel was only a few metres away but when we tried to stand at the door to watch the throngs arriving, a policeman ushered us back in the nicest possible way. In Tehran none of the young people have any time for Khamenei. A taxi driver openly told us of the 'death to Khamenei' chants on the streets after the recent Iran/Emirates football match. Everyone we talked to preferred – even adored – President Khatami and cheered when the European Parliament passed a resolution supporting him.

Back in our hotel in Esfahan – a city a bit like Paris in the desert, a jewel of Safavid architecture, where 'Down With America' is neatly painted on the walls – it is a different story. Late on the night of the Khamenei speech, our young, trendy concierge Ali offers me tea and tells me how important the spiritual leader is. His deep study of the Koran is, for him, a rudder in secular times. The chief threat to the Islamic republic, he says, is that its young people do not know their history and culture: they aren't even aware that Persians are Aryan not Arab. By chance I am reading Robert Byron's *The Road to Oxiana* on this trip. First published in 1937, Byron relates an almost identical conversation.

Even ardent Ali is ambiguous about the West. He is learning English from what he calls a 'book of poems'. When he fetches this it turns out to be a collection of Beatles' lyrics. He opens it at 'Strawberry Fields Forever' and is very surprised when I tell him that it is a song, with a melody. I am, alas, obliged to sing it for him in the lobby. Ali asks about the metaphors in the lyrics but when I offer to send him a tape of the songs themselves he declines at once, suddenly incurious. Later we hear that in his speech Khamenei denounced those who argue that Iran should extend the hand of friendship to America. We brace ourselves for some hostility on the streets as a result of this, but the extraordinary Persian warmth and hospitality is, if anything, even more exuberant in its wake.

Cinema has made an unexpected incursion into Iran's political halfway house. Friends in the know in Tehran are intrigued that George W. Bush has asked for a private screening of Mohsen Makhmalbaf's film *Kandahar*, premiered at Cannes this year. Those of us who have long advocated the philosophical superiority of Iranian directors such as Makhmalbaf scarcely imagined that we would be counting a Republican president of the US amongst our number. Perhaps Bush's request again demonstrates the unpredictability of the political geometry between Washington, Kabul and Tehran.

I would give anything to be a fly on the wall in that screening room. Bush, whose de-clared taste in cinema, like that of Ronald Reagan, is for John Wayne westerns, might find himself somewhat restless in his seat. Whilst *Kandahar* is a denunciation of the Taliban, completed in haste in the spring of this year many months before the attacks on America, its techniques are closer to René Magritte than CNN. Like Magritte's eerily veiled por-traits, the women in the film are photographed mostly in full burkha, the dying light of the sun tantalisingly revealing details of their faces through the elaborate meshes of their out-fits. At one point the travelling sister encounters Médicins Sans Frontières field-workers awaiting delivery of artificial limbs. These are parachuted into southern Afghanistan; the images of them serenely floating earthwards are as dreamlike as anything by Giorgio de Chirico. In another scene, a male doctor tries to diagnose a woman's illness whilst each is screened off entirely from the other's view. A thick blanket hangs between them and only a peephole allows him to see sections of her body and perform his examination.

Some critics in Cannes judged *Kandahar's* denunciation of the Taliban to be stolid, but for me it was a masterpiece and a great piece of surrealism (the other this year being, intriguingly, *Mulholland Dr.* (2001) by David Lynch). In the end, Bush's request to see this remarkable film is a fascinating one. A typically Iranian cinematic meditation on veiled women, solar eclipses and the metaphoric blindness of the Taliban is being pressed into the service of *realpolitik*.

The *Tehran Times* said in an editorial recently that despite Fukuyama, the big questions in history, economics and culture are yet to be answered. Whatever your beliefs on this point, Iran is still debating it and that debate, like the film *Kandahar*, is not taking place solely on a material, secular and verbal level. That speculative quality is what makes this country so open to interpretation, and its cinema so vital.

IRAN

Why are Iranians such good filmmakers? There is a season of Iranian films coming up on British television in early May, the fullest ever retrospective of director Abbas Kiarostami at the National Film Theatre throughout the month, and an installation of his work at the V&A until June. Tehran-based directors have won, per capita, more movie prizes than those of any other country in recent years. In 1995, their feature films made 755 appearances at international film festivals. Britain, which has the same population, didn't manage half that. Some of the best women filmmakers in the world today are Iranian and even the country's teenagers are winning top prizes around the world. Akira Kurosawa, Jean-Luc Godard and Werner Herzog have called Abbas Kiarostami one of the great living filmmakers. An American critic said that 'we are living in the era of Kiarostami, but we don't yet know it'.

How can a country that is not technologically advanced, not rich, was not involved in the invention of cinema, which made no films of consequence before about 1959, whose artists are far from free and whose religion is suspicious of imagery, be leading the way?

The first, unexpected, answer is Islamisation. Like other movie houses at the end of the 1970s, Iranian cinemas showed mostly escapist entertainment films with lots of sex and violence. In one of his first speeches on returning to Iranian soil, Ayatollah Khomeini said that he wasn't against cinema, just the sleazy direction it had taken. Like Lenin, he felt that movies could 'purify' his country, and so his ministry of culture and Islamic guidance put in place a set of prohibitions: Iranian directors could not show women's hair or body parts, sexual touching of any sort, or any anti-government comment. What is less well known is that they also banned 'demeaning behaviour', denigration of people on grounds of ethnicity or creed, or violence. The latter was a bit rich from a regime which was more murderous than the one it replaced, but the irony is that the puritanism of the new Islamic Republic was rather similar to, say, John Grierson's social ambitions for British documentary in the 1930s.

Such ideas can result in cinema of dull worthiness, but it can now be seen that the preference of Khomeini's henchmen for spiritual and community themes over sexual or violent ones has rendered Iranian films graceful and satisfying compared to those of commercial industries. Forbid your filmmakers from representing what is called in film studies the 'male gaze' and you enter new territory, because much of cinema – Hollywood and the French new wave in particular – is based on it. The Islamisation of cinema in Iran decoupled looking and longing. The rest is history.

International audiences saturated in the conventional, hyper-eroticised cinema of Hol-

The groundbreaking, poetic *Khaneh siah ast/ The House is Black* (Forugh Farrokhzad, 1963)

lywood, Hong Kong, Japan and elsewhere have fallen for the Iranian mix of allegory and decency which, rather than skimming the surface of life, looks with patience at its fine grain.

I went to Tehran recently to make a television documentary for Channel 4 to accompany a series of classic Iranian films it is screening in early May. My brief was to make a programme which would sketch the outlines of Iranian cinema history and explain its uniqueness. After three weeks there, however, I discovered an additional, very different reason why the country makes such great films. I had been to Iran before – I drove the length of its West/East diagonal – so was not surprised by the warmth of its people, their lack of hatred of the West, the beauty of the architecture or how quickly at home I once again felt. But I hadn't worked there, and this was the eye-opener. I arrived hoping to interview all the key filmmakers and, in some cases, take them back to locations where they had filmed decades before. Without exception, they all said yes. Every door opened. People made themselves available the day we called, or the next, at our convenience. We shot on sets and in cutting rooms, with the top stars and the landmark directors.

This can-do attitude was a surprise, as was the complete flexibility of filming in Iran. We went there to make one documentary, but came back with three – the planned one, a half hour one in which Kiarostami travels to Karaj to meet one of his former actors, and a 74-minute film for cinema about Kiarostami's famous Rostamabad trilogy. Take a small example of the flexibility involved. A film called *Gaav/The Cow*, made in 1969 by the director Dariush Mehrjui and starring Ezzatollah Entezami, Iran's Sean Connery, was seminal. We suggested that, possibly, these two men might return to the village where it had been made. Neither is young, nor had either been back for 35 years. The trip meant five hours' driving through snowed-up roads. Yet both agreed to go. In Britain, agents, limousines, PRs, PAs and the rest would have been involved.

In Kiarostami's house one day we suggested going to see Babak Ahmadpoor, the man who, as a boy, played the lead role in Kiarostami's landmark film *Khane-ye doust kodjast/ Where is the Friend's House?* (1987). Because we were working with the best people, but also because time isn't so tight there and people are more open to suggestion, he said yes, and our filming became the basis of the second and third documentaries we made.

I have never experienced the degree of freedom we had as filmmakers in Iran to change our minds, to have the spark of an idea, and then realise it. It is the inertia of filmmaking – its resistance to change of plan, its heaviness of foot – which often sucks the life out of it. If, conversely, flexibility of approach is valued in a film culture then the time between idea and realisation is reduced.

True, it was the first time I had worked with new, ultra-portable cameras. But in the weeks since I have returned, I have come to believe that it was a human, rather than an organisational or technical, quality that made this shoot the most stimulating I have ever had. Call it optimism, or maybe commitment. When I rewatch the Kiarostami films in the retrospective, or those coming up soon on television, I will read between the lines, as it were, and look for evidence of the sort of artistic spontaneity we have just enjoyed.

RUSSIA

It's not every day that a big Hollywood star and one of its hottest directors reworks a Soviet metaphysical masterpiece of the 1970s. *Solaris*, starring George Clooney, directed by Steven Soderbergh and adapted from Andrei Tarkovsky's film of the same name, has opened in the US to neither highbrow nor lowbrow acclaim. The film's final reel in particular has been the subject of much head scratching, as it's sort of a happy ending but sort of not.

Solaris will no doubt be equally scrutinised when it opens here in January, but the ambiguity of its ending raises broader questions. The biggest box-office hits in Soviet and Russian cinema have always been tragedies, yet when they are shown in the US, they often have tagged-on happy endings. Nothing surprising in that, you might say. US cinema has conquered the world by being feel-good. Look at Steven Spielberg's *Minority Report* (2002), a splendid work of digital-gothic, ruined in its closing moments when Tom Cruise touches his pregnant wife's stomach.

In fact, the history of US cinema's optimism is more complex than this suggests. The American film noirs which influenced *Minority Report* were visually and tonally dark. *Gone with the Wind* (1939) has a very unhappy ending. *Titanic* (1997), the biggest US box-office hit of all time, is a tragedy (of sorts). Within a few years of Tarkovsky's original *Solaris*, Martin Scorsese made an equally bleak anti-musical – *New York, New York* (1977) – whose centrepiece was an exuberant dance routine called 'Happy Endings' – a homage to Judy Garland production numbers of the 1940s and 1950s. In an astonishing sign of the film world's 1970s ambivalence about utopia, 'Happy Endings' was cut from the film. The spirit of Judy Garland, it seemed, would not wash.

In the same year, 1977, Woody Allen's *Annie Hall* carried the ironic line, 'In the movies you should try to have happy endings, because life so rarely does.' Roman Polanski was closer to the spirit of the times when he had Faye Dunaway, the innocent victim in *Chinatown* (1974), shot through the eye at the end of the film.

Last scenes are so crucial in America that some stock market speculators judge the US mood by the prevailing endings of big movies. But what's even more remarkable is the influence of Russian film, working across a great cultural divide, on the cult of the ending. There are happy endings in Soviet and Russian films too, of course, but, unlike America, tragedy has always been the norm. The obvious reason is that Russia had an infernal twentieth century. Yet in other countries, cinema lightens as history darkens. Betty Grable songs were the biggest thing in the West during the Second World War. US cinema got jollier as the depression deepened. China went through as much as Russia, yet its movies rarely end in so many tears.

It would be easy to pontificate on the bottomless soul of Mother Russia. Yet neither Tolstoy nor Dostoevsky were notably more miserable than French or German novelists of the nineteenth century. No other major filmmaking nation, with the possible exception of Sweden, supports the argument that sombre literature begets sombre cinema. Even Satyajit Ray's adaptations of Rabindranath Tagore – the most serious Indian films ever made – pull their punches somewhat at the end, leaving open the possibility of hope.

Russia's special brand of cinematic gloom may owe something to the fact that when it entered the First World War in 1914, its borders were closed and no international films were shown. The Revolution was three years away, but in this short period, Russian directors started to evolve a unique tone. Tsarist era filmmakers like Evgenii Bauer and Yakov Protazanov made a string of great, sombre movies which have only recently been rediscovered. Bauer directed a scarcely believable eighty films between 1913 and 1917, when he died of pneumonia. With titles like *Posle smerti/After Death*, *Zhizn za zhizn/A Life for a Life* and *Umirayushchii Lebed/The Dying Swan* (in which an artist strangles a ballerina as soon as she falls in love with him) Bauer explored questions of how fate and natural forces foil human desire. Such films were hugely popular.

And just as Russian cinema was cooking on its melancholic gas, a group of US songwriters started to put pen to paper. The work of these men would become the manifesto of Hollywood utopianism. Irving Berlin had his first worldwide hit with 'Alexander's Ragtime Band' in 1911 and after the jazz age he penned classics such as 'Blue Skies', 'There's No Business Like Show Business' and 'God Bless America' for songbirds like Judy Garland, Ethel Merman, Eddie Cantor and Fred Astaire. While 'There's No Business Like Show Business', with its chin up, keep-smiling-through message, became a national anthem of hope, Yip Harburg was writing 'Over the Rainbow', a leftist ballad about self-improvement which anchored *The Wizard of Oz* (1939). Similarly, Al Dubin wrote the lyrics for *42nd Street* (1933), which became cinema's archetypal story of the chorus girl getting a big break and becoming a star.

The songs and themes of Berlin, Harburg and Dubin turned sound cinema into the most optimistic cultural industry anywhere in the world, and in doing so gave America a signature. That signature has become blurred at times and even today filmmakers find it oppressive. But here's the real puzzle about happy endings. Berlin, Harburg and Dubin were all Russians.

AFRICA

This year is the thirtieth anniversary of the release of one of the most interesting movies of the 1970s. It was made in the same year as *The Exorcist*. It hit the screens within months of Robert Altman's *The Long Goodbye* and Terrence Malick's *Badlands*, each of which is cherished by cinephiles. It is better than any of these, yet it has almost never been shown in British cinemas and only specialists are likely to have heard of it.

It is not a particularly difficult film. Like *Bonnie and Clyde* (1967), it is a story about young people on the run. Nor is it overly serious. Like Jean-Luc Godard's *À bout de souffle/ Breathless* (1960), it is playful and beautifully inventive. The reason that its anniversary is not being celebrated, that it isn't even mentioned in most serious film histories, that its brilliant director simply doesn't appear in the main film encyclopaedias, that it has never been shown on British television, that it occurs on almost none of those lists of all-time great films, that few people take it into account when they are writing about 1970s aesthetics, is this: it and its director are African.

Every aspect of American cinema of the 1970s has been poured over, every stone unturned, every seminal filmmaking dinner reported on, every drug-fuelled party detailed, every aesthetic advance celebrated. Peter Biskind's book *Easy Riders, Raging Bulls* should have been the last word in this yet instead it sent people looking under the same stones to retell the same stories. At exactly the time when Biskind's filmmakers – Martin Scorsese, Francis Ford Coppola, William Friedkin and Peter Bogdanovich – were storming the citadel of Hollywood, thousands of miles away from the coke parties and swimming pools of Los Angeles, an equally vibrant film culture was blossoming in Dakar, Senegal. Striking films made by passionate and complex directors were released in such rapid succession that it was hard to keep up, yet nearly forty years after black Africans started making films about themselves, few in the West have even the most basic co-ordinates with which to plot this Senegalese wave of talent.

The first films shown on the continent were British shorts, screened in Johannesburg in 1896. In the subsequent six decades, African cinema consisted largely of Western filmmakers setting their Tarzan movies there, or films like *The African Queen* (1951) which were told from the point of view of a white missionary. No significant black African directors emerged. In 1935, the Misr studio in Cairo became the first of its kind in the Arab-African world and, as a result, an industry developed in Egypt, which has remained the continent's biggest film producer. Its output comprised mostly comedies and musicals but Kamal Selim's *El Azima/The Will* (1939) was the first to bring some kind of social realism to the screen.

The wind of de-colonial change in the 1950s and the Bandung Conference in Indonesia in 1955 began to establish indigenous cultural production as a political imperative, but again it was the north of the continent which led the way. The Egyptian Youssef Chahine produced the seminal *Bab el hadid/Cairo Station* in 1958, which mixed melodrama, tragedy and scenes of a women's campaign against marriage. Its style was as bold as that of the American director Nicholas Ray.

The 1960s started with the Sharpeville massacre and the imprisonment of Mandela but in 1966, exactly seventy years after the first screenings on the continent – and, it should be noted, three years *before* the first major American film directed by a black person – the first black African feature was made, in Dakar. The director was a former Citroên factory worker and novelist, Ousmane Sembène, who had studied filmmaking in Moscow. The film was *La Noire de.../Black Girl*, about the housemaid of a white French family who goes to live in France with them, becomes depressed and commits suicide. Sembène used an interior monologue to let us hear her thoughts and had that monologue spoken by a different actress, the first of many experimental techniques used in African cinema in the next two decades. He studied filmmaking in Moscow, as have many of the greatest directors who followed in his footsteps.

Sembène became the father of black African cinema and, sustained in part by subsidies from the French government, Dakar became its mini-LA. While Francophone Africa would produce a series of master directors in the years to come, Anglophone Africa produced none.

Again in Dakar, the next great director to make his name was Djibril Diop Mambéty who, aged 28, made *Touki Bouki*, the film whose thirty-year anniversary is now so conspicuous by its absence. The title means 'Journey of the Hyenas' in the local language of Wolof, and throughout his career Mambéty used hyenas to symbolise the viciousness of human beings. This caustic road movie was Africa's *Easy Rider* and is the continent's first modernist film. It would be twenty years before Mambéty made his next feature. Called simply *Hyenas*, it was another masterpiece.

Meanwhile, in Mali, Souleymane Cissé released *Baara* (1978) and *Finye/The Wind* (1982). Like Sembène, Cissé studied in Moscow. His work at this time was less fable-like than Sembène's but, as in *Baara* ('the world of labour'), he captures the richness of African city life. In the more spiritual *The Wind*, one character says 'Our knowledge and sense of the divine has escaped us.' In Ethiopia, the UCLA-trained Haile Gerima directed *Mirt Sost Shi Amit/Harvest 3,000 Years* in 1975, a brilliant, slow-moving portrait of farming life, shot rigorously with long lenses. One character dreams of a place 'where there are no flies and no Europeans'. It ends with a local mad man, Kebebe, killing the sadistic black landowner.

Where American cinema started to take a nosedive in the 1980s, Africa underwent a golden age. A film festival at Ouagadougou, the capital of Burkina Faso, to the south of Mali, became its showcase. When Gaston Kaboré made *Wend Kuuni/God's Gift* there in 1982, the continent had another landmark. This story about a mute child adopted by a whole

La Noire de...: the first black African feature film

village had echoes of films by Truffaut and Herzog, but its theme of pre-colonial solidarity made it more powerful than either. Still in Burkina Faso, Med Hondo's *Sarraounia* (1986) was a Kurosawa-like epic about a warrior queen. The following year, Cissé made his best film yet, the astonishing *Yeelen* and Sembène set *Camp de Thiaroye/The Camp at Thiaroye* amongst black infantrymen during the Second World War.

The 1990s continued to produce outstanding films. Dani Kouyaté's *Keita! L'héritage du griot/Keita, The Legend of the Griot* (Burkina Faso, 1995) was the best of many films about African oral traditions, and as recently as last year, Abderrahmane Sissako's *Heremankono/ Waiting for Happiness*, made in Senegal's northern neighbour Mauritania, gave anything made in the West a run for its money. Again, Sissako studied in Moscow.

The contours of African film history are much more rich and complex than this quick run-down can possibly suggest. It is peopled with artists who articulated their countries' modernity as much as Scorsese, Coppola, Schrader, Malick, Bogdanovich or Rafelson. This was not some distant modernity that we in the West who are much closer to the American psyche could only vaguely understand. The portraits of human society and sub-jectivity in the great films of Sembène, Mambéty, Cissé, Gerima, Hondo and Sissako are as relevant to us as those of their American colleagues. That our film magazines, TV and radio programmes, books and festivals do nothing major to explore the film ecology of Western Francophone Africa – to take just this area – and do nothing to mark thirty years of *Touki Bouki* is, in the end, our loss.

African Revenge
(this 2007 article was not written for *Prospect* but expands on the above)

Where would movies be without the fire and phlegm of revenge? It's the driving force in Quentin Tarantino's *Kill Bill* films (2003; 2004) and *Death Proof* (2007). Reprisal is a dish served cold in Korean director Park Chan-wook's trilogy *Boksuneun nauigeot/Sympathy for Mr Vengeance* (2002), *Oldboy* (2003) and *Chinjeolhan geumjassi/Sympathy for Lady Vengeance* (2005). *Gladiator* kicked off the new millennium with Old Testament revenge. And it was the same further back. A 1960s western like *C'era una volta il West/Once Upon a Time in the West* (1968) is a retaliation opera. *The Godfather* (1972–1990) trilogy is a Rembrandtesque study in vengeance. The films of Don Siegel, Jean-Pierre Melville and Robert Siodmak are cratered with revenge. The first commandment of genres like martial arts, horror, grindhouse, gangster and rape revenge is an eye for en eye. Grindhouse and horror seem high on it. Retaliation, in these genres, is narcotic.

It's in pop songs and novels, theatre and opera too. And it's surely no surprise. The desire to hurt someone who's hurt you is a primitive impulse; its moderation or otherwise is the stuff of the great religions.

But in cinema revenge is particularly prevalent, because it has a movie *shape*. A cruel act – a false imprisonment, say, or the murder of a relative – sparks a quest for retribution that is suspenseful because its conclusion will be violent. Revenge isn't multiple, like novels are multiple, but singular, like classic movies.

So how do we explain the fact that the continent of Africa, which has rather more reason to be vengeful than the Anglophone world because of the iniquities of colonialism, has hardly produced any films about getting its own back? Lots of wonderful movies have been made in Africa since the 1960s yet, unlike Tarantino or Sergio Leone or Park Chan-wook, its great movie makers don't seem excited by the idea of filming people hunting down and hurting those who have hurt them. You'd expect centuries of oppression, humiliation and exploitation to have a caused a continent-wide psychological need for catharsis and, indeed, African life has been tragically bloody for decades now. But its movies don't really reflect this.

Take *Dry Season/Daratt* (2006), for example, the last African film released in the UK, made in Chad by Mahamat-Saleh Haroun. In it, a sixteen-year-old youth sets off to find and murder the man who killed his father. He takes a job in a bakery owned by the murderer, watching him every day, choosing his moment. Surely this is a classic revenge situation? Yes, the film broods with *andante* suspense, but in the end the son only pretends to kill the assassin, so *Daratt* is about the dissolution of the impulse to avenge. It looks at retaliation through a fresher lens than bravura western directors like Tarantino.

But what, then, about *Bamako* (2007), the previous African film shown in the UK, in which a trial is held in a courtyard in Mali's capital city? In it, African society is the plaintiff and the legacy of colonialism and the world financial institutions are in the dock. Again the stage is set for a revenge story – the film stares the evils of colonialism squarely in the eye – but what unfolds is witness bearing, not vengeance.

And, further back in the history of African film, when the wounds of colonialism were still raw and so cinematic retaliation might be both more expected and excusable, it seldom appears either. Even those classic African films that seem to be about vengeance, or look as if they will depict it, aren't quite and don't. Med Hondo's *Sarraounia*, for example, made in Burkina Faso and Mauritania in 1986, is one of the continent's angriest movies. It is set in 1899 in the Sudan, amidst French atrocities committed against locals. But it shows resistance to, rather than vengeance for, those crimes. It lacks a time lag and, therefore, doesn't deal with the psychology of delayed anger. The plot of the late Senegalese director Ousmane Sembène's masterpiece *Ceddo* (1977) similarly sounds like a springboard for retribution: in an unspecified past, the Ceddo tribe are threatened by the spiritual colonisation of Arab-Islam and Euro-Christianity, and physical slavery. They must choose between insurrection or integration. Sembène is too busy charting the implications of this choice to look at belated bloodletting.

Egyptian director Youssef Chahine's state of the nation film *al-Asfour/The Sparrow* (1972) climaxes with Nasser's shock announcement of the loss of the Sinai during the Six Day War. His characters are stunned. The matriarch of the film, Bahiyya, runs into the streets, overwhelmed and yelling 'We won't accept defeat!' Chahine's tracking shots of her are amongst the greatest moments in world cinema – passionately melodramatic and moving – yet his film stops short of vengeance.

I could go on, but the point is surely clear. Neither new African cinema nor the great films by founding fathers Sembène and Chahine nor mid-period master directors like Hondo are much about retaliation. Why not? As many of the great African films – and there are loads of them – are co-funded by the French government, it's tempting to think that the former oppressors have baulked at financing films in which wrongdoing is avenged. This may be so – only an analysis of African film projects rejected for French funding would show whether it is – but even if it were, it would only be a partial explanation.

More relevant, I think, is the fact that, with the exception of Egypt, Nigeria and South Africa, the continent's movies have been closer to what we in Europe think of as art cinema, and so have not been an expression of populist rage and resentment.

This is not to say that there's no fury in African movies, just that they aren't, on the whole, populist. It's certainly there – few filmmakers in the world were more militant than Sembène and his brilliant compatriot Djibril Diop Mambéty. But instead of that fury being embodied by lone avengers like Clint Eastwood or Jimmy Cagney, their angry people are likely to be women, in the case of Sembène, or the tone of their movies is likely to be wildly satirical, like Mambéty's *Touki Bouki* or *Hyenas* or Sembène's *Xala* (1975). *Hyenas* seems to be about rage – a jilted former lover, who has since become 'richer than the world bank', returns to her home village to punish the man she loved by promising the villagers that, if they kill him, she will give them all the consumer goods they want. But it is the locals' greed that vexes director Mambéty, not the woman's ire. And the story itself is European, adapted from a play by Friedrich Durrenmatt. After an hour or more of crisp gender satire in Sembène's *Xala*, a troupe of disabled people do circle in on the movie's greedy and self-important central character. They enact a revenge of sorts by spitting on him, the shock of the act coming from the very fact that it is so rare in African movies. Both films are about women, in many ways, and women are just as capable of wanting revenge as men, of course, but the target of their ire in African cinema is as likely to be obdurate black men as domineering white states, so their narratives do not usually have nice clean vengeance contours. And the influence of *griots* – storytellers – on African film stops them being clean-cut eye-for-an-eye movies too. From the mid-1970s onwards, such griots have woven their way through African cinema, turning fact into fable, and interpreting events. This takes some of the raw anger out of the plots, rendering them mythic.

All of the above are relevant but the real answer to why African films are less vengeful than ours comes from Sembène again. In his great book on the director, David Murphy quotes him as saying 'you don't tell a story for revenge but rather to understand your place in the world'. Surely that's it. African cinema is angry, yes, and driven, but not by the need to retaliate. *Daratt* and *Bamako*, *Touki Bouki*, *Hyenas* and Souleymane Cissé's *Yeelen*, *Ceddo* and *The Sparrow* are too busy working out how Africans should live with other Africans – what Edward Said called the move from filiation to affiliation – to deal with the almost decadent matter of revenge. Vengeance is for people with time on their hands. Eastwood and Cagney, Oh Dae-su in *Oldboy* and Charles Bronson's Harmonica man in *Once Upon a Time in the West* had bags of time. African movies in the 1970s looked around at the rubble left by colonialism and said 'OK, now that we've shook them off, where do we go from here?' In the 1980s they turned the clock backwards and told stories of pre-colonial times, to ask 'Where were we before they came? And can we pick up a thread from those times?' These were such brilliant and relevant questions that, in comparison, vengeance stories were for wusses.

Back in the Anglophone West, we have begun a cycle of Iraq movies – *The Kingdom* (2007), Brian De Palma's *Redacted* (2007), etc – that have the feel of apology and atonement about them. It's right to say sorry, of course, but maybe our filmmakers could take a leaf out of Africa's book by not only saying gotcha or sorry, but by making dazzling films about finding a place in the world.

MEXICO

At the Oscars this year, it seemed a dead cert that the best cinematography award would go to one of two Mexicans. Emmanuel Lubezki's photography in Terrence Malick's *The New World* was astonishing, and Mexico City-born Rodrigo Prieto shot this year's hottest film, *Brokeback Mountain*. When neither won, you could feel the disappointment from Baja to Veracruz.

I am in Mexico City as a guest programmer at the city's international contemporary film festival (FICCO), and it has been fascinating to see the complex manner in which the country relates to its cinema. In recent years there has been much to be proud of. *Amores perros/Loves a Bitch* (2000) and *Y tu mamá también/And Your Mother Too (2001)* were international art-house hits. The lead in both – Gael García Bernal – is one of world cinema's hottest stars. Salma Hayek went to Hollywood and made good. Alfonso Cuarón, the director of *Y tu mamá también*, did the same, and ended up helming box-office juggernauts such as *Harry Potter and the Prisoner of Azkaban* (2004). Rodrigo Prieto seems never to draw breath. Hollywood is hoovering up Mexican talent. Such attention boosts the ego, but Mexico's sense of itself as a movie-making nation has always been richer than that of local boys and girls making good.

From the start, movies played a role in the nation. Its 1910 revolution was not only filmed; Pancho Villa is said to have staged some of his campaigns for the camera. In the 1930s, Veracruz-born Fernando de Fuentes was the country's first important director and virtually invented its national cinema. Like Lubezki and Prieto, Gabriel Figueroa was one of the greatest cinematographers of his day – working with de Fuentes in the 1930s, studying with Orson Welles' favourite director of photography, Gregg Toland, then giving the consistently sparkling look to the 1940s films of Emilio Fernández – the country's second great director.

De Fuentes, Fernández and Figueroa together created a national cinema which took a distinctly Mexican approach to subjects like indigenous people, peasant versus city life and religious piety. In terms of actors, Cantinflas and Tin Tan were massively popular comedians in the Chaplin mode. Dolores del Rio became a star in Mexico as well as a mem-

A kiss across a yawning social divide in *Battle in Heaven*

orable character actress in Hollywood. And María Félix was so famous that she seemed to transcend cinema.

By the late 1940s, Mexican cinema was on a roll. But then came Luis Buñuel, guns blazing. The Spanish surrealist made films in Mexico between 1946 and 1965, a sabbatical about which the country is rightly proud, though Buñuel's mockery of Mexican archetypes created mixed feelings. At the parties and discussions at FICCO this year, it was clear that there was a similar ambivalence about the new wave of Mexican cinema that we have so admired in Europe.

Take two of the most distinctive films of this new wave – Cuarón's *Y tu mamá también* and Carlos Reygadas' *Batalla en el cielo/Battle in Heaven* (2005). I could find hardly anyone with a good word to say about either. At first I thought this was tall poppy syndrome, but later it became clear that something more interesting was at play.

Y tu mamá también is about the friendship between an upper-class teenager and his lower-class friend. *Batalla en el cielo/Battle in Heaven* (2005) depicts an intense relationship between a high-class young woman and her working-class chauffeur. Mexico's massive class divisions – a sliver of a cultural elite, another sliver of a middle class and a huge majority of poor people – explained the potent anxiety of both films. Each was made from within the cultural elite. Each imagines the elite engaging with those beneath it.

Each encounter has a sexual dimension. Watching *Brokeback Mountain* in Mexico, you're struck by how many times the script suggests that Mexico is a place of sexual liberty. The Mexican new wave films point to the fallout from such freedom. Encouraged by an older woman they both fancy, the male teenagers from different worlds in *Y tu mamá también* kiss. Afterwards they recoil from the moment and their friendship breaks down. The kiss, and its divisive impact, is a bleak metaphor for the impossibility of class interaction in Mexico. I heard it said several times here in Mexico that the film is too American – yet its pessimistic ending could hardly be less so. I think its portrait of social immobility touched a nerve.

Battle in Heaven's cross-class sexual contact is even more disturbing. The films begins with the rich girl crying as she fellates her entirely expressionless chauffeur. The fact that the scene is so implausible seems to make some Mexicans dismiss the film as fake or patronising. But seen as a pitiless metaphor for the social divisions in the country, the sex scenes are devastating.

In Mexican cinema, elite filmmakers create the aesthetic while a majority social class provides the subject matter. Both form and content reveal the impossibility of social marriage – and the result is remarkably challenging.

It's the question of who gets to tell the story that makes people uneasy. Down the road, the first big-budget film set in the Mayan period is being shot. A key story in Mexico's history is coming to a multiplex near you. Its director? An Australian filmmaker called Mel Gibson.

The People's Republic of China wants to do business with the rest of the world. The rest of the world is falling over itself to do business with the People's Republic. The recent Shanghai International Film Festival showed how one industry – cinema – is trying to handle this heady attraction. Against the roar of a city of 17.5m people rebuilding itself, delegations from Mexico, Finland, Australia, France, America, Britain, Spain – to name just those I noticed – were in town, exchanging business cards, trying to learn Sino-business etiquette. Like a ball scene in a Jane Austen novel, courtships were initiated and discourse was formal. The dance was somewhat macabre, but many of the attempts at connection were sincere. At a seminar on Sino-Hollywood co-operation, Ang Lee insisted that LA and Beijing can make films together if they focus on the inner lives of human beings. I was in Shanghai to publicise the Mandarin edition of my last book and, in interview after interview, I was asked to describe Chinese cinema, as if it really mattered what we in the West thought of it.

Comparison of the hard facts about Chinese and developed-world film shows the complexity of the integration process. Unlike in the modern capitalist economies, the Chinese film market is massively underscreened. There are 38,500 auditoria on the mainland, the same number as in America. If cinema ticket sales reached the level of America's (about four per person a year), and even if they were pegged at just $1 a pop, $3bn extra revenue would be earned each year. And that's cinema alone. Add twice this amount from DVD and you have $100bn in a decade. The Chinese government obviously wants much of this, and some of it will be pocketed by the American multiplexers with whom it has already formed partnerships. But domestic films represent 68.5 per cent of the market in China (the figure is less than twenty per cent for most European countries), and even if this proportion drops to fifty per cent by 2015, the film industry stands to gross perhaps $4bn a year – almost as much as America, in a country with far lower overheads and labour costs.

When the film trade magazines list the most powerful people in the business, the Chinese will soon be at or near the top. Who will these powerbrokers be? In the capitalist economies, a powerful but unconfident LA-based oligarchy sustains but deforms markets around the world by pumping them with cinematic steroids. In China, all film production, exhibition and development decisions must be approved by the State Administration for Radio, Film and Television (SARFT). Such state control means that indie and DV (digital video) filmmakers must work in semi-secret and that approval of completed films can be slow or ridiculously censorious. But SARFT behaves more interestingly than might be expected. Some of SARFT's senior figures are former filmmakers and technophiles, fascinated by the digital era. Hence, perhaps, the fact that the highly funded Beijing Film Academy is one of the world's best film schools. Some $10m has

One of the greatest stars of 1930s cinema: the almost forgotten Ruan Linyu in *Shen nu/ The Goddess* (Wu Yonggang, 1934)

been set aside to digitise a thousand feature films a year in China – creating what will soon be the world's biggest digital archive for film. Martin Scorsese and Steven Spielberg have long campaigned for an increase in digitisation to rescue fading film prints. In one decision, SARFT can authorise such activity on an unprecedented scale. Provided they digitise the right films to the right standard, film history will thank them. If we leave such research and development to the steroid capitalist market, it will be done piecemeal, and only when someone spies a profit.

That could well be the Chinese motive too, and the Chinese state is wrong in much that it does, but its ability to act strategically, to steer change in the film world when digital and delivery convergence demands it, is surely exciting to the film pragmatists in America and Europe.

What was clear in Shanghai was that Chinese top-downism and Western steroid-capitalism are attracted to each other's strengths. It is possible to imagine that, by 2050, for example, China could be the R&D centre of global film. It would provide the world's film studio and post-production needs. It could deliver audiovisual content to cinemas, home computers and handsets around the world. It could be home to a great archive – the film equivalent of the library of Alexandria, endorsed by UNESCO. Europe, America, Africa and the Middle East would provide individual filmmaking voices, writers, directors, actors and stories, and aesthetic ideas, which would guarantee the plurality and subjectivity of world cinema – aspects that China is, for the time being, still struggling to develop.

This is perhaps a pipe dream, and assumes that the courtships that I saw beginning proceed smoothly. It acknowledges that there's stuff we're good at and stuff they're good at. It assumes harmonisation in crucial areas like human rights. But in Shanghai today there are independent production companies, often set up by Vancouver-Chinese, who are fast becoming go-betweens between state and foreign companies. Such diaspora Chinese will surely be the dance masters of the future.

MOSCOW

As I write, the world's press if full of comment about Hollywood's latest blockbuster, *The Kingdom*, in which US government agents, led by movie star *du jour* Jamie Foxx, investigate a terrorist bomb in a Western housing complex in Saudi Arabia.

Yawn. Not only is the plot shop-soiled, the idea that we can see the state of America reflected in Hollywood's latest bauble is, too. Yes, the US is anxious about the Middle East and yes its mainstream entertainments express this anxiety, but *The Kingdom* does this so obviously that there's nothing new to say.

The real story about mainstream cinema lies in another big, flashy entertainment film that opens this week. Its titles begin with the logo of Rupert Murdoch's 20th Century Fox studio. Nothing surprising about that. But the film's name is *Dnevnoy dozor* – *Day Watch* in English. And, box-office wise, it is the biggest movie made in Russia since the fall of the Soviet empire.

But its bigness isn't the story. *Day Watch* got disdainful one- and two-star reviews from the UK's posh critics – the *Sunday Times* called it 'unbearably noisy and deadening' – yet Danny Boyle said that the film to which it is a sequel, *Nochnoy dozor/Night Watch* (2004), would have Tarkovsky spinning in his grave and Quentin Tarantino called it 'an epic of extraordinary power'. And I am considering ending the updated version of my book *The Story of Film* with it. Where *The Kingdom* is tired, *Night Watch* and *Day Watch* excited me, for the first time in ages, about the aesthetics of entertainment cinema. What's going on?

In the 1990s, mainstream American cinema was boring. Then, unexpectedly, came Keanu Reeves as Neo in his big black coat, balletically dodging bullets that caused the air around him to ripple. *The Matrix* (1999) captured the excitement of the dawn of cyberspace. Thereafter, Hollywood returned to rote and my attention wandered to movies from other parts of the world, where innovation made itself less scarce. So exciting were the films I discovered from Iran, Africa, Japan, South America and India that I didn't in the slightest miss my old pal, US movie entertainment.

Flash forward to August 2007. I deign to see a press screening of *Day Watch*. I'd heard that *Night Watch*, its predecessor, was a sci-fi/vampire *Matrix* mish-mash, so gave it a body swerve. I sit in the front row of the cinema, the curtains open and there unspools before me a big, testosterone-fuelled, CGI-engorged, market-sassy film – wearyingly familiar blockbuster elements – that makes the *Lord of the Rings* trilogy (2001–2003) look creatively puny, which it is.

The surfaces of *Day Watch* and *Night Watch*, which I've since seen, are the first things you notice. The films' subtitles respond to the action, splishing on walls, slashed by knives, vibrating when doors are banged. The Manichean world of the story, though unfathomable and probably absurd, has a torque around which everything seems to spin. Contemporary Moscow represents Light (but is still like a film noir) and is contrasted to a Dark parallel world that looks like Fritz Lang's *Metropolis* (1927) mixed with porridge and whizzed in a food processor. Shot and scene transitions are mostly whipping morphs of some form – though they happen so fast (and I was having so much fun) that I couldn't always clock them. About forty minutes into *Day Watch*, a male and female pair of characters swap bodies, and the effect is less *Freaky Friday* than as if Bogie and Bacall had done so – sexy and insolent. The clothes are Helmut Newton meets Jessica Rabbit meets Sergio Leone meets the Wachowski brothers.

The interesting question, I think, is how the movies have come to look so new. Their fortysomething Kazakh writer-director Timur Bekmambetov started off in commercials and music videos – nothing new in that. He debuted as a feature filmmaker in 1994 then, in 2000, helmed the ultra-trash sword and thong soft-core gladiatorial flick *The Arena*, executive produced by the legendary B-movie producer Roger Corman. *The Arena* was hardly an artistic stretch for Bekmambetov, and the acting was appalling, but as long as the breast count is high, Corman leaves you alone, so Bekmambetov had a chance to experiment with digital effects and prepared his CGI palette for *Night Watch*.

Film imagery in the digital age can feel affectless but what gives the *Watch* movies some weight is that, like the great city films before them, their production designer's stylebook is highly responsive to a remarkable piece of urbanism – in this case, Moscow. In 2005, Bekmambetov explained that 'half my mentality is Russian reality – very poor people, lots of problems, very rich oil barons, Roman Abramovich ... and half of me is the filmmaker – vampires, Roger Corman, *The Matrix*, American movies. Stylistically I feel that Moscow is a very grey, very depressing city but our idea was to make a movie that something sharp and saturated was happening [in] ... the 1990s were a very, very strange time in Russia ... the country was broken into two parts, the people older than twenty ... and a new generation that grew up without communism.'

This explains much, I think: the Manichaeism of the *Watch* films, their porridgy look that keeps bursting into fields of colour, their youthful energy, their sense of being haunted by ghosts, their *noir* melancholia, and their escapism. They are daft, and even boring at times, but stylistically revelatory. Bekmambetov's comments suggest that their visual distinction is a result of their Dionysian response to Russia's extraordinary social change.

Bekmambetov has pulled the centre of gravity of mainstream filmmaking eastwards. It would be nice to think that it would stay there for a while, but he has signed a deal with Hollywood and is making an action thriller starring Morgan Freeman, Angelina Jolie and James McAvoy. The company? Universal, who made *The Kingdom*.

AMERICA IN A HUFF February 2007

The new rules for tax relief on filmmaking in Britain that came into effect on 1 January have already caused what in Scotland is called a 'stooshie'. It started on 5 December 2006, when the Department of Culture, Media and Sport (DCMS) published its 'final framework of the cultural test for British film', a point system that scores new movies for Britishness. The new system will make it harder for films like the *Star Wars* prequels, which have no British storyline or cultural relevance but were partly filmed here, to help themselves to some of the £120m in tax breaks doled out to filmmakers. This tougher line, insisted upon by the European commission, has caused grumbles. According to the *Times*, Hollywood responded with a speedy threat to snub Britain as a place to make films.

On the face of it, the new ruling seems sensible. Most people would accept that movies like *My Beautiful Laundrette* (1985), *Billy Elliot* (2000) and *The Queen* (2006) captured something essential about the character of Britain, and so should benefit from state support. Conversely, why should our taxes subsidise Hollywood films? Nor are the new guidelines too strict. The *Harry Potter* films, though made with mostly American money, will still get tax breaks because they are set in Britain, adapted from British novels and full of British thesps. Ditto the Bond films.

But to argue this way ignores the benefit of inward investment. Making *Star Wars* (1977) or *Batman Begins* (2005) or *United 93* (2006) here not only contributes to the economy, but maintains skills and ensures that technicians are at the top of their game for the next British film that needs them. The new guidelines jeopardise such contributions, so Hollywood's threatened snub should be taken seriously.

The solution to the stooshie is obvious: split the cultural and enterprise agendas. Instead of one set of DCMS-Treasury guidelines that scores both the cultural and economic contribution a film will make to Britain, have DCMS rules about culture on the one hand, and an inward investment support mechanism on the other. Two sets of rules, because films create culture and money. Only occasionally does the same film do both, which strengthens the argument for twin tracks.

More interesting, though, is the psychology of America's response to the new rules. If I were a studio honcho and the dollar was this weak against the pound, I'd be alert to, and riled by, the old-world snobbery of cultural testing. The bouncers at the door of European culture like my Hollywood money, but not my dressed-down escapism. Furthermore, I'd argue that it's me and my Hollywood pals who fuel moviegoing internationally: our block-busters – *Jaws* (1975), *Star Wars*, *Titanic* (1997) – enthral people on every continent and put cinema at the centre of world entertainment. I make cinema exciting – and puny, elitist film cultures like Britain's benefit as a result.

These responses are reasonable, but old hat. Since 1918, when Hollywood began to dominate international cinema, its relationship with the rest of the world has been ambivalent. Other countries have repeatedly legislated to limit its influence, as if its products were diseased. Britain's 'Eady Levy', first proposed by Harold Wilson's government and incorporated in 1957, was a tax on cinema tickets to raise money for culturally British films. To the US it looked like an attempt to circumnavigate the global GATT agreement, which prevented direct subventions to the movie industry. When France introduced the idea of *l'exception culturelle* into the 1993 GATT negotiations, and when, in 2005, UNESCO accepted it as a universal means of protecting cultural diversity, America argued that it was economically penalised by such debarring. The ringleaders of the Iranian Revolution argued that US cinema was immoral, and so funded those who wanted to reinvent film as a medium of art. There are many other examples.

Hollywood has, in its view, endured such obloquy for decades now, often from countries whose populations clamour for the new *Star Wars* or the latest Mel Gibson movie. When you are stigmatised and powerless, you sulk or unravel. When you are stigmatised and powerful, you flex your muscles elsewhere. So it has been with Hollywood.

The reasonableness of America's response depends on where you sit. Hollywood cannot see itself as others do. It doesn't get that its often well-intended optimism can not only pall but, in its falsity, freeze the spine. An example proves the point. In 2001, Alfonso Cuarón made *Y tu mamá también*, a brilliantly entertaining road movie about sex and class. It scores 7.7/10 on the Internet Movie Database, as good a guide to popular English-language taste as exists, and took about $30m in cinemas around the world – fantastic for a Mexican film. In the same year, *Pearl Harbor*, *Planet of the Apes* and *Jurassic Park 3* were released. Nearly everyone agreed that they were all very boring. Yet they took at least $450m, $360m and $360m respectively. Hollywood – by saturating advertising sites, film magazines and other media, and by pre-booking the biggest screens in major cities – forced the market into consuming these tedious, inept, formulaic films. It created a wave of maximised awareness and minimised choice.

The point has been made before but, in the light of the British tax stooshie, the paradox needs to be reasserted. The movie free-marketeers have created an unfree market. In psychological terms, Hollywood has a persecution complex. It thinks that everyone is against it, when in fact it gets what it wants – which is sometimes wonderful – most of the time. When what it wants is not wonderful, it should expect to be shunned, and shouldn't get the hump. The DCMS is right to set its cultural test, and should, perhaps, go further.

CANNES 2

June 2007

This year was my sixteenth Cannes Film Festival. Once again it was good for the mind – I saw great films – and bad for the body – waiting in line for films, I was roasted in the Riviera sunshine; I auto-pickled in *Provençal* wine because half the people I know in the film world were on the Croisette, so there was an awful lot of lubricated catching up to do; and I porked up by two kilogrammes. If you've ever considered going to Cannes (it's quite easy), only do so if you prefer your mind to your body. This is not the case for me, but by now I'm far too hooked.

After 2002's festival, I raved about *Russkiy kovcheg/Russian Ark*, directed Aleksandr Sokurov. To my delight, it became an art-house hit in the UK. The 2003 event was a grand stand-off between films depicting an American, violent malaise (Clint Eastwood's *Mystic River*, Lars von Trier's excoriating *Dogville*), and those, made in Asia, that saw human beings as a gentler species. By Cannes 2004, this gentleness had blossomed, in films like Zhang Yimou's *Shi mian mai fu/The House of Flying Daggers* and Wong Kar-wai's *2046*, into a garden of Asian pictorial delights. I had never, in one festival, seen so many gorgeous images. In 2005 and 2006, violence was again the theme (David Cronenberg's *A History of Violence*, Michael Haneke's *Caché*), but the best films came from European directors like Haneke, the Dardenne brothers and Pedro Almodóvar. This year's festival continued some of these ideas: the new Coen brothers movie, *No Country for Old Men*, is about American violence, as is David Fincher's (OK) *Zodiac*, James Gray's (terrible) *We Own the Night* and Quentin Tarantino's (not very good) *Death Proof*. Some of the Asian films – like Hou Hsiao-hsien's *Le Voyage du ballon rouge/The Red Balloon* – were splendid. No nation or region stood out but, for the first time in my memory of Cannes, all the best films, the ones that touched me most, were about human goodness.

Where the Coens' adaptation of the great Cormac McCarthy novel was a pitch perfect illustration of how avarice divides, as was the Korean film *Milyang/Secret Sunshine*, whose Jeon Do-yeon won the best actress prize, the Palme d'Or went to *4 luni, 3 saptamâni si 2 zile/4 Months, 3 Weeks and 2 Days*, Cristian Mungiu's film which everyone seemed to think was brilliant but bleak. It was indeed brilliant but, I'd argue, not that bleak. Though set in the grim half-light of Romanian communism, the film's defining moment is a young woman agreeing to the demand of a sleazy abortionist to have sex with him in order that he will terminate the pregnancy of her friend. Her act is selfless. She gets exasperated with her friend, and scared when she has to dispose of the foetus, but she did a great, complex, generous, ennobling thing, and that, for me, gave the film its hope, and originality.

The German-Turkish director Fatih Akin built his magnificent film, *Auf der anderen seite/The Edge of Heaven*, around two such ennobling things. In the first, a Turkish Professor of German (and how often do we see a Turk play a Professor of anything in a film?) decides to find and pay for the education of a young Kurdish woman whose mother has died. The first part of the movie enacts his quest to do so. As Akin's intricate plot unfolds and doubles back on itself, we watch as the young woman's German girlfriend is accidentally shot dead. Her mother is distraught, travels to Turkey where the shooting takes place and decides to continue the task her daughter had undertaken, which was to try to get justice for the Kurdish girlfriend, who has been imprisoned. Eventually, the Professor and the mother meet. Akin's fine-tooled narrative means that neither knows that their separate quests are so intimately linked. Their scenes together – two quiet, decent, cautious people, a Turk and a German, taking risks in their lives for the sake of someone they don't know – are the best moments I've ever seen in a movie about the relationship between the two countries. Akin's film is as well structured as a Nic Roeg picture, and as moving as *Das Leben der Anderen/The Lives of Others* (2006). When his credits rolled and I realised that the mother was played by that muse of Fassbinder, Hannah Schygulla, I was overwhelmed.

But, for my money, a film in Cannes 2007 by Aleksandr Sokurov, he of *Russian Ark*, was even better. *Alexandra* is about the eponymous eighty-year-old grandmother who travels, with great difficulty, to a Russian army camp in Chechnya to visit her grandson, who is a soldier there. Just as Shakespeare's Henry V, on the night before Agincourt, wanders, disguised, through his soldiers' camps, listening to their chat, their faces lit by flickering campfires, 'a little touch of Harry in the night', so Alexandra goes on a similar night-time wander and then a second stroll, to a local village market, where she meets Chechen women her own age. One of them sees that her feet are sore, and that she is tired from the heat, so takes her to her home in wrecked Grozny (which is a shell of a city, like Berlin after the Second World War), for some tea and a rest. An act of simple human kindness.

As Alexandra potters, she experiences sensory overload – especially regarding the smell of the young men and the steel and iron of their weapons and tanks – and, in the hands of Sokurov, who is a master at depicting rumination, such sense perceptions become nothing less than a Joycean odyssey. Alexandra is a curmudgeon and insufficiently thankful when a Chechen lad, filmed as if he was in a Pier Paolo Pasolini film, escorts her right back to the Russian camp, but she emerges, I think, as the most distinctive character I've ever seen in a war movie. The idea of the film is so simple – a granny in an army camp – yet because of the performance of the legendary, 81-year-old opera singer Galina Vishnevskaya (soloist at the Bolshoi, stripped of her Soviet citizenship in 1978), and because of the fact that behind the camera is a director who, unfashionably, doesn't strive for depictions of character or psychology, but metaphysics, *Alexandra* is profoundly moving, deeply original and uplifting – as great a work of art as cinema has produced.

Many agreed (though the festival's jury didn't give it a prize), but there was accord, between the Anglophone critics at least, over the fact that Christophe Honoré's musical *Les Chansons d'amour/Love Songs* was a turkey. Which it wasn't. I have always believed that the cinematic musical genre (not its Andrew Lloyd Webberian theatrical cousin) has the unique potential to marry the truth about real life with rococo fun. I adore, for example, how Jacques Demy's *Les Parapluies de Cherbourg/The Umbrellas of Cherbourg* (1964), which stars Catherine Deneuve, takes place in a pink, lime and yellow universe and has gorgeous Michel Legrand harmonics, yet refers to the Algerian War and is about the painful dissipation of love. I love, too, how *Cabaret*'s (1972) swirl of choreographed, permissive love is lacerated by scenes of Nazism, and how Martin Scorsese's great musical, *New York, New York* (1977), interrupts its long depiction of human incompatibility with musical moments of real rapture. My own experience is that the amplitude of life is large, it soars, then plummets, then repeats the cycle, and that singing and dancing (on the street at dawn, if necessary) are an integral part of it. Most modes of cinema – realism, comedy, adventure, melodrama, etc – are aesthetically too much of a monotone to capture the absurd, giddy range of lived experience.

Honoré's *Les Chansons d'amour* did so for me, triumphantly. A girl dies, and her lover spends most of the rest of the movie grieving. The setting is a microcosm – Paris's undistinguished tenth *arrondisement*. Yet, like a puppeteer who understands the tragedy of the situation (the film is based on the director's own experiences of bereavement), Honoré insists on lifting his grieving marionettes up into moments of recovery and happiness. Whereas in the Mungiu, Akin and Sokurov films, the generosity is on-screen, in Honoré's it is in the form of the film itself, the idea that grief can be seen through the prism of the musical genre, that that genre can refract sadness and despair into the colours of the rainbow. Don't believe the Anglo scribes (many of the French critics loved it), *Les Chansons d'amour* is a joy.

JESSE JAMES

Right from the earliest days of the movies, audiences must have felt like shouting 'Look how much I can see!' The phrase, and its exclamation mark, express the pleasure of discovering new *categories* of visual experience in cinema: moving image travelogues of camels at the pyramids or Tsarist splendour in Russia in the late 1890s; close-ups of the luminous faces of something called a movie star in the late 1910s; sweeping Technicolor fantasies of the 1930s; the 'liquid metal' computer visual effects in *Terminator 2: Judgement Day* in 1991, and so forth. The cinema image began as a pale, fuzzy, flickering, monochrome imitation of the brilliance of human sight, and has been on a march towards verisimilitude ever since.

In recent years, thanks to digital technology, that march has speeded up to the extent that I want to shout 'look how much I can see!' at least once a year these days. Shooting and projection technologies are accelerating the rush towards visual mimesis. Zeno's paradox of Achilles and the tortoise cautions that no matter how fast the former runs, the latter will always, in the same period, have moved on a bit, so perhaps speeding cinema will never catch up with neuro-retinal complexity, but boy is it getting close.

I say this because I've just watched *The Assassination of Jesse James by the Coward Robert Ford*, which stars Brad Pitt as James and Casey Affleck as Ford. As soon as it started I felt that someone had washed my windscreen or given me better contact lenses. I was seeing the texture of bark on tree trunks, the weave of the characters' clothing and the pores in the actors' skin, in remarkable detail.

The technical reasons for this are worth mentioning because they show that cinema is half way through its great transition from photochemistry to digital. The movie was shot by Roger Deakins on super-35mm, a method whereby the area of the 35mm negative reserved for the soundtrack is instead allocated to the image, allowing about a third more visual information than standard 35mm, still the industry norm. Then the film was scanned onto a computer, creating a digital intermediate. As some of the scenes were shot in low light, this allowed Deakins and his team to improve this intermediate, adding light to faces and other elements that might otherwise have been only partially visible. Finally, in the screening I attended, the film was projected digitally, thus removing any of the small wobbles ('gate movement' or 'weave') that sometimes occur in a film projector and are magnified on-screen, and ensuring that the focus is pin sharp throughout.

Neither super-35mm, digital intermediate nor digital projection are completely new in themselves but add them together and you get an unprecedented visual crispness and clarity. Compared to any frame of *Jesse James*, Terrence Malick's beautiful *Days of Heaven* (1978) looks like a movie drawn in soft pastel crayons.

But the technology's only half the story. *The Assassination of Jesse James by the Coward Robert Ford* is based on a novel of the same name by Ron Hansen which, says Deakins, is 'full of detail and really sets you in the world'. The film's New Zealander writer-director Andrew Dominik was determined to mirror this detail and set us in the world in a number of ways. Scenes are long. There are pauses between lines of dialogue. The camera is often close in on the faces of Pitt and, in particular, Affleck. We see the actors think before they speak. We see not only their facial movements but even the tiny muscles around the edges of their eyes. Affleck's character is the super-fan of the now legendary Jesse James. We watch, close-up, as he almost swoons in James' presence, his eye-lids drooping woozily, ecstatically, as in Bernini's sculpture *The Ecstasy of St Theresa*. Dominik didn't only want to film key dramatic moments in this famous encounter between two men that has fascinated filmmakers for decades. He was interested in the fine-grained micro-psychology of their time together, sitting around tables or campfires. The meaning of the book was in its detail – cinema today can photograph detail like never before – and so Dominik forced a studio star system that loves dash, fast editing and car chases, into an uncustomary, patient, pointillist portrait of two men slowly realising that each's destiny is in the hand's of the other. The detail 'sets you in the world'.

Perhaps it's the slow pace that has caused this $30m film headlined by one of the world's most famous movie stars to take less than $4m in the US. Perhaps it's its arty title. The fact that it's about the pathology of fandom must make it an edgy watch for Brad fans, especially as he seems to be playing himself. However, despite the moaning from many US and UK critics that it's slow and boring, *The Assassination of Jesse James by the Coward Robert Ford* is a masterpiece and a small landmark in the history of cinematic humanism. From *La Passion de Jeanne d'Arc/The Passion of Joan of Arc* of 1929 at least, movies have tried to take us elsewhere, into the minds of characters, by sustainedly looking into faces. The technology of the movies is allowing us to do this looking, and visit this elsewhere, more clearly than ever before. In the era of Facebook, face films are astonishing.

ANTI-INTERNATIONALISM   August 2003

One of the themes of my writings in recent years has been the need for an internationalised understanding of films – where they come from, what they deal with, how they mean to affect us. So it might come as a surprise to regular readers that this month I argue that the flow of movies outside their own country should be stopped. Dead. Soon.

Yet this argument is, in fact, a rational proposal to stimulate world cinema. It would work like this: for two years, say 2008 and 2009, no country would export its films or import any foreign films. The mutually agreed closure of borders would be fixed five years in advance in order to allow national film industries to plan for the drastic change in domestic market circumstances. Two years of closure should be enough time to change the way producers think. It would be a period of inwardness – a detox. By 2010, after this voluntary isolation, world cinema would be immeasurably better.

It's obvious why this won't happen, but here are three compelling reasons why it should: Germany in the late 1910s, Russia in the 1910s and 1920s, and Iran in the 1980s and 1990s. Only when Germany isolated its film production between 1916 and 1921 did its filmmakers begin to become distinctive. Unable to rely on new aesthetic models from abroad, they took a think tank approach to their own work, and within a few years, world-class talents such as Fritz Lang, Robert Wiene, F. W. Murnau, and G. W. Pabst emerged. Faced with empty screens, they were forced to invent.

This is what I mean by detox, the equivalent of a writer sitting down at a keyboard and asking him or herself the question, 'What do I really think?' German filmmakers asked themselves what they really thought. Despite the coercions of Bolshevism, that is what Russian and Soviet directors did too. Before 1914, Russian cinema was dominated by French product. When the country entered the First World War, most international film companies closed their Moscow offices. Almost immediately, the country's filmmaking became more distinctive. After the revolution and inspired by its iconoclasm, a group of now famous directors – Lev Kuleshov, Dziga Vertov, Sergei Eisenstein, Vsevolod Pudovkin – answered the question, 'How can we make our national cinema different from others?' by changing the way films are edited. After the Islamic Revolution in 1979, Iranian directors saw few Western films. The most innovative of them drew on the traditions of Persian poetry and philosophy – not cinema at all – and came up with a unique paradocumentary approach and some of the great films of the 1990s.

The idea of isolationism makes many people bristle, but I am proposing just a temporary period of celibacy. The effect on twenty-first-century cinema would be as great as that on Germany, Russia and Iran in the twentieth. Without its imports from the US, the British film industry would have four times as much screen time to fill and, assuming that people continued to go to the movies, four times the income. Pessimists will argue that the result would be the same lowering of standards as seen when television went satellite, but if you accept that the reality of UK film culture today is a lot of stalled talent unable to get on and evolve – which it is – then surely that talent would blossom. Small-scale digital production would accelerate the process. The British equivalent of the Coen brothers might emerge. The big James Bond sound stages could be given over to Danny Boyle, Gurinder Chadha, Michael Winterbottom, Stephen Frears, Terence Davies, Marc Evans and Lynne Ramsay, who would have five years to plan big, imaginative, entertaining films.

Nearly every other country would undergo a similar change. The question would not be how to dilute the current creativities of the film worlds of Spain, Italy and Greece, for example to fill a much larger amount of screen time, but how to draw in new people and look to new national, social and personal themes to expand the reach that those some-what hampered industries now achieve. With the exception of Denmark, each European country is currently punching well below its weight. Australasian cinema's two peaks were in the 1970s and 1990s, when filmmakers confidently dealt with a diverse range of ideas – racism, landscape, theology and sexuality. Faced with the imaginative and commercial gap left by the temporary disappearance of US, Asian and European film, that continent's filmmakers would again be forced to look at their own societies and pleasures and find stories and styles to express them. Ditto South American cinema. The art-house directors of Taiwan, South Korea, China and Japan would suffer from the loss of their international advocates but, as in Europe, the clear demarcations between art and commercial cinema would be redrawn and new genres – think *Wo hu cang long/Crouching Tiger, Hidden Dragon* (2000) – could emerge.

Perhaps only India would remain unaffected. Though it exports to the Middle East and now Europe, its lower production budgets and complex regionalism has made it almost self-sufficient. Its current aesthetic moribundity needs a different kind of shake up – perhaps along the lines of the mega Goa Film Festival in which Delhi has just heavily invested.

Since America is a vast net exporter of cinema, it would be the first and most powerful country to veto the two-year detox. This would be a shame because it too could benefit. The US movies which do best at the international box office are the Ur-action ones – the high-octane, Arnie and Stallone vehicles which exist in parallel universes of killing machines and abstract power. Given five years to anticipate the cessation of revenue from these, the studios would need to look to other markets within their own country: middle-aged and old people, middle-class Hispanic, black and Asian audiences, even intellectuals. US independent cinema addresses these to some degree, but a blurring of the line between independent and mainstream would occur. Multiplexes would be forced to broaden the range of people they attract through their portals.

The bonus of my proposal would come on 1 January 2010. After two years of denial, imagine the pleasures of rediscovery and re-acquaintance. Immediately after the Second World War, French moviegoers were able to catch up on the treasures of American cinema, seeing *Citizen Kane* (1941), *The Maltese Falcon* (1941), *The Little Foxes* (1941), *Double Indemnity* (1944) and *The Best Years of Our Lives* (1946) all in the single month of July 1946. January 2010 could be even better.

conclusions

DOUBTS

The very first article I wrote for *Prospect* magazine, in April 2001, argued that there's something inherently right-wing about cinema. Five years and more than fifty articles later, I argued that, in the wake of 9/11, the rise of documentary and digital imagery, cinema had shifted somewhat leftwards.

When *Widescreen: Watching. Real. People. Elsewhere* was mooted, I thought these two pieces could book end it, as it were. Start with an argument about rightness, read five years of short essays that attempt to chart changes in film culture, then end with a longer piece trying to show that together those changes constitute a crab-like movement in film culture, in the direction of the social.

Then, quite late into Guy Bingley's edit of this book, I re-read my original 'Film is Right' piece and found it harsh and somewhat smug. It read as if I was trying to catch the eye of my new editors, and their readers, by making bold statements. I was right, I think, to compare Travis Bickle in *Taxi Driver* (1076) to Wyatt Earp in *My Darling Clementine* (1946), but wrong when I didn't indicate that there's a difference between painting a brilliant portrait of someone, as De Niro and Scorsese did of Bickle (or Francis Bacon did of Pope Pius XII), and endorsing that person's approach to life. This seems obvious now. I was right that rage coursed through the veins of 1970s filmmakers in America, but wrong to think that the filmmakers' rage and their characters' rage were one and the same thing. Rather, they were two separate ingredients of that heady cocktail on which much of innovative US film culture got drunk around 1970 and from which it woke up around 1980, hung over and gasping.

My first instinct was to rewrite the 'Hollywood is Right' piece, but then realised that that would be dishonest. My second thought was to ask my editor to excise it, but that would be to tell a different kind of untruth. And there's a lot in the piece that is still valid. So, instead, we've agreed to remove it from the front of the book and place it here, in the penultimate slot, beside its update, against which it looks immature in some ways, which perhaps it was.

FILM IS RIGHT

April 2001

Democrat Tom Hanks is number one box office just about everywhere in the world. Democrat Steven Spielberg has recently been knighted. Robert De Niro and Barbra Streisand were friends of the Clintons. This year's best film Oscar nominees *Traffic* and *Erin Brockovich* are the latest in a long liberal tradition in mainstream Hollywood dating back through *Schindler's List* (1993), *Philadelphia* (1993), *Wall Street* (1987), *One Flew Over the Cuckoo's Nest* (1975), *Guess Who's Coming to Dinner* (1967), *In the Heat of the Night* (1967), *Spartacus* (1960), *12 Angry Men* (1957), *Casablanca* (1942) and *Citizen Kane* (1941). Few stars graced George W. Bush's inaugural ceremony.

And further back things weren't much different. Bacall turned Bogie into a Democrat. Gene Kelly, John Garfield, Olivier and Danny Kaye marched on Washington against McCarthy. The icons Monroe, Brando, Dean, Clift, etc, were all Democrats. It's the same outside the US. In Britain, Thatcher could muster almost no movie supporters. In Spain, cinema exploded after Franco. We all know about outcrops of reaction in the movie world like Ronald Reagan and Charlton Heston but they were the exceptions.

Or so we have long assumed. In fact there's an interesting political secret to be pulled out of the Hollywood cupboard, and it does not concern merely the mild conservatism of many mainstream blockbusters, or the frontier values of the old western and its modern successors. Look, rather, into the very heart of American counter-culture and you will find films like *Blue Velvet* (1986), films which penetrated the mainstream with a spirit of the avant-garde. Yet at the core of their innovative visions there is also a spirit of right-wing libertarianism and rage against modernity. They are reactionary films, and the left has never appeared to notice, or mind.

It may be that in the very flickering nature of its medium, cinema is simply too transient for its politics to stick. The major art form of the twentieth century could ultimately prove to have been merely shallow, exploitative, formulaic, sentimental, jejune, sensationalist and kitsch. But it could also be that these are the ingredients that have made cinema, at heart, a right-wing form. No book in the English language has addressed the theme of the right-wing tradition in American cinema. And to my knowledge, no major article has mapped the terrain. The right-wingness of cinema needs to be outed.

The left has had no difficulty identifying the corporate-capitalist nature of the film business. But no one seems to have done the more specific job of pointing out where individual films reinforce right-wing values. Maybe, as Hanif Kureishi wrote recently in this magazine, we are living in 'politically torpid' times. But that would explain only why there's no recent treatise on conservative and reactionary cinema, not why there has never been one.

However, in a short critical essay on Francis Ford Coppola written in the 1970s, David Thomson hinted that there was a lot more to be said: 'I am being tough on Coppola,' he wrote, 'for the very reason I have been hard on Frank Capra and John Ford. These are three men of remarkable talent. They shoot riveting, ravishing films … But that genius is not enough. There is a talent in American films that makes for adolescent attitudes, veiled fascism, and a work that leads one to recognise the proximity of talent and meretricious magic.'

'There is something in the best of American films,' Thomson went on, 'that is not good enough and that is dangerous.' So much American cinema is spawned from the idea of an individual winning out against the adversity of a harsh world, that the exhilaration of the moving image comes to be the natural vehicle for a universalised struggle for liberty. There's nothing necessarily either left- or right-wing about that. But the celebration of freedom, taken to an extreme, becomes blind libertarianism. It refuses any concept of solidarity or community, or engagement with other values. It is the liberty of the right.

Let's start with David Lynch, cult director of the TV series *Twin Peaks* (1990) and the film *Twin Peaks: Fire Walk With Me* (1992), *Blue Velvet* and *Wild at Heart* (1990). His films are the pinnacle of the avant-garde in the mainstream. Martin Scorsese and Bernardo Bertolucci say that he is a master. *Blue Velvet* was his breakthrough, but *Eraserhead*, nine years earlier, reveals more about his underlying political ideas. It's about a man in a disturbing urban landscape who gets impregnated by his girlfriend and gives birth to an embryonic mutant. Lynch told me in an interview two years ago that it came out of his time living in Philadelphia. In contrast to his own small-town upbringing, he found Philadelphia 'festering with a sickness'. He hated its cityness, its industry, its modernity. In films such as *The Straight Story* (1999) and *Blue Velvet*, he envisaged what he calls 'floating' small towns, or islands from the world. Of the rest of the real world, with its interfering social demands, he has a paranoiac distrust.

In 1965 a young Lynch went to Europe on a planned three-year trip to art schools, in what would become a formative experience. He came back after 15 days. He found Europe, 'too clean to paint'. Philadelphia was too dirty, Europe was too clean. America has an 'isolationist' tradition in foreign policy, but it can claim a much purer cinematic expression of the same sentiment in Lynch's attitude to the rest of the world.

Embedded in films like *Blue Velvet* is Lynch's Dostoyevskian belief that you can find the wisdom of the cosmos without moving from the small town where you were born.

But surely you can't discover everything by staying put. How, for example, do you find out about other cultures? 'Other cultures,' he said, 'are just the same as ours underneath.'

The more you think about Lynch, the less surprising it seems that he accepted an invitation from Ronald Reagan to dine at the White House. Isabella Rossellini went too. This does not go down well with those who interpret Lynch's avant-gardism as politically progressive. The point here is not to tarnish Lynch's reputation, rather it is to say that it is his very illiberality – his to-hell-with-you go-it-alone libertarianism – which is the source of his artistic frisson. He is untouched by the ironic fringes of liberal culture and this explains why his portraits of Alvin Straight and John Merrick (the Elephant Man) are so open to feeling and, oddly enough, so humane.

The isolationist right in cinema, of which Lynch is the contemporary standard bearer, goes way back. Frank Capra, who co-wrote, produced and directed *It's a Wonderful Life* (1946), is its patron saint. In that film, James Stewart plays a young man desperate to get away from small-town life. Things do not go the way he planned; he never leaves, considers suicide, is talked out of it by an angel and is eventually saved from financial ruin by contributions from the townsfolk. The famous ending of the film, where the locals pool their small savings and defeat a heartless loan shark, is surely progressive. Isn't it? Didn't Capra intend his film to be leftist and anti-materialist? Isn't that why it plays on television at Christmas?

The truth is not so palatable. Harry Cohn, Columbia studio boss, could see Capra's true colours. The filmmaker was an anti-Semite, who shared the Jewish mogul's enthusiasm for Benito Mussolini. In *Mr Smith Goes to Washington* (1939), Capra portrays the American capital as a place of fancy ideas, detached from ordinary people, intoxicated with power. This is our old friend – hatred of cosmopolitanism.

These facts cast *It's a Wonderful Life* in a harsher light. Its collectivism starts to look like right-wing populism. Its final message is that there's no place like home. There is no need for elsewhere; a patriot will find everything he needs in home, family and small-town American life.

The isolationist instinct represents a thick seam in classic American cinema especially, of course, in westerns. Another key figure in the pantheon is Howard Hawks, director of *His Girl Friday* (1940), *To Have and Have Not* (1944), *The Big Sleep* (1946), *Red River* (1948), *Gentlemen Prefer Blondes* (1953) and *Rio Bravo* (1959). A splendid career, all things considered. It is often pointed out that the best Hawks films have no social context. *Rio Bravo* tells the story of a sheriff (John Wayne) and his team (Dean Martin, Walter Brennan and Ricky Nelson) withdrawing into a prison house, waiting for the arrival of a marshal. They are cooped up, relaxed, making jokes, relying on each other when it comes to the crunch. Often voted one of the best films ever made, it has seldom been pointed out that *Rio Bravo* is the ur-movie of isolationism, a filmic, Shangri La fantasy of right-wing brotherhood.

And *Rio Bravo* was conceived for a specific political reason. John Wayne and Howard Hawks had been angered by blacklisted writer Carl Foreman's script for another western classic, *High Noon* (1952), which had been seen by many as a liberal response to McCarthyism. Hawks in particular hated the way Gary Cooper's sheriff showed indecision and needed the help of other people, even his wife. So Wayne's sheriff in *Rio Bravo* was given a scene where he says something like 'How good are you? Are you good enough to take the best man they've got? If not, I'd just have to take care of you.'

So there you have one type of movie rightism, seen in the work of Lynch, Capra and Hawks, three of the greatest directors America has produced – a blue artery of right-wing isolationism running through the culture. More recently, America's 'greatest living filmmaker', Martin Scorsese – who in real life is a sincere supporter of liberal causes – has also shown himself obsessed with right-wing rage and what can be called 'frontierism'. Just as Lynch draws from Capra, so Scorsese draws from western director John Ford.

There's no doubt which flag Ford flew. When the American Film Institute gave him his lifetime achievement award, he eulogised the then President Nixon who was in the audience. The director was dying, but this was August 1973. Ford's movies, like those of Capra, can at first appear progressive. Setting aside the slight matter of the depiction of the slaughter of native Americans in his work from 1917 to 1964, his emphasis on a kind of community and on comradeship could seem leftist. The impression fades on consideration. In *My Darling Clementine* (1946) Henry Fonda's Wyatt Earp, former marshal of Dodge City, comes to Tombstone on a cattle drive. He finds an uncivilised, disordered place. His cattle are rustled and his younger brother is killed. As he did in Dodge City, he becomes a lawman, fights the Clantons at the OK Corral and restores order.

Tombstone is morally corrupt, but it's on the way to modernity and cityhood. Fonda arrives and like an Old Testament patriarch, is disgusted by the immorality, and restores the law. The wildness is tamed. The frontier is made orderly. The film makes him a hero, yet Ford, who knew Earp in real life (the latter didn't die until 1929), must have known that the marshal was far from that.

Ford built his whole system of values on the contrast between solid Earp and the coughing, drinking, dapper Doc Holliday, played memorably here by Victor Mature. Mature's urban, overdressed, troubled, neurotic man is also an intellectual, a New Yorky combination in Ford's eyes, a type he didn't know or trust or understand. *My Darling Clementine* dreads the coming of city life as much as Lynch hated Philadelphia, as much as Heidegger hated modernity.

At first it seems impossible to call Scorsese a frontier rightist in his work when he lives and breathes Manhattan, but play *Taxi Driver* (1976) against *My Darling Clementine* and the connections start to show. New York is Tombstone a century on. De Niro's Travis Bickle is precisely a type of Earp. He is disgusted by the immorality of the city gone rancid. He is repelled by the blacks, the fags, the whores and the pimps. Like Dante with

Beatrice he falls for angelic blondes, sees in them brightness and purity. He has a Catholic sense of what hell is (Manhattan) and what goodness is – the virginal women (Jodie Foster and Cybill Shepherd) who obsess him. *Taxi Driver*'s screenwriter Paul Schrader talks explicitly of the religious contours of the film. While his own Calvinism doesn't practise worship of the Virgin Mary, Schrader wrote a story for Scorsese, so he once told me, that did.

Of course to show that the film is Catholic does not in any way demonstrate that it is right wing. But *Taxi Driver*'s type of Catholicism, its revulsion at certain types of people, is reactionary. To quote David Thomson again, it is true that Scorsese 'shoots riveting, ravishing film'. And, as in the case of Lynch, it is the fact that Scorsese's and Bickle's revulsion is expressed so ravishingly that makes the film such a head spinner, especially for young men.

There is often a complex moral ambiguity about a naturalistic art form like film. In sympathetically portraying Bickle, Scorsese wants us to understand the many real people like Bickle out there, but not necessarily to agree with them. But the truth is that *Taxi Driver* dignifies immature fears about other people and makes glorious the inglorious instinct to kill what you hate. *Taxi Driver* is very good, but it is also not good enough.

It's not much of a jump from Travis Bickle to vigilantism. Few would seriously doubt that the money-spinning *Death Wish* films are of the vigilante right. In them Charles Bronson, a New York businessman, takes the law into his own hands after his wife and child are mugged. The first three films were directed by Michael Winner. The second film's rape scene is revolting. As a quintet the films are an orgy of social reaction. And so was the case, to a much lesser extent, with Clint Eastwood's films of the 1970s, which were routinely accused of fascism. Eastwood's most famous character, Harry Callahan, appeared in five films (*Dirty Harry* (1971), *Magnum Force* (1973), *The Enforcer* (1976), *Sudden Impact* (1983) and *The Dead Pool* (1988)). He was a misanthropic maverick policeman in 1970s flower-power San Francisco. He had no time for feminism, civil rights and the like. Ronald Reagan, who was a friend of Eastwood, took to using Harry's catch phrase 'Go ahead, make my day'. This was backlash vigilantism gone mainstream. The *New Yorker* called it 'fascist medievalism'.

Eastwood's first western as a director, *High Plains Drifter* (1973), is an even clearer depiction of right-wing vigilantism. He plays a stranger who destroys a town for no apparent reason. *High Plains Drifter* detests urban culture. One French critic went so far as to call the film 'a *Mein Kampf* for the west', and even John Wayne had problems with it, writing to Eastwood – in a surprising defence of townies – 'That isn't the people who settled this country'.

If *Dirty Harry* was one of first signs that Hollywood would try to revise the history of the 1960s counter-culture, it wasn't until 1994 and *Forrest Gump* that it really got its teeth into the flower children. This hugely successful film featured Tom Hanks as a simple-minded southerner who goes to Vietnam, becomes a hero, meets presidents, and inspires Elvis to sing and John Lennon to write 'Imagine'. Despite the liberalism of its star, Tom Hanks, it was the most important right-wing film of modern times. Among its most vocal supporters was presidential candidate Pat Buchanan. Gump himself is named after a Klan ancestor and the anti-war movement is shown as rowdy, druggy and incoherent. Gump's girlfriend, Jenny, gets seduced by the counter-culture, becomes drug-addicted, performs songs naked and gets an unnamed 1980s disease from which she dies. The arc of her life runs smoothly from political action to immorality and death.

The revisionist right is, of course, a symptom of culture in general rather than cinema in particular, but several key films of the last thirty years share that desire to reclaim the past. Another of Reagan's favourites, *Rambo: First Blood Part II* (1985), found an inventive way for it to be OK for an American to go into Vietnam again with all guns blazing. The excuse was to rescue soldiers missing in action. But the film helped to reverse guilt about the war. *Apocalypse Now* (1979) did the same. Where *Rambo* was gung-ho, and nakedly reaction-ary, *Apocalypse Now* did something more subtle and powerful. It aestheticised Vietnam. The war was transformed in the national psyche from a vast political mistake to a vast op-eratic experience. This case is strengthened by the fact that the film's first screenwriter was John Milius, self-confessed 'Zen fascist', writer of *Dirty Harry* and *Magnum Force*, director of *Conan the Barbarian* (1982) and *Red Dawn* (1984) and admirer of Ford and Hawks. He had outright contempt for the 1960s. His key idea is the glory of America, its mythic past, its anti-communism, its idealised surfer culture. There is no doubt that *Apocalypse Now* is glorious, but it has no political analysis. It is massive and not very grown-up.

One of its leading actors, Dennis Hopper, is an arch rebel. *Easy Rider* (1969), which he directed, is such a pure expression of the 1960s counter-culture that surely, with Hopper at least, we're in safe liberal hands. No. Hopper thinks government is too big, voted for George Bush Snr, and once told me that he is proud that he's the first of his family to switch from Democrat to Republican. I asked him why he had wanted a former boss of the CIA for president, and he replied that it was exactly because Bush Snr held that post that he thought he would be good. 'All the other presidents have been paranoid about the CIA,' he said. 'Bush wouldn't be because he ran it.'

Even a signficant slice of gay cinema refuses to fly the progressive flag. Paul Morrissey directed the Andy Warhol films *Flesh* (1968), *Lonesome Cowboys* (1968) and *Heat* (1972). Aesthetically austere and socially anarchic, their homoeroticism broke new ground with their worship of Joe Dellasandro's naked body. Yet Morrissey is a right-wing Christian Re-publican. And the forefather of gay cinema was Vichy-accommodating Jean Cocteau.

So, much of great American cinema since the 1970s, the stuff that dominates movie magazines and cable channels, is right wing, and draws from a deep tradition of conserva-tive American film. Big, illiberal, thoughtless tendencies have been the force behind the aesthetic grandeur of some of the most memorable American films of all.

And even in the 1990s, there was a lot to please George W. Bush. Quentin Tarantino's postmodern gun operas did not come from a rightist perspective, but the Bruce Willis story in *Pulp Fiction* (1994) certainly did and the Tarantinisti lack their master's sophisticated mockery of male rage. David Lynch's window continued to close with *Wild at Heart*, whose two main characters had retreated so much from the world that it was as if they had regressed to memories of Elvis and *The Wizard of Oz* (1939). Scorsese's frontierism continued with *Casino* (1995), a bloody re-enactment of the time when the mob still ruled Vegas, before the corporations moved in to democratise it.

Vengeance à la *Dirty Harry* and *Death Wish* wasn't absent from 1990s cinema either, and *Falling Down* (1993), about a stressed-out middle-class white male on a spree killing Koreans and others, was its high point. Michael Douglas starred in that film and also in *Basic Instinct* (1992), a right-wing bisexual *cause célèbre* whose filming was picketed by gay groups yet whose director, Paul Verhoeven, has hardly ever made a purely heterosexual film. The reactionary rightism of Paul Morrissey was alive and well. Coming up to date, punk rightism took a new twist in David Fincher's muddled *Fight Club* (1999), and the pre-modern spirit surfaced in Terrence Malick's extraordinary war film *The Thin Red Line* (1998).

But isn't it too easy to indict American cinema in this way? Maybe to list the reactionary tendencies of classic American cinema stories isn't really to get to the crux of cinema's relationship with the right. What about the form of movies as well as their content? Isn't it, after all, the very form of *Apocalypse Now*, its operatic structure, that glorifies war?

It is a staple argument of the best writers on cinema that movies are inherently worshipful. To photograph something that's five foot tall and project it onto a screen which is forty foot tall is to make more of it. Photograph De Niro's eyes moving slowly in close-up in *Taxi Driver* and project them onto a cinema screen and they move twenty feet. Nothing in human culture – apart from the Sphinx or Mount Rushmore or the Buddhas of the Far East – giganticises physiognomy as cinema does. And it makes it look as if De Niro or Garbo live forever and glisten on the screen, as if they have transcended ordinary human life. To put them on the big screen is to worship them like pagan gods. Even realist cinema and documentary makers centralise the people or places that they feature. To see old footage of your hometown or of distant historical events is to marvel at how precious are these glimpses of the past. They have been kept alive by the footage and are therefore special. Think of the most purely cinematic moments. Gene Kelly in the rain. The white picket fence and Technicolour flowers of *Blue Velvet*. Shirley MacLaine running in *The Apartment* (1960). The slow-burning napalm in *Apocalypse Now*. The death of the girl in the red coat in *Don't Look Now* (1973). The opening of *Raging Bull* (1980). The song 'My Forgotten Man' from *Gold Diggers of 1933*. De Niro looking in the rear view mirror in *Taxi Driver*. Everyone can supply their own. They aren't necessarily great plot twists; they are reified, an apotheosis of the moment. The secret of Garbo, says David Thomson, is that she was photographed. Rilke wrote that what a poet does is 'praise'. That, I think, is what the camera does to the things it photographs.

Even leftist filmmakers seem to understand this. Ken Loach's minimally lit and designed films make heroic the Peter Mullans, Crissy Rocks and Robert Carlyles of their stories. Jean-Luc Godard's interrogations of the language of cinema in the 1960s and 1970s were still about the glories of the faces of their actors. One of the few great filmmakers who could also write well about films, Pier Paolo Pasolini, said that cinema is 'the sacred language of reality'. For Pasolini, to film a face was to make it almost religious, like a Fra Angelico painting. If something inherent in cinema means that it praises, reifies, sanctifies, makes epic, then this means that what movies can't do very well is criticise in a rational way. They are temperamentally unable to be objective, to analyse a social situation, to go to the root of problems without finding the hero of the situation. In other words, they are not very good at being left-wing.

The most famous right-wing filmmaker of them all was happiest when she sanctified. Leni Riefenstahl, Hitler confidante, inspired documentarist, photographer and nonagenarian snorkeller, made *Triumph des Willens/Triumph of the Will*, about the Nazi Party rally in Nuremberg in 1934, and *Olympiad*, about the 1936 Olympic Games in Berlin. For Riefenstahl, the athletes and Hitler alike are heroes. They have superior souls and she films them as if they have superior souls. She is not interested in a Balzacian account of their real social lives. She isolates her characters and worships them with her camera. Here, then, is the uncomfortable truth about Thomson's ravishing filmmaking 'that is not good enough and that is dangerous'.s Scorsese films De Niro, Coppola films Martin Sheen and Brando, Morrissey/Warhol film Delassandro, with some of the awe with which Riefenstahl filmed those athletes.

Is filmmaking then, in the very nature of its medium, inherently right-wing? The answer turns out to be a very un-Hollywood one. In its tendency to glorify, in the way it transcends, in its preference for emotion over reason, in how close it performs to the spirit of Heidegger – yes. It is.

FILM IS LEFT

Five years ago, I argued in *Prospect* that despite Democrat-inclined movie stars and liberal directors, movies have always been essentially right-wing. This applied even to 'new Hollywood' movies like *Apocalypse Now* (1979).

No writs arrived. No rebuttals. Maybe that's because my piece was largely about cinema's past, about the way mainstream cinema has been about escape. As the standard-bearer of permissive capitalism, Hollywood has always whispered in our ears that we must lie back and enjoy the ride. And so we do. We buy a ticket for *Gladiator* (2000) or *Wo hu cang long/Crouching Tiger, Hidden Dragon* (2000) to play truant in imagined lands, places that leave our own lives unchallenged and unchanged.

But things have changed since my piece in April 2001. The real world has given us Enron, Sharon, 9/11, the war in Iraq, the Madrid bombing, the tsunami, 7/7, Ahmadinejad and Hurricane Katrina. A lot of reality in five years.

In contrast, the popular movie world has fled into the deep space of CGI-inspired fantasy films. Its headline trends were the emergence of international children's trilogies (*The Lord of the Rings* (2001–2003) and *Harry Potter* (2001–2004)), the revival of animation (the *Shrek* films (2001; 2004), *Ice Age* (2002), *Finding Nemo* (2003), *The Incredibles* (2004)) and horror (*Saw* (2004–2006), *Dawn of the Dead* (2004)). It has ransacked comic books (*Hulk* (2003), *Sin City* (2005), *Superman* (2006)) and recycled television shows (*Charlie's Angels* (2000; 2003), *Scooby-Doo* (2002), *Starsky and Hutch* (2004), *Bewitched* (2005)).

Just as in the Second World War, when Betty Grable musicals and Bob Hope comedies served up escapist respite to embattled nations, so in our own tough times movies turned their backs on politics and did what they do best: distract, dazzle, elude. In the last five years, movies and reality seem to have moved apart. Films have rejected the opportunity to engage with political realities.

Or so it seems. Look a little deeper and it becomes clear that this isn't true. A complex convergence has occurred, with the result that in some ways films are less right-wing than they were.

To understand why, it's first worth noting the significance of this five-year time frame. It is exactly how long it took for the first major 9/11 fiction film, Paul Greengrass's *United 93*, to be considered, commissioned, made and released. If the movie world has a cycle – a block of time in which it digests a world event and presents it as memory and myth – five years now seems to be it. It was eleven years before the first big Vietnam movie (*The Green Berets* (1968), very right-wing) appeared; the first major AIDS movie (*Long-time Companion* (1990), pretty bland) came nine years after the first diagnoses; and *Hotel Rwanda* (2004) ten years after the massacres. This might explain the reports of Los Angeles audiences yelling 'too soon' when the *United 93* trailers were screened. But as there has been an acceleration in every other aspect of cinema – cutting the time between cinema and VHS/DVD releases, for example – it might be expected that movies would also start catching up with reality, as it were.

And it has been hard not to notice that in the last five years, despite the blockbusters, cinema has been bucking its escapist tendencies. The most obvious trend is that for the first time, documentary has become a major player in the world of cinema. Films like *Être et avoir/To Be and To Have* (2002), *Spellbound* (2002), *Touching the Void* (2003), *Capturing the Friedmans* (2003), *Fahrenheit 9/11* (2004), *La Marche de l'empereur/March of the Penguins* (2005) and *Grizzly Man* (2005) have been seen, discussed and have performed as if they were fiction films. The noun 'movie', as commonly used, has stopped meaning fiction.

And a rash of recent political movies from America provide further proof of a new engagement with reality: *Crash* (2004), *Silver City* (2004), *Syriana* (2005), *Good Night, and Good Luck* (2005) and *Munich* (2005). George Clooney, it is said, is a twenty-first-century Robert Redford, using his power as a movie star to make socially concerned films like *Syriana* and *Good Night, and Good Luck*, just as Redford fronted the Watergate movie *All the President's Men* (1976).

But we should not get carried away. First, only Steven Spielberg's *Munich*, the most conventional of these films, is 'Hollywood'. The others were made with new, liberal, private equity unconnected to the studio oligarchy. *Syriana* and *Good Night, and Good Luck*, for example, were part funded by eBay's Jeff Skoll, through his company Participant Productions. Its website's strapline says: 'Our films raise awareness about important social issues, educating audiences and inspiring them to take action', a creed so un-Hollywood that it sounds like a send-up.

Second, there is a major difference between Hollywood in the 1970s and now. Back then, some of the studio bosses – Robert Evans at Paramount, for example – were on the side of the arty liberal directors. They were cine-radicals too, and changed the tone and language of Hollywood from the inside. Nowadays, bean-counters run the oligarchy.

Instead, what the Clooney films and others point to is a re-engagement of the American indie scene. Galvanised by the Patriot Act, a supine media and war on terror sophistry,

American indie filmmakers have dumped their kooky, slacker self-regard for something more oppositional. In interviews and films alike, Clooney has tried to wrest the cornerstone idea of patriotism from under the feet of Republicans and neocons.

The remarkable success of *Brokeback Mountain* (2005) showed that leftfield American filmmaking can do well at the box office and begin to form its own liberal mainstream. *Brokeback Mountain* missed out on the best picture Oscar, but has won more than a hundred prizes. It cost about $14m to make, but recouped that and more in Britain alone. Its $90m and counting at the US box office is therefore pure profit. Its production company, Focus Features, is owned by Universal, so, ironically, much of this is likely to pile up for those studio bean-counters, but the point remains that *Brokeback Mountain* is a new high-water mark of success in political cinema.

In fact, the more closely you look at the spectrum of world filmmaking in the last five years, the more signs of re-engagement you find. As I have said before, Western cinema's historic blindness to Eastern cinema has come to an end. As Chinese cinema broke through in the Anglo-Saxon world, as arty Japanese horror taught Western directors how to portray anguish more truthfully, so English-language cinema grew up a bit. The films we see and make in the West need to internationalise further, but we are moving in the right direction. DVD has helped. DVD distributors' ransacking of cinema's past has also brought a revival of interest in radical films which have, historically, been hard to keep in distribution. Emile de Antonio is back in the repertoire. His anti-McCarthy film *Point of Order* (1964) and Vietnam-themed *In the Year of the Pig* (1968) have been long talked about by cinephiles but little seen, by my generation at least.

There have been quite a few films about the Middle East over the years, but in the last five, the number by filmmakers from that part of the world has grown rapidly. Two festivals of Palestinian cinema have taken place in Britain this year. Palestinian auteurs, such as Elia Sulieman and Hany Abu-Assad, have emerged. Abu-Assad's film about suicide bombers, *Paradise Now* (2005), was the first Palestinian film to be nominated for an Oscar. And through the documentaries of directors such as Avi Mograbi and Amos Gitai, Israel has become a centre of excellence for non-fiction filmmaking.

Just as the fault line of the Cold War – and, therefore, the setting of Cold War cinema – ran along the Iron Curtain, after 9/11 the armistice line in Israel-Palestine became the world's hottest border. A new bogeyman, Osama bin Laden, emerged. Arab characters and themes became issues in Western dramaturgy. In reaction, indigenous Arab filmmaking flourished. Arab and Arab-looking actors were in demand.

Before 9/11 you could count on the fingers of one hand significant British films that dealt with Islamic themes. Afterwards, in rapid succession, came, among others, Michael Winterbottom's *In This World* (2002), Kenny Glenaan's *Yasmin* (2004), Antonia Bird's *The Hamburg Cell* (2004) and Winterbottom's *The Road to Guantánamo* (2006). Paul Greengrass, director of *United 93*, is also British, so Britain has more than played its part in putting Islam on-screen.

Mention of Michael Winterbottom brings up another, unrelated area in which recent cinema has become, in a sense, more real. Despite showing genital close-ups, erections and ejaculation, his film *9 Songs* (2004) was passed for an 18 certificate in Britain. When Patrice Chéreau's British film *Intimacy* (2001), which also featured explicit sex, was given a similar rating, it felt as if the new millennium had ushered in a more tolerant attitude to explicit consensual sexual activity on-screen, and so it had. Encouraged by French films like *Baise-Moi* (2000) and *Anatomie de l'enfer/Anatomy of Hell* (2004), both made by women, the taboo on showing erections in mainstream cinema just seemed to fade away.

The list could go on, but the point is surely made that in many small ways film has taken a step closer to reality in the last five years. What happens when you turn this proposition on its head, however? What if we ask not if movies have moved closer to life, but the converse – if life is moving closer to the movies? Life did feel like a disaster movie in the days after 9/11, prompting Belgian ultra-realist directors Jean-Pierre and Luc Dardenne, who have won the Cannes Palme d'Or twice, to observe: 'Today's paradox is that the aestheticisation of reality requires the de-aestheticisation of art.' And it is not only realist directors who feel this. Michael Haneke, who had a recent art-house hit with *Hidden*, explains the intensity of his work by saying that reality is losing its realness.

If they are right, then the very thing that the earliest filmmakers fell in love with – a camera's ability to hoover up reality and re-project it in motion and detail on a big screen – is not quite as valuable as it once was. The best European filmmakers today – Haneke, Lars von Trier, Bruno Dumont, Claire Denis, Pedro Almodóvar, etc – are equally sceptical about film as a medium of social realism.

So where does this leave us? With a less definitive answer than five years ago. Then it was possible to say that there was a 'right-wing quality' at the heart of Western cinema, derived from the mythology of the frontier, the loner and the vigilante, which has interested some of the best Western filmmakers – Scorsese, Coppola, Eastwood, David Lynch, Howard Hawks, John Ford. For them, although we sit with others in the cinema, we are basically on our own, looking up at a screen. In those conditions, the best thing to put on that screen is another person on their own, in a big landscape or dazzling cityscape – John Wayne in westerns, Robert De Niro as Travis Bickle or Jake La Motta, Martin Sheen in *Apocalypse Now*, Kyle MacLachlan in *Blue Velvet* (1986), Clint Eastwood as Dirty Harry. The great, disconnected, anti-social, right-wing men in modern American cinema.

The solitary condition of watching movies hasn't changed – if anything, DVD probably means that we are more often literally on our own when we watch films – but the movie world has lost some of its love for loners. Even CGI fantasies like the *Toy Story* films (1995; 1999) and the *Lord of the Rings* cycle (2001–2003) are about teamwork. So if it is going too far to say that movies are more liberal than they were, they are at any rate less socially empty. Reality, it seems, no longer 'pops you out of the story', as they say in Hollywood. We don't mind seeing it now and again on the big screen, especially if our daily lives don't always feel that real.

But to put this in perspective, it is worth looking back to the 2001 Oscars to see what was nominated in the year before 9/11. One of the biggies was *Traffic*, a film about duplicity in the US war on drugs, that won four Oscars, including one for Steven Gaghan as screenwriter (Gaghan later co-directed *Syriana* with Clooney). Another was *Erin Brockovich*, about a single mother who takes on and beats a corporation, for which Julia Roberts won her Oscar. The political strain in cinema was there then – it always has been. The question is whether it will only ever be a strain.

CINEMA MATTER

March 2008

My partner's a therapist who treats people who have suffered sexual assault, torture and other major traumatic experiences. I am a movie guy. When we go somewhere I am, therefore, the light relief. She gives me gravitas, I give her a hint of showbiz, a bit of bling. We're a bit like the Sarkozys in reverse.

I'm used to being the bauble. My column, 'Widescreen', nestles beside articles on economics, essays on science and medicine, foreign policy and the environment. How can I not feel a bit *frou frou* against all that? These big, serious subjects tool human experience. I might not be here if doctors had not treated the jaundice I caught as a child. Politics build the tracks on which we run. Science, economics, education, religion, transport, agriculture and philosophy shape how we live and think. In comparison, cinema is a tiddler. It's just 113 years old. And it's entertainment too. It is small, young and disposable. It can't extend lives or treat pain or build bridges or grow cabbages.

But cinema, at its best, is an art – an *arriviste* art – and art matters. It's also a multi-billion dollar business. And money certainly matters. In a fuzzier sense, movies seem to shape aspiration and desire. Some would say that they were twentieth-century America's most striking export and an exertion of its soft power. Certainly they seem responsive to national psychology. If you want to know what we are scared of, look at our movies. I have argued before that they function like Freudian parapraxes.

This all makes me feel less shallow. If what I write about is an art and a major business, if it influences how people think and plays a role in the zeitgeist, then it is powerful and, therefore, matters. It isnae just bling and I'm not just a bauble. I can hold my head high in society. Hooray. A cheer indeed. But cinema is often talked about as art, as zeitgeist and as aspiration, and I'm bored of such vague talk. I'm on a long flight from Beijing to Dubai as I write this. In the six hours to go, I'm going to try to think a bit more about whether movies matter. To do so, I'll start with a magnifying glass trained on the fine grain of the role cinema has played in one individual life. For convenience sake, that life, albeit a somewhat battered 42-year-old bauble, will be my own.

I was a nervy little boy. Being brought up in Belfast in the 1970s, during the Troubles, made me somewhat more so. The world felt both generally and, because of the Troubles, specifically, a bit scary. When I went to the movies, just sitting in the auditorium, before the lights went down, before the film started, I could feel my nervous system ease. Those almost empty, dark movie houses, which would soon light up with projected vistas and faces, made my voltage drop.

This is a feather in cinema's cap, but does not take us very far. The human nervous system has always, surely, enjoyed a vicarious thrill and the melting away of fear – whether through reading novels or riding rollercoasters, attending the opera or even, so I'm told, cracking open a tinny to watch Arsenal on the box. Cinema hasn't created radically new psychological experiences. It has just been extremely good at upgrading old ones. It's claimed sometimes that we live in an escapist age and, if cinema is very good at escapism, and very popular, then Hollywood and Bollywood are partly to blame, but this is to forget that Christianity, Hinduism and Islam, for example, are star systems and story factories too, as were Egyptian cosmology and the Greek deities. It would be easier to argue, in fact, that post-Enlightenment humanity is somewhat less escapist than ever. If, therefore, the physical experience of watching the screen hasn't changed human experience at all, what about what appears on the screen? Surely the ubiquity of cinema makes the issue of how it represents real life a matter of concern? Indeed, and hundreds of books and film studies courses worry over the ethics and politics of film. Many of them start with things like fashion. In the jazz age in particular, when cinema was highly designed and massively attended, the cupid's bow lips of Clara Bow, pill-box hats, pencil skirts and box jackets leapt straight from the screen to the girls on Broadway and Mayfair. Bauhaus-influenced black and white sets, polished floors and nipped-in waists told millions of people what utopia might look like. Bernardo Bertolucci once told me that much in his film *Il Conformista/ The Conformist* (1970), re-released recently, depended on the length of actress Dominique Sanda's skirt. In my own case, after seeing Dennis Hopper's film *Colors* (1988), I immediately bought a pair of mirror shades like those sported by Sean Penn in the film, and wore them for weeks. Why? To try to look as good as Penn, I suppose. Because I misrecognised myself in him. In order to nick some of his attitude and pass it off as my own. Such borrowings happen all the time and tell us something about human narcissism or the instability or acquisitiveness of identity. The most striking example I know of such elision of the difference between movies and life is that several generations of men in India, when they dance at weddings, do so in the manner of Indian megastar actor and producer Amitabh Bachchan. Another example from my own life is more embarrassing. I can't remember at what age I first saw Martin Scorsese's film *Taxi Driver* (1976) but I do recall that when Robert De Niro took off his shirt I immediately decided that his chest hair was *exactly* how chest hair should be. That mine isn't exactly like his has been a small disappointment throughout my adult life.

Unedifying, I know, but at least I can use such an irrational fact about me and chest hair to make this point: if circumstances had been different I might well have seen a shirtless man in real life and made the same aesthetic judgement, but I doubt if it would have pricked me so much. The power of cinema made the moment stick and the realisation of this points to the fact, which Luis Buñuel and Alfred Hitchcock knew, that cinema has a hot line to our subconsciousnesses. It dials in quick.

Sex is but a block away from such things. I'm sure the fact that I was watching Kim Novak in *Vertigo* (1958) and Tippi Hedren in *The Birds* (1963) as I was going through puberty fixed some elements of my erotic imagination. At such formative times, of course, many things are grist to the erotic mill but, again, it was surely the power of film and its seemingly direct dial to my brain stem that locked in the sexual buzz of a well-tailored suit and heels. The fact that I was an equal opportunities luster – I wanted to be with Novak or De Niro – triangulated things in heady ways. From talking to friends I could see that they weren't bisexual (I rued their disadvantage) and, it began to dawn on me, neither was the world in general. Yet cinema, it seemed to me, most definitely was. When Hitchcock photographs Novak in a state of undress, her hair hanging down, in *Vertigo*, he doesn't invite just the men in the cinema to imagine the moment we have not seen – James Stewart taking her clothes off – but the women too. When De Niro takes his shirt off in *Taxi Driver*, women and men see his body from the same distance and with equal privilege. It is quite possible to imagine a film in which the screen splits at such moments of erotic appeal, the left half being for people who fancy women, the right for those who fancy men, but I have not seen this done. For years film theory talked about how movies coerced viewers into gendered responses to sexual display – Cameron Diaz's slow-motion appearance in *The Mask* (1994) makes us all lusty guys – but for me, in my early teens, I was both a boy and a girl in the cinema and that was great.

Looking back, this was part of why cinema mattered to me. It made the world legible. The Northern Ireland in which I was growing up was wrong about sex, and cinema was right. If I had had to learn about the vectors and valencies of sexuality from the Ballymena of Ian Paisley and the St Louis nuns who ran the school I attended, I would have been seriously screwed up. Theirs was an impenetrable medieval lexicon of sex whereas cinema spoke plain erotic English.

This was exciting. Cinema was like one of those websites in which you input a paragraph in a foreign language and it translates it into your own. I haven't heard this point made before. The closest I've come to it is in the memoir of the autistic, American, cattle-handling machine designer Temple Grandin, in which she says that as a girl, when she heard the word 'underneath' she had to translate this into a little video in her head of her getting underneath a table. Then she understood the word. I'm not saying that I was autistic or that movie lovers in general are, but I know that cinema did something like that translation for me. And judging by my conversations with cinephile directors like Martin Scorsese and Bernardo Bertolucci, and the filmmaker Tilda Swinton, it did so for them too. Novels could never have unscrambled life for me in the same way. Scorsese would never have been a novelist. Cinema matters because it unlocked life for people like him and Swinton and me.

Which is only to say that it matters to those for whom it matters. And even then only in a vague Chomskyan, 'my brain is structured like cinema' kind of way. To get back to something more concrete, how about this for a claim? Cinema stopped me being racist. Where I grew up was almost exclusively white. I had no opportunity to observe the agency, subjectivity or volition of non-white people. I've read novels by Naguib Mahfouz, Toni Morrison and J. M. Coetzee, and most of James Baldwin's. The writing of Franz Fanon and Edward Said made me stand back from my own whiteness and Westerness. And yet none of this particularised non-white people for me like the movies of (deep breath) Djibril Diop Membéty, Ousmane Sembène, Youssef Chahine, Soulymane Cissé, Haile Gerima, Idrissa Ouedraogo, Safi Faye and Med Hondo in Africa; Wu Yonggang, Bu Wancang, Fei Mu, Yuan Muzhi, Xie Fei, Chen Kaige, Zhang Yimou, Tian Zhuangzhuang, Wong Kar-wai, Lou Ye, King Hu, Hou Hsiao-hsien, Tsai Ming-liang, Edward Yang, Cecile Tang and Anne Hui in the Chinese-speaking world; or Yasujiro Ozu, Kenji Mizoguchi, Mikio Naruse, Akira Kurosawa, Nagisa Oshima, Hiroshi Teshigahara, Shinsuke Ogawa, Shohei Imamura, Noriaki Tsuchimoto, Kazuo Hara or Hirokazu Kore-eda in Japan. I read back these names and they sound like a song. It's not just that I've gotten to know the world through these 35 directors. When I first started meeting people from Ethiopia, for example, I could see behind their subjectivity, those unforgettable, passionate, thinking, dreaming people in Gerima's movie's.

I take whiteness and blackness as my example because it is so visible, but the same applies to other differences. I had spent no time with middle-class people until I went to Scotland when I was 18. I first met openly gay people at the same time. Yet cinema direct-dialled things about both into my adolescent mind as I sat in the dark, or at home at night watching a movie on BBC2.

Film has had a dodgy effect on my sense of sunglasses and body hair, but it has provided also a translation service for life for me, and kicked Northern Ireland's stupid ideas about sexuality into a hat, and made me fall in love with Africa and Iran, Japan and South America. Overall, that's pretty good I'd say. In the fine grain of my own life, cinema not only matters, but it shines.

What happens, however, when we move beyond my bailiwick, and ask whether movies amount to a hill of beans for broader groups of people or even nations? Consider the film *Gregory's Girl* (1981). Seeing it for the first time was like looking in a mirror. The details of Gregory's goofy, adolescent crush on the girl in the football team were all too familiar. And, having lived in a new town, the film's setting in Cumbernauld, one of the great experiments in new town urbanism, was very much so. But when I talked to Scots, it was clear that Gregory was theirs, and his new town stage was theirs, and his humour and hairstyle and manner of speaking was theirs. The film's success boosted the confidence of the Scottish cottage film industry. But, more than that, the fact that a lad from Cumbernauld was up there, on the silver screen, where James Dean and De Niro live, legitimised 1980s, working class, diffident Scottishness. It put it at the top rather than the bottom. It made it something you boasted about rather than hid.

Success in football and pop music can reinforce group identities in similar ways but not to the same degree. David Beckham is inspiring but non-narrative. The confidence of young English lads – and lads around the world – is boosted by his meritocratic example. But Beckham soared up and away from his background like a rocket. Gregory, being fictional and cinematic, takes his 1980s Scottish world with him when he bursts into life on the big screen. Or perhaps that's back to front: when *Gregory's Girl* is screened, it's a time and place that we see and then, only then, one of its most likable citizens, Gregory. The film is such a capsule of time and place that, as part of a piece of work I am doing for the Scottish Government, I am hoping to screen it in China as a way of showing, there, what Scotland is.

The film *Walkabout* (1971) reinforced a strain of Australian identity just as *Gregory's Girl* did in Scotland. There had been Aboriginal characters on screen before it, but the wise, beautiful, taciturn youth who the two white children meet in the outback not only launched the acting career of the extraordinary David Gulpilil, but took aboriginalism from a current affairs issue into the realms of recognition and fulfilment. Likewise *Gadjo Dilo* (1997), made by Tony Gatlif, an Algerian director of Romany descent, made Romany people proud and others interested. Gregory, Gulpilil and Gatlif created performed selves in the symbolic, charmed, exciting realm of cinema for three marginalised identities. These and countless other examples show what a great witness-bearer cinema can be, and that matters.

Zoom out further, from groups to whole nations, and it's immediately clear that cinema's record as witness-bearer is mixed. Let's look at the plus side first. In *Cinema of Unease* (1995), a documentary he made about New Zealand's film history, actor Sam Neill argued convincingly that success in cinema was central to the country's growing confidence as a nation. To see the first good indigenous New Zealand movies on the big screen was to think, my God, at last. In Britain, films like *In Which We Serve* (1942) and Humphrey Jennings' documentaries, depicted the wartime common cause across class divides – the British spirit – which, though idealistic and somewhat contentious, played a part in the slow erosion of class barriers which was one of the stories of Britain's twentieth century. In a recent lecture, Jean-Michel Frodon, the editor of the film magazine *Cahiers du cinéma* that helped launch the French New Wave, argued that for André Malraux, France's most effective culture minister until Jacques Lang, cinema was 'a diplomatic tool that enhanced the shining of France in the world' – hence the country's heavy promotion of French cinema abroad. The poetic humanism of Iranian cinema since the mid-1980s has, for those who have seen it, stood in winning counterpoint to the audio-visual clichés of the country on Western television.

These are 'good' examples of film helping a nation to find a place in the world but, obviously, cinema can reinforce beliefs in far less edifying ways. The list is depressingly long: Africans in *Tarzan* movies, Jewish people in Nazi cinema, African-Americans in Hollywood cinema until the 1960s, Chinese people in Japanese film, and vice-versa, middle-class people and intellectuals in Maoist and Soviet movies, Mexicans in American cinema until the 1970s, etc. These slurs were not invented by cinema, but it took to them with alacrity. To detail such misrepresentations would take far longer than a flight from Beijing to Dubai. Suffice to say that movies have been far too willing conspirators.

Nearly everything I've said so far has been about cinema as an identity machine. What has become clear is that cinema matters because it is magic at first-person, it fuels it, it is an SSRI of first-person, it is an identity steroid – whether that identity is the individual self, the ethnic or social group, or the nation. But what about when it isn't boosting types of selfhood? Does it have an impact on other aspects of social or political life?

Yes, but usually in alliance with its sometime sparring partner, TV. In the UK, Ken Loach's *Cathy Come Home* (1966) is regularly cited for the outrage it generated about homelessness and the fact that it helped create the charity Shelter. I've written before in *Prospect* about *Heshang – The River Elegy*, a series of Chinese documentaries that not only benefited from the relative freedom of thought in China in the 1980s, but helped broaden that freedom until the Tian'anmen clampdown. In these and many other cases, the language of film told disruptive stories, but it was TV's ability to deliver these stories to mass audiences that created the impact. Other films changed the world without having to rely entirely on TV broadcasts – Michael Moore's *Bowling for Columbine* (2002) convinced Wal-Mart to stop selling certain types of bullets and Marcel Ophüls' *Le Chagrin et la pitié/ The Sorrow and the Pity* (1969) convinced France to confront its wartime collaborationism. Japanese activist film in the 1970s was particularly effective in setting up alternative exhibition circuits, in community halls, village venues and schools, to challenge the government on issues such as environmental damage and transport.

And there's a final lens, beyond questions of individuals, groups, nations or specific social change, in which cinema's impact can be looked at: its imaginative fidelity; the degree to which it has told the truth, or effectively conjured the themes of our lives.

Take war, for example, since I mentioned Northern Ireland's low-level one earlier. I believe that because cinema looks like real life and watching a movie feels like watching a parallel universe very like our own, but a bit more glamorous and structured more like a story, movies almost inevitably fail to capture the immersive agony of war at its worst. As well as Belfast I was in Sarajevo during its siege and in both cases the feeling was of drowning in war, being in the conflict like a fish is in water. Cinema certainly hasn't shied away from trying to depict war – as either a heroic stage or an ignoble mess. And yet I can think of only two sequences in the whole of movie history that have given me that fish in water feeling: a celebrated scene in Elem Klimov's Soviet film *Idi i smotri/Come and See* (1985), when a boy and girl escaping the Nazis in Byelorussia wade through and almost drown in a black bog that sucks at their bodies; and the first flashback Omaha Beach sequence in *Saving Private Ryan* (1998). And in each case, I'd argue, it's the physicality rather than the 'war-ness' of the scene that creates its impact.

Cinema, I believe, inevitably understates the most intense real experiences. Yes, documentaries about Vietnam introduced a dose of reality into America's national perception of its misadventure there, and that is to the great credit of those films, but they could only do so because Washington and TV had painted such a fake picture of the fighting in the first place. The Vietnam documentaries marched America halfway back from its self-deluding untruth, but only halfway. Years ago, when I had photographs I'd taken in India developed, I realised a blindingly obvious fact. Photography doesn't capture smell. My pictures of the slums of Mumbai, the biggest in Asia, did not convey how terrible they are, partially because of my limited skills as a photographer, and partly because the medium itself is 'optimistic' in the sense that it can't convey just how bad troubling things really are. A still or moving image of Mumbai's worst living conditions, even with sound, will always fail to capture their cacophony, their sensory overload, their enduring effect. Apply this thought to the question of war in cinema and words like 'glamorise' and 'sanitise' seem to be appropriate.

Which is, of course, to indict the medium I love. And no art form is really up to war – not *Guernica*, not *War and Peace*, not Britten's 'War Requiem', not Owen's 'Dulce et Decorum Est', not Sun Tzu's *The Art of War*. Take other themes, however, and cinema scores more highly. It is very good at travel and wanderlust – think road movies and westerns. It is excellent at psychological flashback, trauma and fear – in movies as diverse as *The Pawnbroker* (1964), *Trois couleurs: Bleu/Three Colours: Blue* (1993), *Sous le sable/Under the Sand* (2000) and the *Blair Witch* trilogy (1999–2002). Like TV, it is rather good at making us laugh by creating comic situations that then 'live on' in real life: the Coen brothers' film *The Big Lebowski* (1998) seems to me to have not only found the essence of what is funny about slackers in the real world but also to have invented funny things about its fictional central character – The Dude/His Dudeness/The Duderino – which real people then incorporated into their own personalities. I'm sure that there were people like The Dude before the Coens made their film but, due to its cult success, there are, I believe, more.

And consider another theme, loneliness. Movies, the kingdom of shadows, are its Mecca. I think of the films that sit in piles around my desk in my study at home: the Bill Douglas trilogy (1972–78), Billy Wilder's *The Apartment* (1960), Satyajit Ray's *Devi* (1960), Robert Bresson's *Pickpocket* (1959), Wong Kar-wai's *Fa yeung nin wa/In the Mood for Love* (2000), Ingmar Bergman's *Nattvardsgästerna/Winter Light* (1962), Ken Loach's *Kes* (1969), Mikio Naruse's *Nagareru/Flowing* (1956), Ernst Lubitsch's *Ninotchka* (1939). Aren't these all in some way about loneliness? Stick an individual up on the big screen, put a frame around them, watch them in the dark, and the experience, as well as whatever else it's about, is often about being alone. Whilst it is defeated by war, the art of film is well placed to capture, to depict and to celebrate things like human fear and loneliness. And, therefore, it matters.

Dubai is looming. I can see it glowing in the distance because there's a TV screen in the seat in front of me, on which two cameras are showing the view from the front of the plane. Emirates Airlines provides a film jukebox even for economy passengers like me, so I could have watched a classic Egyptian musical, a Hong Kong action movie, or *The Philadelphia Story* (1940) and then its remake *High Society* (1956). It was watching these last two films back to back many years ago that taught me something about the speed of cinema, its economy and rapture. But instead I wrote this, in which I discovered what? That when it sticks close to questions of self, confidence and eros, of who rather than how; when it's about medium-sized things like aloneness and fear; when it doesn't bite off more than it can chew; when it does these things, film matters.

Barak Obama is now on the news headlines on the TV screen in front of me. I heard recently that he is a fan of the films of American independent filmmakers John Sayles and his producer Maggie Renzi. This is no great surprise. No white filmmakers anywhere in the world have written, directed and produced a more nuanced range of films about ethnic and social diversity than Sayles and Renzi. Imagine Obama's relationship with those films – *Brother from Another Planet* (1984), *City of Hope* (1991), *Passion Fish* (1992), *Men with Guns* (1997), *Honeydripper* (2007). He will have responded to them because they depict worlds he knows are out there. But, also, I'd guess, because they describe worlds – a smalltown Alaska in the case of *Limbo* (1999), the magic realism of an unnamed Latin American country in *Men with Guns*, a well-to-do home in the bayou of Louisiana in *Passion Fish*, a fishing village in Donegal in *The Secret of Roan Inish* (1994) – that he has never experienced but, through the Sayles/Renzi films, was glad to. If – a big if – Obama will soon be the most powerful person in the world, I am glad that the Sayles/Renzi films have direct-dialled into his brain. A very specific way in which films matter.

**Related titles from Wallflower Press.
Please also visit
www.wallflowerpress.co.uk
to receive online discounts
of up to 20%**

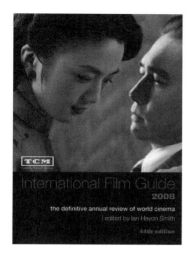

INTERNATIONAL FILM GUIDE 2008
(44TH EDITION)
The Definitive Annual Review of World Cinema
Ian Haydn Smith (ed.)

First published in 1963, the *International Film Guide* enjoys an unrivalled reputation as the most authoritative and trusted source of information on world cinema. Now relaunched by Wallflower Press, the 2008 (44th) edition is a special double edition covering the films and festivals of 2006 and 2007, via a 'World Survey' section encompassing the output of over a hundred countries. Other features include coverage of five 'Directors of the Year' (Fatih Akin, Suzanne Bier, Guillermo del Toro, Paul Greengrass and Jia Zhangke), a detailed country focus on Germany, industry analysis on documentary and the growth of DVD production, and a comprehensive listing and description of all major international and smaller local film festivals from all over the world. Written by expert local correspondents who present critical reviews assessing new films, trends and industry developments covering features, documentaries and shorts, this new incarnation of the International Film Guide heralds the return of a much-respected annual volume encompassing all aspects of contemporary global cinema.

424 pages
978-1-905674-61-9 (pbk) – £19.99

'The *International Film Guide* traces without prejudice the ties between cultures, countries, filmmakers, the past and the present.'

Bertrand Tavernier

'After a one-year hiatus, the *International Film Guide* is back, and that's very good news for film aficionados everywhere … Needless to say, the amount of information is staggering and anyone with the smallest interest in film will add dozens of titles to his or her "must see" list. The selection of experts is first rate as well … It is a delight to browse, and read. An indispensable addition to any film lover's bookshelf.'

Wout Thielemans, *Moviescope*

'It is impossible to find so much important data about the most recent film production compressed and collected in one place … This heavy volume will certainly deliver its money's worth … For the sheer number of intriguing titles I first found out about here, this book cannot be compared to any other.'

Dejan Ognjanovic, *Beyond Hollywood*

DEKALOG
the new home for serious film criticism

The Dekalog series is a new list of bi-annual publications, released each March and September, dedicated to presenting serious and insightful criticism on a wide range of subjects across the full spectrum of contemporary global cinema.

Each issue is a guest-edited specially-themed volume including the writings of a diverse collection of authors, from academic scholars, film critics, filmmakers and producers, and personalities involved in all kinds of institutionalised cinephilia such as film festival directors and film museum curators.
The intention, therefore, is to include the multiple voices of informed and complementary commentators on all things cinematic in dedicated volumes on subjects of real critical interest, especially those not usually served by established periodicals or book-length publications.

In addition to specially-commissioned essays, each issue also includes an exclusive 'Dekalog Interview' with a leading figure related to the theme in question, and a 'Dekalog Re-View' section where readers' feedback will be edited by respective guest editors and published in subsequent editions. All readers are therefore very much invited to participate in the discussions by contacting any of the series' guest editors at dekalog@wallflowerpress.co.uk.

FORTHCOMING ISSUES IN THE DEKALOG SERIES:
Dekalog 2: On Manoel de Oliveira – guest-edited by Carolin Overhoff Ferreira
Dekalog 3: On Film Festivals – guest-edited by Richard Porton
Dekalog 4: On East Asian Filmmakers – guest-edited by Kate Taylor

AVAILABLE NOW:

Dekalog 1: On The Five Obstructions
guest-edited by Mette Hjort

156 pages
978-1-905674-75-6 (pbk) – £12.00

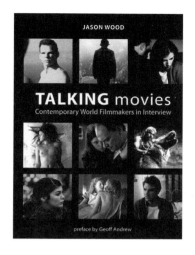

TALKING MOVIES
Contemporary World Filmmakers in Interview
Jason Wood (Preface by Geoff Andrew)

A culmination of more than ten years of interviews, *Talking Movies* is a collection of conversations with some of the most audacious and respected contemporary filmmakers of the present generation. Several of these in-depth discussions have already featured in publications such as *Vertigo* and *Enthusiasm*, and there are over fifteen interviews exclusive to this book. The names included here are those at the cutting edge of cinematic style the world over, those whose work has defined how images are processed and appreciated by modern audiences. Directors frankly discussing their craft and the social, political and technological forces that inform it including Claire Denis and Bertrand Tavernier (France), Guillermo del Toro, Alejandro González Iñárritu and Carlos Reygadas (Mexico), Hal Hartley and Richard Linklater (USA), Stephen Frears and Andrew Kötting (UK), Nuri Bilge Ceylan (Turkey), Atom Egoyan (Canada), Lucrecia Martel (Argentina) and John Hillcoat and Nick Cave (Australia).

224 pages
978-1-904764-90-8 (pbk) – £16.99
978-1-904764-91-5 (hbk) – £45.00

About the author

Jason Wood is a film programmer, documentary filmmaker and writer. Recent publications include *Nick Broomfield: Documenting Icons* (2005) and *Contemporary Mexican Cinema* (2006). His journalism has appeared in *Vertigo*, the *Guardian* and *Sight and Sound*.

Reviews

'*Talking Movies* is an indispensable volume that should be considered a set text for arts journalists (both budding and professional) trying to master the methodology behind achieving the most revealing and entertaining interviews possible.' ★★★★★

David Jenkins, *Time Out*

'The strength lies in Wood's questions; never generic or glib, his inquiries always demonstrate an assured insight into the director's work … *Talking Movies* could have been a cursory collection of existing pieces, but instead it has the cohesion of an original book.'

Moviemaker

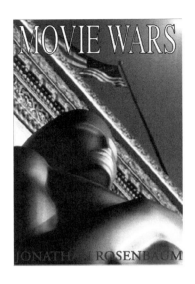

MOVIE WARS
How Hollywood and the Media Limit What Films We Can See
Jonathan Rosenbaum

Contrary to what a number of disillusioned critics have written and what appears to be the pervading conventional wisdom, Jonathan Rosenbaum believes that cinema is very much alive and well. The problem is, he feels, that all too often we just do not get the opportunity to see the best of it. In *Movie Wars*, America's leading film critic explores the production, distribution and promotion of mainstream contemporary cinema and how, at every turn, the industry treats the viewer with contempt. Using examples such as Miramax's buying of films solely to keep them out of the hands of competitors with no intention of distributing them, the American Film Institute's narrow championing of Hollywood studio product in their 'Best 100 Films' list, and the mainstream media's unquestioning acceptance of the Hollywood PR machine, *Movie Wars* is a damning critique of corporate cinematic culture and a no-holds-barred call to arms for those looking for life outside the multiplex.

192 pages
978-1-903364-60-4 (pbk) – £12.99

About the author
Jonathan Rosenbaum is film critic for the *Chicago Reader*, author of *Movies as Politics* (1997), *Essential Cinema: On the Necessity of Film Canons* (2004) and *Discovering Orson Welles* (2007), as well as a frequent contributor to *Film Comment*, *Cineaste*, *Cahiers du Cinéma España* and *Film Quarterly*.

Reviews
'Jonathan Rosenbaum is the best film critic in the United States – indeed, he's one of the best writers on film of any kind in the history of the medium.'

James Naremore

'A book I can't recommend highly enough to anyone who wants to learn about the generally corrupt overlaps and sweetheart deals between film festivals, distributors, mainstream film critics and allegedly independent filmmakers.'

John Patterson, *The Guardian*

'Rosenbaum's impassioned, compellingly argued polemic reminds us that film exists not just in the movie world but in the real world too.'

Jonathan Romney

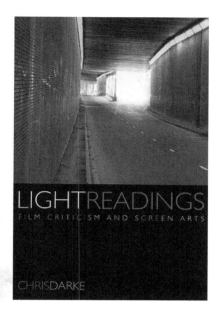

LIGHT READINGS
Film Criticism and Screen Arts
Chris Darke

In *Light Readings: Film Criticism and Screen Arts*, leading film critic Chris Darke re-visits his writing over recent years to address important questions emerging out of the changes effecting film and digital media. Was the 1990s the decade in which cinema as a medium and collective experience finally became subsumed within a converging universe of multiple media? Should the cinema be reconsidered to accommodate the new possibilities of the moving image? This insightful collection of reviews and essays also includes interviews with Atom Egoyan, Bill Viola, Olivier Assayas, Jacques Audiard and Xavier Beauvois.

.

208 pages
978-1-903364-07-9 (pbk) – £12.99

About the author

Chris Darke is a regular contributor to *Sight and Sound*, *mute* and *The Independent* and the author of *Alphaville* (2006). His other activities include screenwriting, cinema programming and producing arts reportage for television.

Reviews

'An inspired collection of essays on the interface of new medias and their mutual interfaces.'

Film Comment

'Darke establishes his credentials as a cineaste … Compulsive reading for serious film students.'

Hotdog

'The writing is clear, informative and frequently perceptive. Darke is also a skilled and imaginative wordsmith and always a pleasure to read … The present anthology will serve as a useful reference for students and amateurs of the moving image.'

Contemporary magazine

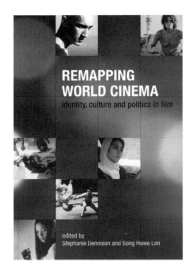

REMAPPING WORLD CINEMA
Identity, Culture and Politics in Film
Stephanie Dennison and Song Hwee Lim (eds)

With films such as *Crouching Tiger, Hidden Dragon* (2000), *Oldboy* (2003), *Goodbye Lenin!* (2003) and *The Motorcycle Diaries* (2004), the state and popularity of world cinema has rarely been healthier. Through 16 chapters contributed by leading international film scholars, including Dudley Andrew, Lucia Nagib and Michael Chanan, *Remapping World Cinema: Identity, Culture and Politics in Film* explores many of the key critical and theoretical approaches and debates to this fluid and ever-increasing field of study, including race, stardom, post-colonialism as well as national cinemas' relationship with Hollywood. Covering a broad scope, this collection examines the cinemas of Europe, East Asia, India, Africa and Latin America. It will thus be of interest to scholars and students of film studies, cultural studies and post-colonial studies, as well as to film enthusiasts keen to explore a wider range of world cinema.

224 pages
978-1-904764-62-5 (pbk) – £16.99
978-1-904764-63-2 (hbk) – £45.00

About the editors
Stephanie Dennison is director of the Masters programme in World Cinemas at the University of Leeds. She is the co-author of *Popular Cinema in Brazil* (2004).

Song Hwee Lim is Senior Lecturer in Film at the University of Exeter and the author of *Celluloid Comrades: Representations of Male Homosexuality in Contemporary Chinese Cinemas* (2006).

Reviews
'At last a book that will really support and inform the study of world cinema as both practice and concept. This is a highly accessible but also original collection, filled with concise and compelling polemical pieces as well as detailed studies of national and regional cinemas from around the world ... *Remapping World Cinema* is an essential addition to the burgeoning study of international films and film cultures.'

Catherine Grant, University of Kent

'*Remapping World Cinema* is a valuable contribution to the critical interrogation and understanding of an increasingly important and central concept in cinema studies.'

Duncan Petrie, University of Auckland

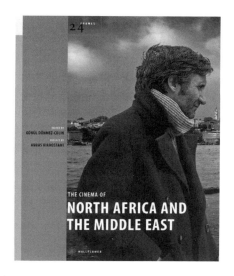

24 FRAMES

The 24 FRAMES series is a major publishing project consisting of 18 volumes providing comprehensive overviews of national and regional cinemas from all over the world. Each volume focuses on 24 key feature films or documentaries that serve as entry-points to the appreciation and study of the history, industry, social and political significance, and key directors and stars of every national cinema around the world. These collections are each edited by renowned experts in their respective areas and offer a unique, text-centred insight into the history of global cinema.

Forthcoming in the 24 Frames series in 2008 are volumes on the cinema of Germany and India, with volumes on China & South-East Asia and Southern Africa to follow in 2009 and 2010…

THE CINEMA OF NORTH AFRICA & THE MIDDLE EAST
Gönül Dönmez-Colin (ed.)
978-1-905674-10-7 (pbk) – £18.99
978-1-904764-11-4 (hbk) – £50.00

THE CINEMA OF CANADA
Jerry White (ed.)
978-1-904764-60-1 (pbk) – £18.99
978-1-904764-61-8 (hbk) – £50.00

THE CINEMA OF RUSSIA & THE FORMER SOVIET UNION
Birgit Beumers (ed.)
978-1-904764-98-4 (pbk) – £18.99
978-1-904764-99-1 (hbk) – £50.00

THE CINEMA OF FRANCE
Phil Powrie (ed.)
978-1-904764-46-5 (pbk) – £18.99
978-1-904764-47-2 (hbk) – £50.00

THE CINEMA OF AUSTRALIA & NEW ZEALAND
Geoff Mayer and Keith Beattie (eds)
978-1-904764-96-0 (pbk) – £18.99
978-1-904764-97-7 (hbk) – £50.00

THE CINEMA OF SCANDINAVIA
Tytti Soila (ed.)
978-1–904764–22–9 (pbk) – £18.99
978-1–904764–23–6 (hbk) – £50.00

THE CINEMA OF THE BALKANS
Dina Iordanova (ed.)
978-1-904764-80-9 (pbk) – £18.99
978-1-904764-81-6 (hbk) – £50.00

THE CINEMA OF BRITAIN AND IRELAND
Brian McFarlane (ed.)
978-1–904764–38–0 (pbk) – £18.99
978-1–904764–39–7 (hbk) – £50.00

THE CINEMA OF SPAIN AND PORTUGAL
Alberto Mira (ed.)
978-1–904764–44–1 (pbk) – £18.99
978-1–904764–45–8 (hbk) – £50.00

THE CINEMA OF ITALY
Giorgio Bertellini (ed.)
978-1–903364–98–7 (pbk) – £18.99
978-1–903364–99–4 (hbk) – £50.00

THE CINEMA OF CENTRAL EUROPE
Peter Hames (ed.)
978-1–904764–20–5 (pbk) – £18.99
978-1–904764–21–2 (hbk) – £50.00

THE CINEMA OF THE LOW COUNTRIES
Ernest Mathijs (ed.)
978-1–904764–00–7 (pbk) – £18.99
978-1–904764–01–4 (hbk) – £50.00

THE CINEMA OF JAPAN AND KOREA
Justin Bowyer (ed.)
978-1–904764–11–3 (pbk) – £18.99
978-1–904764–12–0 (hbk) – £50.00

THE CINEMA OF LATIN AMERICA
Alberto Elena nd Marina Díaz López (eds)
978-1–903364–83–3 (pbk) – £18.99
978-1–903364–84–0 (hbk) – £50.00

DIRECTORS' CUTS

The DIRECTORS' CUTS series focuses on the work of many of the most significant contemporary international filmmakers, illuminating the creative dynamics of World Cinema. The series includes monographs as well as edited anthologies. Forthcoming titles in 2008 include volumes on John Sayles, David Cronenberg and Sally Potter. Many more are planned for 2009 and beyond, including titles on Michael Haneke, Guy Maddin, Aki Kaurismaki, Clint Eastwood, Takeshi Kitano, Michael Mann, the Dardennes brothers, Gus Van Sant, Eric Rohmer, Robert Altman, Istvan Szabo, Raul Ruiz, Michael Winterbottom, Wong Kar-Wai, Steven Soderbergh, Béla Tarr, Sidney Lumet, Catherine Breillat etc...

THE CINEMA OF JAN SVANKMAJER
Dark Alchemy (second edition)
Peter Hames (ed.)
978-1-905674-45-9 (pbk) – £16.99
978-1-905674-46-6 (hbk) – £45.00

THE CINEMA OF ANG LEE
The Other Side of the Screen
Whitney Crothers Dilley
978-1-905674-08-4 (pbk) – £16.99
978-1-905674-09-0 (hbk) – £45.00

THE CINEMA OF NEIL JORDAN
Dark Carnival
Carole Zucker
978-1-905674-41-1 (pbk) – £16.99
978-1-905674-42-8 (hbk) – £45.00

THE CINEMA OF TODD HAYNES
All That Heaven Allows
James Morrison (ed.)
978-1-904764-77-9 (pbk) – £16.99
978-1-904764-78-6 (hbk) – £45.00

THE CINEMA OF LARS VON TRIER
Authenticity and Artifice
Caroline Bainbridge
978-1-905674-43-5 (pbk) – £16.99
978-1-905674-44-2 (hbk) – £45.00

THE CINEMA OF STEVEN SPIELBERG
Empire of Light
Nigel Morris
978-1-904764-88-5 (pbk) – £16.99
978-1-904764-89-2 (hbk) – £45.00

THE CINEMA OF TERRENCE MALICK
Poetic Visions of America (2nd edition)
Hannah Patterson (ed.)
978-1-905674-25-1 (pbk) – £16.99
978-1-905674-26-8 (hbk) – £45.00

THE CINEMA OF ROMAN POLANSKI
Dark Spaces of the World
John Orr and Elzbieta Ostrowska (eds)
978-1-904764-75-5 (pbk) – £16.99
978-1-904764-76-2 (hbk) – £45.00

THE CINEMA OF WERNER HERZOG
Aesthetic Ecstasy and Truth
Brad Prager
978-1-905674-17-6 (pbk) – £16.99
978-1-905674-18-3 (hbk) – £45.00

THE CINEMA OF JOHN CARPENTER
The Technique of Terror
Ian Conrich and David Woods (eds)
978-1-904764-14-4 (pbk) – £16.99
978-1-904764-15-1 (hbk) – £45.00

THE CINEMA OF MIKE LEIGH
A Sense of the Real
Garry Watson
978-1-904764-10-6 (pbk) — £16.99
978-1-903364-90-1 (hbk) — £45.00

THE CINEMA OF NANNI MORETTI
Dreams and Diaries
Ewa Mazierska and Laura Rascaroli
978-1-903364-77-2 (pbk) — £16.99
978-1-903364-78-9 (hbk) — £45.00

THE CINEMA OF KRZYSZTOF KIESLOWSKI
Variations on Destiny and Chance
Marek Haltof
978-1-903364-91-8 (pbk) — £16.99
978-1-903364-92-5 (hbk) — £45.00

THE CINEMA OF DAVID LYNCH
American Dreams, Nightmare Visions
Erica Sheen and Annette Davison (eds)
978-1-903364-85-7 (pbk) — £16.99
978-1-903364-86-4 (hbk) — £45.00

THE CINEMA OF ANDRZEJ WAJDA
The Art of Irony and Defiance
John Orr and Elzbieta Ostrowska (eds)
978-1-903364-89-2 (pbk) — £16.99
978-1-903364-57-4 (hbk) — £45.00

THE CINEMA OF GEORGE A. ROMERO
Knight of the Living Dead
Tony Williams
978-1-903361-33-7 (pbk) — £16.99
978-1-903364-62-8 (hbk) — £45.00

THE CINEMA OF ROBERT LEPAGE
The Poetics of Memory
Aleksandar Dundjerovich
978-1-903361-33-7 (pbk) — £16.99
978-1-903364-34-5 (hbk) — £45.00

THE CINEMA OF KATHRYN BIGELOW
Hollywood Transgressor
Sean Redmond and Deborah Jermyn (eds)
978-1-903364-42-0 (pbk) — £16.99
978-1-903364-43-7 (hbk) — £45.00

THE CINEMA OF WIM WENDERS
The Celluloid Highway
Alexander Graf
978-1-903364-29-1 (pbk) — £16.99
978-1-903364-30-7 (hbk) — £45.00

THE CINEMA OF KEN LOACH
Art in the Service of the People
Jacob Leigh
978-1-903364-31-4 (pbk) — £16.99
978-1-903364-32-1 (hbk) — £45.00

THE CINEMA OF EMIR KUSTURICA
Notes from the Underground
Goran Gocic
978-1-903364-14-7 (pbk) — £16.99
978-1-903364-16-1 (hbk) — £45.00